MW01286806

Jack & Helen Frye Story

Randall D Reynolds

Published by Sedona Legend, 2015.

While every precaution has been taken in the preparation of this book, the publisher assumes no responsibility for errors or omissions, or for damages resulting from the use of the information contained herein.

JACK & HELEN FRYE STORY

First edition. March 27, 2015.

ISBN: 978-1543148534

Written by Randall D Reynolds.

Dedicated to the friends and family of Jack and Helen Frye, and especially, Rosie Targhetta Armijo. The Frye story is greatly enhanced with rich and colorful anecdotes graciously shared by these invaluable witnesses to history.

Also dedicated to my partner of 21 years who has supported me through thirteen years of endless research, graciously tolerating the required dedication to complete this indepth historical narrative.

JACK & HELEN FRYE STORY
By

Randall D. Reynolds

Chapter 1

<u>Tapestry of Threads</u>

'1979'

On this autumn day in November of 1979, at the Wings of the Wind house, a terminally ill Helen Frye rests in her comfortable armchair with an oxygen tank and tray of medicine paraphernalia at her side. The endless crimson vistas of Helen's beloved Sedona Frye Ranch spread out below her, as seen through the plate-glass windows of her hilltop home.

With her eyes closed, and in a trance, Helen listens to Jo Stafford singing, "...Fly the ocean in a silver plane." Helen's caregiver enters the large room and pauses as she observes the record player. She smiles softly as she looks over at Helen. Walking over to Mrs. Frye, she adjusts the colorful shawl on her lap. "It's time for your pill," she says gently as Helen opens her eyes. The weary woman reaches up with shaking hand and takes the medication uttering, "I'm only 71, yet I feel the doctors are correct, I haven't that long to live." "Yes, there, there, Mrs. Frye," says Helen's caregiver soothingly. "You've had a long and wondrous life, everything will be fine." The kindly woman leaves the room as Helen slips into a beautiful dream serenaded by 'You Belong to Me.'

Jack Frye appears in the mist of Helen's mind standing next to a silver twin-engine plane with Transcontinental & Western Air, Inc. stenciled on the fuselage. He beckons to Helen and smiles warmly as Helen strolls out to the plane, dressed in heels, seamed-stockings, and a full-length mink coat. Excited and full of anticipation Helen rushes to Jack's open arms. He sweeps Helen's petite figure into his massive embrace, they kiss as he lifts her off the ground and spins her in a circle. Jack's breath is warm on Helen's cheek and the scent of his lime shaving soap permeates her senses. Helen awakens with a jolt, exclaiming to herself, "My God what a vivid dream, so real, like I was actually with him again!" Helen's heart races as she whispers, "Not yet Jack, not yet."

The next day, Helen's dearest friend Rosie helps her dress saying, "I always loved that House of Apache Fires you and Jack built. Such spectacular views and beautiful rock work! I still remember when we all moved up there in the summer of 1948." Wistfully, Helen replies, "Just a dream, nothing more than a broken dream Rosie, but I have to see it just one more time." The day is crisp and sunny, a beautiful Sedona morning, and Helen is eager for this last final gesture.

Within an hour, a station wagon filled with Native Americans navigates the red dirt road through the ranch and up to the rear entrance of the Indian Pueblo mansion. Once parked, the passengers exit while several help Helen out of the car and up to the rear door of the sprawling red rock dwelling. Helen reaches into her pocket pulling out an old tarnished silver key, as she unlocks the door, one of her Native American friends helps her push on it. The massive door protests and groans with a mournful creak, swinging inward. Musty dank air, like that escaping a long-sealed tomb, washes over the group, who all step back sharply as if in reverence. One of the Native Americans mutters to his companion, "House of Spirits!"

Stepping into the entry of her dream home, a flood of emotion permeates Helen's body; she shivers and reaches out to a wall to steady herself. Mrs. Frye asks her friends to leave her alone now as she starts her journey from room to room. First though, Helen pauses as she pulls out a jeweled cigarette case and lights a cigarette. She draws on the cigarette like an old friend. As she exhales slowly, the blue smoke flows through the house like a foggy mist.

"This house looks empty, but it's not empty to me. It's filled with all my most precious memories, my hopes and dreams," says Helen with a wisp of a smile. She continues as she whispers to the shadows, "I know you're here Jack, but not yet my darling, not yet." Helen takes a moment to gaze around the master bedroom suite. Suddenly, a flashback scene confronts her, overwhelming her senses. She reaches out to grab the log fireplace mantel, steadying herself, while a spectral vision flashes across the room transporting her back in time...

'Red Rock vistas of vibrant color unfold around Jack and Helen as they place down markers flagging the corners of the House of Apache Fires building site in 1941 Sedona. They are dressed in western regalia; two saddled stallions graze nearby on the edge of a red rock cliff overlooking a verdant creek. Suddenly, Jack and Helen turn to each other with love and accomplishment in their eyes. The surreal Sedona vista opens up in a massive sunset panorama beyond them. Standing on the edge of the cliff facing west, the two are silent, as they hold hands, both in awe of the view as the golden rays of the setting sun spray out over the pinnacles and spires. Helen exclaims with a grand sweep of her arm, "This is our legacy Jack, our life together, this place called Sedona!" At that, Jack draws Helen into an embrace and whispers with his Texas drawl, "I love you Helen darling, I love you!"'

The scene fades quickly. Helen, quite overwhelmed, puts her hand over her mouth, her eyes wide. The dreary interior of the House of Apache Fires with its crumbling plaster and empty hallways reappears before her. "This house IS truly haunted," Helen exclaims shakily as she continues through a dark corridor to Jack's TWA home office. Helen peeks into the shadowed room with its scenic corner windows. Again, a menagerie of flashback images washes over her, images, which envelop the room.

'Helen and Jack, with Howard Hughes are at the Ambassador Hotel Cocoanut Grove Club at Los Angeles. Excitedly they pour over plans for a revolutionary new airliner at a private corner table overshadowed by indoor palm trees.' This scene fades, as another appears, filling the void.

'Jack and Helen, Harriet Appelwick, their private TWA Hostess, and Howard Hughes ride the grand vistas of the Sedona Ranch. Helen and Jack show their companions the building site and views their new home will enjoy. At sunset, they all ride across the highest bluff of the ranch—Eagle's Nest. Passionately they regale each other about TWA flying 'round the world' after the war. "The men have the experience transporting the troops overseas with the Connie. Soon we'll have our routes and start passenger service," Jack exclaims proudly! Howard smiles in agreement saying, "You're doing a fine job with TWA Jack! We will be the biggest and the best!" Helen chimes in confidently, "The war-work, darling, just a first step in the scheme of your grand vision!" She and Jack both smile warmly at each other, their faces filled with love. For a moment, Helen notices Howard looking at her with lust in his eyes, his heart seemingly filled with envy and desire. Quickly he looks down.' Another scene washes over the room.

'Wearing a full-length mink coat, Helen attends the TWA Constellation Celebration, April 17, 1944, at Washington National Airport, Washington D.C. Adjoining Helen, on the left and the right, are Jack's personal secretary Beverly Dille, and Helen's friend Austine Bootsie Cassini (later Mrs. William Randolph Hearst Jr.).

A thousand onlookers, military dignitaries, and press fan out behind the fashionably dressed trio. Helen scans the horizon. A massive Constellation airliner, tail number NC310310, trimmed in crimson TWA logo, flashes overhead and banks around, sweeping in for a perfect landing. As the plane moves closer, Helen spies Jack in the left seat as pilot, and Howard Hughes in the right seat as co-pilot.

Within moments, the Lockheed taxis up to the viewing area as Jack waves out the cockpit window. The crowd greets him with a deafening roar of welcome! The sleek airliner pulls up to the staging area with brakes screeching and massive radial engines throbbing at idle. After the quad engines are shutdown, the fuselage door swings open; the two pilots dressed in sport jackets and ties exit. The men wave with smiles of accomplishment as they descend the boarding ramp. The crowd showers the two with cheers and applause. A newsreel camera pans around to Helen at the forefront of the throng. Her eyes misty and filled with pride, she smiles radiantly at Jack, like a movie star. With a grand gesture, Helen blows Jack a kiss with her leather-gloved hand; again, the crowd erupts with a roar.

Airline passengers consisting of reporters and other officials trickle out of the plane, waving to the crowd. Jesse H. Jones, United States Secretary of Commerce, greets Jack Frye and Howard Hughes as they approach the radio mikes. Helen watches with admiration from the sidelines; she and Jack exchange loving glances.

After welcome ceremonies and speeches are complete, the crowd awaits as the TWA Constellation prepares for a preview flight. The first V.I.P. to board is TWA President's wife Helen Frye. Helen strolls graciously through the gathered dignitaries, past Howard Hughes, and up the boarding ramp stairs, where she pauses in front of the entry door. Helen turns to face the throng with a radiant smile, as Jack who has followed at her heels joins her side smiling. On Jack's face is evident the accomplishment of a lifetime, the creation of the first Trans-Atlantic airliner, all in the name of TWA!

In a grand gesture, Jack turns to Helen and sweeps her in his arms, kissing her passionately on the lips while the spectators explode with a frenzied roar. Shutters click and newsreel cameras spin, all focusing on the romantic embrace. After a moment, Jack releases Helen and turns to the crowd with a grin. They both step into the plane's passenger cabin disappearing from view. Other passengers proceed to climb the ramp to the airliner.'

The cheering fades away to silence as Helen stands alone in Jack's TWA office. Helen is stunned as she looks around, expecting to see yet another spectral vision; however, only shadows and gloom reach out to touch her as the silent Apache Fires house descends on her like a shroud. Helen feels something wet on her cheek, she reaches up with her finger and finds she has been crying. She pulls out a hanky embossed with 'H.F.' and dabs at her eyes gently.

Suddenly, Helen hears a sound. She turns, her eyes urgently search the empty hallway, "I feel your presence," she whispers, "you ARE here!" A deep, soothing masculine voice, filled with love, resonates out of the shadows, "Yes, I'm here Helen, don't be afraid my darling. I'm waiting for you, it's time for you to join me." Helen whispers to

Jack, as a tear rolls down her face, "Not yet Jack, please my darling, not yet." With that, Helen begins to weep softly.

Helen composes herself as she continues down the stone stairs into the massive living room wing to the expansive picture windows, which frame the valley below. Proudly she exclaims, "Yes, this is 'My' Sedona!" Helen's eyes scan the horizon coming to rest on the Wings of the Wind house high on its pinnacle across the valley. "If only you could have shared that with me Jack," she says emotionally.

With tears streaking her weary face, Helen makes her way slowly to the front door of the house. Suddenly, she clutches her side, her face grimaces with pain. "This is the last time Jack. I can't come back here again." As she passes through the front door, her hand caresses the frame lovingly and gently. Helen has the overwhelming feeling she is somehow leaving her essence behind; she feels empty and hollow. In Helen's mind, she accepts the reality that among the shadowed rooms of the Apache Fires House rest the culmination of her life-path and dreams.

Helen's friends join her as she exits the sprawling home. Gently, they lead her around the house into the courtyard, where they help her in-to the waiting station wagon. In a cloud of red dust, the vehicle pulls away, down the hill and across the ford through the verdant valley and up to the Wings of the Wind house.

Later that afternoon, at sunset, a long red Cadillac ambulance pulls up to the Wings of the Wind with red and white lights sweeping 'round and 'round. A group of people standby in solemn reverence in the amber rays of the setting sun. Two are religious-like in long white robes, others are Native Americans—and one, a young man, watches broodingly from the shadows.

Two male attendants in white uniforms gently lift a stretcher with the lifeless Helen and slide it into the back of the ambulance. Helen's friend Rosie chokes back tears as she leans heavily on Faye Crenshaw who helps her into the back of the ambulance where Rosie takes a seat next to Helen. Faye calls after her, "I'll follow you up in my car!" Rosie nods, by now she is sobbing uncontrollably. She reaches over and takes Helen's limp hand. Kissing it, she says with emotion, "I've always loved you so much Helen, you were like a second mother to me."

An attendant steps in and sits at the other side of Helen, while the driver shuts the big door and walks around the ambulance, stepping into the driver's seat. The engine leaps to life, slowly, the ambulance pulls away down the juniper-lined red dirt driveway, rocking and lurching on the uneven road. As the vehicle gains speed, rust dust swirls up and around obscuring it in the red dusty glow of its red rooftop strobe.

From an overview, the emergency vehicle with red and white beacons sweeping and siren wailing, makes its way along Red Rock Loop Road, turning onto Highway 89A, proceeding on through the grand vistas of Sedona. Onlookers pause and stare as the ambulance passes through the quaint little town, parting traffic, as it heads north up Oak Creek Canyon. The vehicle's siren cries mournfully, as the ambulance crosses Midgley Bridge, disappearing under cave-like canopies of overgrowth and rock overhangs. After 30 minutes, the Cadillac approaches the Emergency entrance to the Flagstaff hospital.

In the harsh light of fluorescent lighting, Helen rests in a hospital bed with crisp white sheets. An exasperated doctor with poor bedside manner lectures her, "You've waited too long to be admitted and you require surgery immediately!" He pauses for a moment as he studies Helen. Then he snaps at her again, "And stop that smoking woman!" The room is silent as Helen reaches for another cigarette. Calmly, she lights it, exhaling in the doctor's direction. After a moment, she taps it in an ashtray on the bedside table.

Finally, Helen responds, "I hate hospitals and you've offered me no cure—no recovery!" The doctor responds defensively, "But Mrs. Frye we are the only ones who *can* help you now!" Then he adds dramatically, "You will die if you leave this hospital!" Helen quickly snaps back with a dismissive wave of her hand, "If I stay I will die! Now get out, get out of my room!" The doctor retreats as he shakes his head, he joins a nurse who timidly awaits in the hallway. All alone now in the stark sterile room, Helen whispers, "Not yet Jack, please not here my darling, not here!"

Outside the Flagstaff hospital, gloomy black clouds gather as a brilliant flash of lightning illuminates the hilltop location, accompanied by an ear-deafening boom of thunder. A misty rain falls gently, the smell of wet ponderosa and aspen permeates the air. Native American youth and several Hopi Elders start to appear out of a swirling mist, amid a grove of aspen, at the far end of the parking lot. They continue to walk up the path to the main entrance of the hospital while passersby turn and stare.

The Hopi, dressed in full native regalia, pass through the hospital entrance, while the young boys respectfully assist an old frail medicine man who leans on them. Gently, they push through a small group of people standing in the waiting room. Patients and visitors watch this procession with their mouths agape whispering to each other. A receiving nurse looks up suddenly, observing the unusual group moving through the entry area toward the Intensive Care wing. Alarmed, she jumps up and rushes over to them, "Stop, stop, you can't enter this area, its off-limits to visitors! You must return to the waiting room immediately!" "Spirit invites us," states one of the Native Americans mysteriously, in a confident kindly voice. He repeats, "Spirit calls us," his voice trails off. The Hopi push gently past the agitated nurse who retreats to her station. She grabs the phone and calls security, "Come at once!" she pleas urgently.

Native Americans dance and swoop in Helen's room. The loud chanting and melodic drums echo out into the hallway of the normally silent hospital. The medicine man is administering to Helen with herbs and talismans. Helen sits on the bed with her arms extended and palms out, her eyes closed, on her face a smile of serene peace and love.

Suddenly, the hospital staff bursts into the room, interrupting the healing ceremony. One of the youth rushes to block them from Helen, "This ceremony is for a revered and beloved member of the Navajo-Hopi Nation. She will be healed, you must not interfere, Spirit is at work!" Helen's doctor pushes through the room, in a livid voice he exclaims, "Get these savages out of my hospital, who do you think you are?" He continues heatedly, "This is a medical facility. *You* cannot possibly help Mrs. Frye!" At this, Helen reaches out to one of the Hopi, her voice weak and tired, "Please, please, get me home, I cannot," her voice fades to a whisper as the Native American youth leans in closer, "I cannot die here, not in this place. I have to get home to my ranch, and to Jack."

The next day, Helen's wheelchair is at the hospital admittance desk. A nurse holding a clipboard with discharge papers watches Helen shakily sign release papers. Within moments, Rosie pushes Helen out to the aspen-lined parking lot and helps her into a station wagon where a couple of Native Americans await. The vehicle pulls out onto the road and winds its way down the forested canyon toward Sedona. After 45 minutes, the car passes portals and gates, which read, 'Frye

Ranch'. The car continues up the red dirt drive to a dead-end, stopping in front of Wings of the Wind and the adjoining cliff. Helen, who is sitting in the front passenger seat, turns to the driver with joy in her face saying, "At last, I'm home! This is where I want to spend the last days of my life with Jack, on the land we bought together as soulmates."

Chapter 2

The Aviator-Entrepreneur

'1923'

High above 1920's Los Angeles, a two-seater Jenny bi-plane with pilot and passenger swoops and dives, dropping in low over downtown Los Angeles, a woman peers out of the cockpit watching the frenetic scene below. Hundreds of cars, shoppers, and business people scurry through the congested city, past a corner drugstore at the base of a twelve-story brick building.

Seventeen-year-old Jack Frye stands behind a soda fountain, attired in the crisp white cap and apron of a soda jerk. Caught in a trance, he stares out at the hubbub of Los Angeles outside the front windows and listens intently as a sputtering plane passes low overhead. Several customers are at the counter enjoying coffee, sandwiches, sodas, and ice cream sundaes. "Jack, stop that daydreaming and take care of your customers," admonishes a kindly proprietor who has taken the teenager under his wing. "Someday, my boy, this drugstore can be yours!"

However, Jack doesn't hear, his attention is focused on a Model T coupe, which slips through the jumble of traffic outside the drugstore, screeching to a stop at the curb. The sound of the horn, 'Ma-Goo-Ga' assaults the afternoon. "I'm off," says Jack to the old man excitedly as he throws down his apron and white hat, running out the door to the coupe. The old proprietor smiles and shakes his head. Turning to a cashier girl he says, "A young boy's heart is hard to tame, hard to tame." She smiles, as they both watch Jack jump into the jalopy with his pal. The run-a-bout leaps away, disappearing into a jumble of Los Angeles motorists. With a mechanical chug-a-chug, the jalopy navigates the confusing jumble of autos and streetcars, southeast, toward Inglewood, where all the local airstrips are located.

After about 30 minutes the two pull up to a dusty field, with an old Army surplus Curtiss JN4 'Jenny' parked next to an old flight operation shack. A wooden sign hangs over the door displaying, 'Flying Lessons'. The men jump out of the car, while the driver, an older man, named Burdett Fuller, turns to Jack and says, "Well, what'd you think?" With a face full of excitement, the good-looking 6-foot-2 boy surveys the landscape. He observes planes parked for miles across the countryside and gazes up, watching a couple planes zooming by overhead. Finally, he turns to Burdett and exclaims, "I'm on fire, this is my destiny, I just know it is!"

With a pounding heart, Jack accompanies Burdett over to the little office. "Not much here," Burdett says, almost apologetically, "but, the gold's in the air!" Jack whirls around, and with the passion of a God creating a new world he says, "This is the future of flight Burdett. We're on the threshold of the dawning of commercial aviation and

I'm going to create it!" With that, they walk out of the little shack to Burdett's two-seat Curtiss Jenny. Jack looks it over from front to back. Barely able to contain himself he turns to Burdett and exclaims, "Let's go!"

Burdett gets the plane started with a sputter. A rush of hot air permeated with oil and petrol fumes engulfs the two men. Jack climbs into the forward cockpit, while Burdett climbs in the back. With engine roaring, the plane swings around and speeds down the runway in a cloud of dust. As the two lift off, the heady scent of citrus fills the cockpit. Into the blazing California sun they fly, out over Los Angeles and the coastal hills. Jack looks down, observing the autos like matchboxes, tiny ant-like people swarm to and fro; he's filled with an innate sense, a premonition, that the world of air travel is about to be busted wide-open!

Back on the ground, Jack signs up for flight lessons. After buying a half-interest in the Jenny, he learns to fly. At the end of his instruction, unbeknownst to his first paying passenger, Jack is completing his solo flight with the ease of a seasoned professional. (Jack is so strapped for cash he engages the passenger to help pay for his solo-flight fuel.) Jack is very familiar with these Army trainers, as he had served in the Army Reserve for 1 year, at the age of 16.

Jack and Burdett expand Burdett Flying School. Within a year, Jack and two business partners, Walt Hamilton and Paul Richter buy Fuller out. Soon after, they found Aero Corporation of California (1926). In operations, which include all manner of air service, Jack launches the first Los Angeles-Phoenix-Tucson passenger service in 1927, with Standard Air Lines. He also flies the first load of passengers, as president of the fledgling company. At the same juncture, Arizona bestows Frye with the first Arizona 'Private Pilot's License'. Shortly after, Arizona issues Jack the State's first 'Commercial Transport License' for interstate passenger service; Arizona was the only state to issue such a certificate at the time. By 1928, this visionary aviator launches the first air-rail service for the United States from coast to coast. Later still, in conjunction with Transcontinental & Western Air, Inc. (T&WA), launched in 1930, Jack oversees the nation's first transcontinental passenger air service!

Inside a simple bungalow at Inglewood, California Burdett Field aviators Jack Frye, Bon MacDougall, Paul Richter, and Ken Nichols, found the '13 Flying Black Cats' aerial stunt team over the Frye kitchen table. Jack's wife Debbie Greer pours coffee as Jack and Paul Richter show the other men a diagram of stunts they want to perform. The Black Cats soon thrill audiences at air shows around Los Angeles, and all over the Southwest, from 1925 to 1929. Later, Jack and his Black Cat pals fly stunts in the Howard Hughes epic, 'Hell's Angels', among other films. This is when Jack and Howard Hughes become life-long aviation friends.

Jack's sister Sunny recalled in an interview those carefree days when she lived with her brother Jack while attending high school in Los Angeles. One night at dinner, Jack regaled her and a friend, along with Debbie and their brother Don, with stories of the future of aviation. "Someday," Jack related, "there will be cross-country sleeper flights that serve dinner in route." "Imagine that!" said Sunny. "My brother was such a visionary, what a thought in 1925, of course we thought he was nuts!"

Sunny palled around with one of Jack's best friends, a young pilot who had his own plane, a real luxury for the day. The aviator would take Sunny for flights whenever she would appear. Sunny related they would have great fun diving at the ships in the harbor, roaring through haystacks, hedgehopping, and buzzing up and down the Los Angeles coast, all at full throttle! At the time, these areas were all open sandy land, devoid of the current gridlock of Los Angeles homes and boulevards.

Jack trusted Paul with his sister, perhaps blindly so, not having any idea what aerobatics they orchestrated once airborne. Luckily, Paul and Sunny had no mishaps and Jack was never to find out the mischief they sought. Surely, a grounding would have been in store, if the wild duo was ever found out. Sunny related Paul lived in a big house down on Sunset Boulevard, at that time, an area sparsely built up.

Sunny closes her eyes; she remembers. The shadows clear and orange groves appear. A 2-seater, sputtering in the sunset materializes, spewing fumes of petrol and oil that overwhelm her senses. Amid the heady scent of Los Angeles valley citrus groves, Sunny climbs in the bi-plane in front of her trusted aviator-friend, N. Paul Whittier. With engine roaring, the plane speeds down the primitive dirt runway of Burdett Airport in a cloud of dust, climbing up and away, out over the bejeweled California coastline. For hours, Sunny and Paul fly through the intoxicating evening air, over the small town of Los Angeles, swooping, diving, never wanting to land, immersed in the constant sound of the engine and whistling breeze, pilot and passenger are free from earth's gravity, free from life on the ground.

'Summer of 1926'

Cloistered in the drawing room of the Max Whittier Mansion at 1001 Sunset Boulevard in Beverly Hills, Jack and Paul Whittier review aircraft blueprints. Spread out on a large desk the documents read, 'Thunderbird Aircraft'. Jack is pleased as he exclaims, "Paul we have ourselves a real winner here. Theodore did a fine job!" "Yes, I agree," answers Paul, "Woolsey is a wiz; I could never have done all this!" "Well, the best thing we did was to hire him to design it," says Jack, "and of course you to back it," Jack winks at Whittier. "W.F.W. Company- 'Woolsey, Frye and Whittier', I like it! We'll accomplish great things!" Just then, a maid comes into the closed room. "Excuse me, Master Paul. Can I bring you boys something, perhaps some sandwiches and a couple sodas?" "Yes, that would be nice, thank you," says Paul sheepishly, as he looks over at Jack. Jack looks at him and starts to laugh, "Master Paul! I can't wait to tell all the flyboys out at the field that's your real name!" Paul gives him a defiant look saying, "Don't you dare Jack Frye or I'll tell everyone you're afraid of heights!" "You would," Jack says shaking his head, "at least I'm not afraid of flying, and hey, I taught you to fly didn't I?" "That you did, Jack old boy that you did!" Paul laughs as he continues, "By the way, when will the prototype be finished?" "Sometime in June," Jack replies, "and I can't wait!"

'July 11, 1926'

Jack's Aero Corporation Field is the location of a press conference revealing of the Thunderbird speedster, with chief pilot Jack Frye demonstrating the new plane. Champagne is broken over the landing gear, by movie star Alberta Vaughn, as assisted by Frye.

The plane's designer, Theodore (Ted) A. Woolsey is a guest of honor. Although history does not notate such, it is likely N. (Nelson) Paul Whittier was a V.I.P. guest as well. After the press excitedly pours over the new speedster, Frye takes off to demonstrate its maneuverability to the several hundred aviation enthusiasts. For over 15 minutes, Frye swoops, dives, and performs various daring stunts for the crowd. Upon landing Jack offers complimentary flights to the spectators, the first being Mrs. N.W. Henderson. Media reports on the event, with a photo of the sleek speedster, accompanied by Frye and Vaughn.

Jack envisions the Thunderbird to serve as a speedy passenger-express plane. With a shroud-enclosed engine hiding all but the exhaust tips, the sport plane, which is noted for its speed and stability, is fast and sleek, leaving all other planes in the dust. The three aviators had truly created a masterpiece in aero design!

In the first week of August 1926, Police Chief Charles C. Blair swears in pilot Paul Whittier, as an officer of the Beverly Hills Police Department. Whittier, whose father was a founder of Beverly Hills, fills the position for the new division titled the 'Beverly Hills Police Aerial Patrol'.

The agency is set up to patrol the skies over Beverly Hills, a task Paul Whittier dutifully performs, with an official police pursuit emblazoned with 'Beverly Hills Aerial Patrol' on the side of the fuselage, coupled with two police shields on the bottom of the lower wings.

For several weeks, Whittier patrols the airspace and hills over Beverly Hills, aiding in the recovery of stolen cars, thwarting crime, and serving as a fire-spotter. For history's sake, Nelson Paul Whittier was indeed the first official aerial patrol officer of the State of California, and perhaps even the entire United States.

'August 14, 1926'

As a public demonstration of this new civic service and a promo of sorts for the equipment used in the air-patrols, Chief Pilot of Aero

Corporation of California, 22-year old Jack Frye, races in low over Beverly Hills at an ear-pounding elevation of 600 feet performing aerial stunts well below the legal ceiling of 1000 feet! At the time, it's accurate to say Beverly Hills, among other communities, enacted the elevation limit to protect its citizens from the many Los Angeles aviators who were terrorizing people on the ground with their new-fangled aero-contraptions. Not that Jack Frye was such an offender. As Frye drops in over Beverly Hills, N. Paul Whittier, who just happens to be nearby in the air, swoops in after Frye in hot pursuit, with red light blazing and siren howling. Whittier uses his ship to force the violator Frye down for a quick landing in an empty field.

The result is an air 'pull-over' of the law-breaking and discourteous Frye, forcing him to land at a very public and visible location. Awaiting is a crowd of citizens, movie people, and reporters. In this transparent effort, staged for public education and the press, this new police agency shines gloriously. The equipment utilized, interestingly enough, is no other than the new Thunderbird speedster manufactured at the Thunderbird Aircraft Factory by Frye, Woolsey, and Whittier.

Intriguingly, the Beverly Hills Police 'Thunderbird' is also serviced and hangared at Frye's Aero Corporation Field, this, a field noted as the largest airfield in Southern California. After Frye lands, he is ordered out of his plane and promptly arrested by Whittier for breaking the law. To the bemusement of jeering spectators, Whittier transports Frye to the Beverly Hills jail and locks him up.

In conclusion, we have the first 'sky officer' and the very first arrest of pilot Frye on August 14, 1926 at Beverly Hills California. Frye posts a bail of $100.00 and the judge orders him to appear Monday morning on August 16 for arraignment. Beverly Hills Judge, Seth Strelinger presides over this landmark case, the first-ever air violation to appear before a judge in a California court. Most likely, all charges were dropped as this was an initial case, a first offense, and a publicity promo-event.

'September 8, 1927'

In an unprecedented display of pyrotechnics over downtown Los Angeles, Jack Frye performs aerial aerobatics, welcoming the new 1927 Cadillac models displayed at Don Lee Cadillac LaSalle at 7th and Bixel. The Cadillacs, available in 26 variations, are part of the 'Cadillac-LaSalle Style Salon of Southern California' promo, from September 8, 1927, for 10 days, with a daily schedule of exciting events. In this extravaganza (not unlike the premier of Howard Hughes' Hell's Angels at the Grauman's Chinese Theatre in 1930) Jack Frye entertains throngs of spectators.

Don Lee was the state's largest Cadillac-LaSalle dealer; his fame though was more so in supplying Hollywood celebrities with posh luxury-mobiles as the nationally famous 'Dealer to the Stars'.

As the sun sets over the Pacific Coast, two powerful Klieg spotlights began sweeping the night sky. Suddenly, the sound of a throbbing engine approaches out of the southern sky as a large plane appears from the dark void. A phosphorescent flare descends from the sky illuminating the crowd. A Fokker airliner piloted by Jack Frye swoops in low over 7th Avenue, in-between blinding searchlights, as the crowd watches with anticipation and awe!

In the artificial light of the brilliant phosphorescent flare, Frye's plane appears ablaze, highlighted by exploding bursts of fireworks! At the height of this dramatic display, Frye releases pyrotechnics, positioned along the trailing edges of the wings, in the colors of the Cadillac trade emblem of red, gold, blue, and white. Jack swoops and circles for the roaring crowd; finally, the display spent, the legendary pilot and his Fokker disappear into the darkness as the engine fades out over the horizon.

'September 19, 1926'

At another air show, Art Goebel, in his famous Jenny 'No. 27' soars 2000-feet above Clover Field merrily performing aerial escapades above an excited crowd, when suddenly one of his wheels falls off and plummets to the ground! Rather than land and damage the ship or himself, Art continues circling the airshow waving frantically to the ground, "Help, Help!"

Famous aviatrix, Gladys Ingle and Jack Frye are watching closely and jump up from the sideline to save the day! Frye quickly darts to his Jenny, starts the engine, while Gladys runs to a hangar and grabs a spare tire for Goebel's stricken ship. In no time, Gladys scrambles into the passenger seat of the waiting Jenny as Frye guns the engine. In a flash, they're off the ground and in pursuit of 'No. 27'.

Jack Frye expertly navigates his ship close enough for Gladys to lower herself down on to the wing of 'No. 27' with the spare tire strapped to her back. As the Frye plane falls back and maintains a close vigil nearby, Gladys climbs down below the fuselage of 27 and proceeds to replace the wheel—but not as quickly and easily as one might surmise, as the axle has slipped! Gladys secures the wheel to the ship, and then climbs down to wrestle with the axle. She encounters quite a struggle sliding it back in, but finally, success! Gladys anchors the wheel with an axle nut and cotter pin. Nicked up, bleeding, and covered with axle grease, the shaken Ingle clamors for the cockpit and the two planes quickly descend and land. Once safely on the ground, Goebel heartily thanks Gladys and Frye with hugs and backslapping. A pressing crowd of over 500 enthusiast spectators inundates the heroes and their ships!

'September 27, 1926'

Shortly thereafter, Jack Frye spearheads the organization of the first Aerial Sheriff's Squadron of Los Angeles, as based and launched from Jack's Aero Corporation of California Field at 104th and Western at Los Angeles. The air-patrol, managed by Los Angeles Sheriff William I. Traeger, enlists the aid of five Aero Corporation-Burdett Airport aviators as officers. These fliers include William John (Jack) Frye, Richmond A. Edwards, Lee Wiley, Paul E. Richter, Jr., and Walter (Ham) A. Hamilton. All men, after sworn in as aerial sheriffs, are required to respond on call to the Los Angeles Sheriff's Department—anytime night or day, assisting in emergencies and aiding in law enforcement. Other duties consist in recovering stolen cars, missing persons, and aiding in the capture of bandits. The aviators, thoroughly trained as police officers, all pass tests in regard to criminal code and procedures. The pursuit planes are fitted with powerful spotlights for nighttime use.

Throughout the mid to late 1920's, young Jack Frye, an accomplished and popular west-coast aviator, is the hit of many Southern California air shows, winning trophy after trophy for his aerial expertise, namely, dead-stick landings.

At one event, a plane goes up for a stunt with a big one-inch cotton rope tied with loops hanging from the fuselage. A stuntman, climbing up the swinging rope, finds himself trapped when the loops tighten around his foot. In his struggle, he hangs upside down as the plane circles around in front of the shocked crowd. The pilot tries to get him to jump, with a low pass over the airfield, or even dropping in low over the ocean, but the trapped man cannot get free of the noose. Who will rescue this poor man? Jack Frye, who is watching from the ground, takes off with a roar in his plane, which is equipped with a fast and powerful engine. Jack maneuvers his Jenny under the trapped man who is able to grab a hold of Jack's plane and untie himself. The two land amid a roaring crowd of jubilant spectators!

'November 28, 29, 1927'

On February 3, 1926, Aero Corporation of California is founded, serving as holding company for Standard Air Lines, launched in 1927. Standard was the catalyst for Jack's dream of the first regularly scheduled passenger air service between Los Angeles-Phoenix-Tucson. Years later in 1936, Jack tells a reporter, "The plane wouldn't hold enough gasoline to fly it all the way to Phoenix, so I regularly sat down on the highway at Desert Center, California, taxied up to a filling station and took on fuel. We never knew in Los Angeles whether the plane reached Tucson or not, but there was an understanding that if it didn't, the pilot would send us a telegram." The plane was a 6-seat Fokker cabin ship; over one day, back the next, with the other two pilots being Paul E. Richter and Lee Willey. Continuing Jack said, "My grandfather made two annual trips to Dodge City in covered wagon days in freight provisions to his Wheeler County farm, the trip took three weeks each way. Now our planes make the trip in an hour, carry about the same amount of cargo, and operate for about the same cost that my grandfather and his freight wagon knew."

'March 13, 1928'

Jack is hired to fly over the failed St. Francis Dam disaster, so officials can access the damage. On other overflights, photographers for the Examiner and Times take front-page photos leaning out of Jack's Fokker. This is the second largest disaster in the state of California, the first being the great San Francisco earthquake of 1906.

'February 4, 1929'

Standard Air Lines (passenger subsidiary of Aero) launches First U.S. Coast-to-Coast Transcontinental plane-train passenger service from Los Angeles-Phoenix-Tucson-Douglas-El Paso-St Louis-New York. At this juncture, Standard Air initiates service to Douglas and El Paso.

Please note: Contrary to spin seen in vintage publicity, Transcontinental Air Transport, TAT (The Lindbergh Line) was not the 'first' to provide cross-country air service on July 7 and 8, 1929! This is misleading publicity of the day and 'oft repeated.

'August 4, 1929'

Standard Air Lines Inc. launches exclusive 'luxury Fokker tri-motor air passenger service'. Jack Frye, again, as president-pilot of Standard, flies the first load of passengers from California to Arizona on this commemorative occasion.

Chapter 3

Transcontinental & Western Air- a Vision of Greatness

'1930'

By the end of the 1920's, amid the great depression, Frye spins his airline into a merger with Western Air Express (WAE). He assumes the role of 'Vice President in Charge of Operations' for the fledgling company. Before the end of the year, Jack helps develop this company into another giant air concern called Transcontinental & Western Air, Inc. (also known as T&WA or TWA.)

'March 31, 1931'

A tragic accident ends the life of legendary Notre Dame football coach Knute Kenneth Rockne, on ill-fated TWA flight 599 transporting 6 passengers and 2 pilots.

Shortly after the T&WA Rockne accident, Jack Frye personally flies to the accident scene near Bazaar, Kansas, on the morning of April 2, 1931. Piloting a TWA Northrop Alpha mail-plane, Jack sets down on a rocky scrub patch next to the wreck site with passenger (Tony) Anthony Herman Gerhard Fokker. After surveying the wrecked Fokker airliner, Frye and Fokker take off again for Wichita, Kansas.

This is not the first time Jack had been at the wreck site. The previous day, April 1, 1931, Jack spent the entire day examining the aircraft wreckage, piece by piece. Tired and cold, Jack returned to Wichita well after dark to meet with Fokker, whereas Tony Fokker had boarded a TWA plane from Los Angeles to Wichita earlier that day. Jack was waiting when the eastbound Fokker tri-motor landed with Rockne and seven other passengers.

In the aftermath of the Knute Rockne tragedy, Jack knew he had to solicit a totally new revolutionary design in commercial air transport, one that would appease the fearful public and maintain the success of his airline.

This monumental effort, hammered out between Frye, TWA, and Douglas Aircraft Company, resulted in the development of the infamous Douglas Commercial transports: the prototype DC-1, and the production versions, DC-2 and DC-3. This practical and safe series of airliner was an aviation milestone, and a direct result of Frye's vision of aircraft design.

From General Manager, to Vice President, to President, Frye was the 'Heart and Soul' of early T&WA.

'Spring of 1931'

Several months later, Jack taxis out of Grand Central Air Terminal at Glendale in his private TWA Lockheed Vega 5 NC624-E, a custom executive-charter speedster. By the mid-1930's, Frye flies in and out at airports around the U.S. in a variety of company planes; however, the private planes Frye utilizes most frequently for his management of TWA were two of three Northrop Gamma 2D's TWA owned, NR13757 and TWA sister test ship NC13758.

'February 10, 1934'

Hard times loom for TWA when the United States government blunders and announces a desire to cancel current airmail contracts with civilian airlines and reassigns them to the United States Army Air Force (U.S.A.A.F.). Jack Frye, Vice President of Operations for TWA, is well aware of the ramifications of this decision, as the mail contracts are his airline's bread and butter.

On just one of several protest flights to various cities, Jack Frye arrives in Albuquerque, New Mexico on the new TWA showboat, Douglas Commercial 1 (NC223Y), the sleek aluminum twin-engine passenger transport Jack himself is responsible for creating.

Jack's intent with this visit is to extol the foolishness of the U.S. Government in reassigning all airmail contracts to Army pilots, who Frye states publicly are not qualified to undertake such hazardous operations. On this occasion, held on Saturday and Sunday, Frye underlines the ability of the airlines to carry the mail more efficiently and without loss of pilots. Frye also candidly discusses the detrimental effect this move on the government's part will have on airports and employees all across the nation, to include Albuquerque, in cutbacks, etc.

Traveling with Frye is the (then) president of T&WA, Richard W. Robbins; D.W. Tomlinson as Assistant to Robbins; Paul E. Richter, TWA Regional Superintendent; and TWA special guest Wiley Post, among other officials. The futuristic new airliner arrives from Los Angeles on Saturday, and after completion of several exhibition flights for excited airport visitors over the weekend, it continues to Kansas City (TWA's Operation's Center) by Sunday evening.

Soon after the Albuquerque presentation, Frye comes up with another public exhibition idea. He contacts his good friend Edward (Eddie) Rickenbacker, Vice-President and General Manager of Eastern Air Transport, a division of Northern American Aviation (soon to become Eastern Airlines by 1938). Jack reveals his plan to Rickenbacker, a plan executed the day before the current mail contracts are due to expire (February 19, 1934). With this grand cross-country gesture, Jack intends to prove to the United States Government that civilian airlines can carry the mail safer and faster!

'February 18, 19, 1934'

At 11:56 P.M., TWA's brand-new DC 1, christened the 'City of Los Angeles' is loaded to the bulkheads with U.S. Mail, this the last load of eastbound mail TWA is allowed to transport per the new decree by the U.S. Government.

After TWA ground crews notify Frye the transport is fueled and ready, Jack boards the one-of-a-kind futuristic airliner and settles in the left seat, along with his (honorary) co-pilot Captain Edward Rickenbacker in the right seat. Also on board are a contingency of TWA pilots to include Paul Richter and D.W. Tomlinson, both pilot the plane for short intervals. A lucky group of reporters board as well to document the cross-country flight.

Once in flight, Frye shares this cross-country record with Eddie Rickenbacker; however, Frye is actually the pilot for the majority of the flight, this because Rickenbacker does not possess a transport pilot's license, his time in the left seat is only a brief courtesy.

This last cross-country gesture by Frye convinces the U.S. Government, once and for all, to surrender 'delivery of the U.S. Mail' to the capable and efficient airlines.

'May 13, 1934'

Undeterred by dangerous thunderstorms in the west- chilling snow fronts and icing in the east- Jack Frye flashes from coast-to-coast, from Los Angeles to Newark (12-min stop at Kansas City for fuel and mail). Jack claims a transcontinental record with his new Northrop Gamma 2D, 11 hours 31 minutes, cruise-speed 227 M.P.H., peak speed 275 M.P.H., over 2609 miles. The Gamma carries 355 pounds of U.S. Mail and 85 pounds of express. With this second record-breaking flight, Frye drives his point home, yet again proving TWA can deliver the mail proficiently and swiftly! After Jack sets his Gamma down at Newark and taxies to a stop, excited reporters rush the plane.

The Northrop Gamma, built by John Northrop, is designed for fast efficient mail and express transport, with one pilot and a payload of 1000 pounds. Jack Frye was onboard with the development of these early Northrop designs. The rugged TWA Gamma is revolutionary and well suited for cross-country transport of mail and express—day or night.

Unfortunately, for the Gamma, the multi-use Douglas Commercial soon eclipses this capable speedster. The Gamma is short-lived only because of its limited size, the DC series airliners enable the airlines to fly the mail (and passengers) in a more efficient and profitable application.

These stalwart displays of leadership clearly demonstrate why it's Jack Frye who is remembered as the 'Father of TWA', as it is Frye who is always front and center, a tireless bulldog in the preservation and promotion of the airline he built up and nurtured in those early turbulent years. Time and time again, Frye steps up to the plate without hesitation, proving he is the 'heart and soul' of early Transcontinental & Western Air, Inc. from 1930-1947.

On December 6, 1934 (at just 30-years-old), Jack Frye is promoted to President of Transcontinental & Western Air.

Headline- 'Airline Head Missing In Snow Storm'

'Friday, January 11, 1935, 8:00 P.M.'

At the Albuquerque airport, ground personnel in white TWA overalls load express packages into the cargo-hold of Jack's 31-foot TWA Northrop Gamma mail plane, in route from Kansas City to Los Angeles. Meanwhile, buffeted by a cold icy front, 30-year-old Jack shivers, as he stows his briefcase and thermos in the cockpit.

Finally, one of the men shuts the forward hatch saying, "You're loaded, fueled, and ready Mr. Frye." "Thanks," Jack replies, as he climbs into the cockpit. Within moments, the massive SR 1820, 710 H.P. Wright Cyclone radial engine turns over and settles into a rumbled din. Jack motions for a ground crew member to pull the chocks and he slowly taxis out onto the dirt-pack runway. With clearance and landing lights illuminating the high desert runway, Jack's Gamma lifts off and disappears over the dark horizon, westbound for Los Angeles.

'8:40 P.M. Zuni Reservation- Arizona'

Punching through a blinding snow front, the TWA Northrop Gamma NR13757 descends low over the desert, as its momentum diminishes. Worriedly, Jack looks out each side of the cockpit while he studies his gauges carefully. The airspeed indicator shows 200 M.P.H. but it's dropping off fast. Jack plays with the choke; he listens with a keen ear as the radial starves for fuel, cutting out for seconds at a time. Jack exclaims over the whistling wind, "God damn it, that experimental carburetor deicer has failed, I won't make Winslow! Damned if I'm going to have to set her down, and in this blizzard too!" Jack scans the ground, looking from side to side, "I know Deep Lake Emergency Field is out here, but where?" he questions frantically, peering down at a sea of white. Jack monitors his altimeter and airspeed gauges closely, as the plane drops like a rock, the engine now sputtering at idle.

Finally, at 1000 feet, Jack throws back the cockpit slider and looks out toward the ground; however, nothing but darkness confronts him amid pelting snow and sleet. He reaches down and flips on the landing lights, which reveal a blinding white curtain of snow all around him. Jack guides the plane closer and closer to the desert floor, while studying his altimeter gauge closely. Finally, the engine fails completely and the prop winds to a stop. Jack frantically tries to restart the engine to no avail. It's too late though, as the Gamma's landing lights begin to illuminate juniper trees, sagebrush, and snow. Quickly, Jack looks at his gauges and calculates he is at about 105 M.P.H. As the Northrop drops to about 20 feet, Jack pulls back hard on the stick, which jerks the Gamma's nose up, the plane contacts the ground within seconds.

The silver TWA Gamma skids across the snowy desert floor like a sled, plowing up dirt, brush, and trees as it slides. At one point, the ship shudders and sinks in on one side, as the port pant and landing wheel tear off. At this, the 48-foot wide plane suddenly spins around and sloughs to a halt.

Within moments, a dazed Jack climbs out, slips on the wing, and falls into the snow piled up around the fuselage. Brushing the snow off, Jack pulls himself together, walks around the plane and accesses the damage—bent prop, broken landing gear, and juniper tree branches tangled in the undercarriage. "Damn it!" Jack exclaims, "I have to be in Los Angeles Monday morning!" Jack starts to gather wood and clears an area for a signal fire, which he successfully starts. Returning to the plane he tries to contact TWA at ABQ or WIN; however, his battery is weak, and he is not sure his transmissions are received. Finally, he retreats to the fire; standing with his back to the blizzard, he tries to warm his numb body. Jack pulls his aviator jacket close and secures his leather flight cap tight around his face, while coyotes yip in the distance after a late-night kill. The icy stars, like diamonds, spread out in a canopy over Jack's head, in between the fast-moving storm clouds of swirling snow.

'Saturday Afternoon, 3:27 P.M.'

Jack waits near his campfire. He cleans the snow off his Gamma to increase the visibility of the plane from the air, but he knows the silver plane will be hard to spot lodged in a sea of white. Jack looks down at his watch, "17 hours and yet I haven't seen a plane all day," he mumbles. Just then though, he cocks his head as he hears the sound of multiple Pratt and Whitney engines on the horizon. A moment later, Jack spots a TWA Ford Tri-motor approaching slowly from the west.

The airliner descends low over Jack's crash site and the signal fire. Jack waves at the ship with both arms as the pilot dips his wings to acknowledge a visual. After another pass, the plane slows and lands on a flat section of land. Unfortunately though, the ground has thawed and the plane bogs in before it rolls to a stop. Jack trudges through the snow over to the plane just as the pilot steps out. They both make their way around the ship while Jack kicks at a tire. "There's no way we'll get this ship out of this mud," states Jack disappointingly. The pilot, TWA's Major A.D. Smith says, "I'll radio for a truck from Winslow, now that we know your position. You'll be out of here in no time Mr. Frye." "The Gamma will have to be trucked out," says Jack. "Come on with me sir," says Smith, "I have some warm food and coffee for you from Winslow."

Later, after arriving in Winslow late Saturday evening, Frye checks into the La Posada Harvey House Hotel, where he regroups from his ordeal. On Sunday morning, he continues his journey to Los Angeles on a TWA airliner, with no doubt, an interesting tale of survival to share. Luckily, Jack is unharmed, except for what he describes to the press as a "rather bad cold" which he attributes to his exposure to the harsh elements. He also states his location was hard to pinpoint due to the signal fire fuel being too dry and emitting little smoke.

In Los Angeles, Jack connects with his French-born wife, Jean La-Coste. Within 15 days, they're winging their way back east on a TWA airliner, with stops at Winslow and Albuquerque. Life returns to status quo for Frye and TWA.

Headline- 'Hindenburg Departs Today, Millionaire's Flight, 6-State 10-Hour Tour. Passengers- Wealthiest Industrialists in Country'

'October 9, 1936'

The gargantuan Zeppelin Hindenburg moored at Lakehurst, New Jersey dwarfs a line of limousines and passengers preparing to board the massive airship.

Jack steps out of a long black 1935 Cadillac Fleetwood with his secretary who is carrying his briefcase and a valise of paperwork. The secretary stands back for a moment in awe as she gazes up at the ship, "My Lord, Mr. Frye, I've never seen such a ship!" Jack, dressed in a long camelhair topcoat and fedora, looks up at the massive ship and then over at his secretary, "It's big alright, that's a fact, but it won't ever rule the skies, not in this country!"

Later, in mid-flight, Jack stands in the port promenade with other V.I.P. passengers, while uniformed stewards serve drinks and hors d'oeuvres off sterling silver platters.

Numbered at 80, the other passengers are identified, in part: Nelson Rockefeller, grandson of the founder of Standard Oil; Winthrop W. Aldrich, C.E.O. of Chase Manhattan Bank (New York); John D. Hertz, transportation czar; Alvan T. Fuller, president of Packard Motor Company (Boston); Karl Lindemann, chairman of the board Hamburg-Amerika Line (North Bremen, Germany) and officer of Standard Oil Corporation; Dr. Hans Luther, German Ambassador to the United States; Rear Admiral William H. Standley, No.1 Sailor- Navy; Admiral A.B. Cooke, chief of the Bureau of Aeronautics, Commander Charles E. Rosendahl, Lakehurst Naval Station; Paul W. Litchfield, president of Goodyear Tire and Rubber (Akron Ohio); Capt. Edward (Eddie) V. Rickenbacker, general manager Eastern Air Lines; Eugene Luther Vidal, director of Air Commerce; Juan Trippe, Pan American Airways; Byron C. Foy, De Soto Motors president; Lucius B. Manning, Cord Automobile Corp.; and Thomas N. McCarter, president Public Service Corp. of New Jersey. N.B.C. is onboard as well, broadcasting live interviews with the V.I.P. passengers.

On a personal tour of the airship, Jack stands at the helm of the Hindenburg as Captain Ernst A. Lehmann coaches him on the art of navigation. Frye, speaking with a cigar at the corner of his mouth states, "She handles like a dream! You know Captain, if per chance this ship never makes it back to New Jersey, the entire commerce of the United States will be wiped out." They both smile cautiously at each other as Captain Lehmann replies confidently, "I can assure you Mr. Frye this could never happen. The Hindenburg is the safest airship in the world. She has a perfect safety record!"

On a country road bordered by trees dressed in autumn splendor, children run and cheer as the behemoth transport casts a shadow over them as it drones past overhead. The youngsters wave to passengers who are holding glasses of champagne as they peer down from the airship's open windows.

'March 1, 1938, 9:30 P.M.'

A twilight glow shrouds a heavily forested clearing in the High Sierras, just below the treacherous 9,698-foot Buena Vista Peak. Heavy snow is falling with a maddening pace, adding to the already yards of accumulation. In this hushed scene, the distant sound of radial engines approach, faintly, then louder and louder. From a viewpoint of tree level, a silver TWA DC-2 bursts through a bank of low clouds at full throttle, with its massive dual landing lights piercing the gloom from the nose.

The sleek aluminum plane flashes overhead at 200 M.P.H., the clearance and cabin lights cast an eerie glow over the snow-laden trees and icy meadow. As the ice-encrusted plane flashes by, a teenage boy and girl peer out of a backlit cabin window with a look of fear and desperation. The airliner disappears as quickly as it arrives into the snowy shroud. The engines, encased in ice, swirl the falling snow in vortexes at the plane's wake. As the foreign sound of the throbbing radials fade out over the horizon, silence returns to the hushed snow-covered forest.

Within 5 minutes, a massive explosion reverberates through the valley, accompanied by a small orange flash high on the horizon of Buena Vista Crest; then nothing further but stony silence and the frigid whistling wind.

**Headline- 'TWA Airliner Disappears In 'Storm Of The Century'
Over Treacherous Sierras. Massive Search Launched For 9-Miss-
ing Passengers & Crew'**

'March 2, 1938'

In the early dawn of Kansas City, a Cadillac coupe pulls up outside
the TWA executive offices at the municipal airport. As the auto
lurches to a stop, Jack Frye jumps out and rushes into the building,
pushing through a crowd of reporters. Jack's secretary is waiting in
the lobby and Jack motions for her to follow him. As the two reach
the door to his office, he turns to the reporters who have followed
him stating, "No comment men, I'll let you know as soon as I find
out what's going on out there. My secretary can give you the list of
passengers and crew in a moment."

Jack and his secretary enter his executive office and shut the door behind them. At his desk, Jack turns on a chrome reading light shaped
like a Douglas Commercial airliner. He turns back to his secretary
and says, "Clear my schedule, I'm leaving for Fresno immediately to
head the search. Time is of the essence." "Yes sir, Mr. Frye," she says.
"Should I book a westbound flight for you?" "No, too slow, I'll take
the Gamma. Have it ready and on standby. Call Boulder and tell
them I will be passing through." "Certainly, Mr. Frye," she replies as
she rushes from the office to meet with the reporters.

Soon after, a silver TWA Northrop Gamma NR13758 with lettering
'Experimental Overweather Laboratory' displayed on the fuselage,
lands at the Fresno Airport amid snow flurries. After the plane taxies
to a stop, Jack throws the cockpit slider back and steps down from
the plane.

Reporters inundate the magnanimous TWA president, who starts fielding questions. "Yes, I think we have a good chance of finding the plane in-between storm fronts." "What are their chances?" shouts a reporter from the rear. Frye looks out at the mountains before replying, "Very grave I fear, very grave boys." Another reporter steps forward, "Mr. Frye, we understand you're taking control of the search. Will you be searching for the lost passengers personally?" "Yes, I just flew in from Kansas City, via Amarillo and Boulder, as soon as my plane is serviced and fueled, I'll be taking off for the mountains. Now please, please, I have to go over the maps with the other men and coordinate the search." With that last comment, Jack heads off to the operations center.

Within an hour, Jack rushes out to the Gamma, starts the mighty cyclone engine and roars off toward the snow-laden Sierras. Frye returns well after dark, tired and disheartened; he and his men find no trace of wreckage.

'March 8, 1938'

Several days later, after many searches by air with no trace of the DC 2, let alone passengers or crew, Frye returns east with a heavy heart, back to the management of TWA. Only in June, as aided by a spring melt, is the plane finally located with no survivors. Frye pays a reward of $1000 to the hiker who eventually locates the wreck.

By the end of the 1930's, TWA has become one of the most successful airlines in the country. With two record flights under his belt, one with the Gamma from Los Angeles to Newark, and the other in the DC 1 with Eddie Rickenbacker from Los Angeles to New York, Frye had accomplished great things. This, aside from the research he completed with TWA Chief Test Pilot Tommy Tomlinson, (who also worked with Paul Richter), which opened the airline routes 'above the weather', a concept developed by Frye and TWA to avoid flight-path turbulence.

By 1938, Jack Frye and Howard Hughes join forces to purchase TWA, with Hughes' financial backing. Motivation is to enable Frye to operate the airline without interference from the current TWA Board of Directors. One of the first projects is the further development of the pressurized Lockheed Constellation airliner, already underway, which when completed will enable Transcontinental & Western Air, Inc. to pursue transatlantic passenger service.

Chapter 4

Innocence Lost

'Clarksburg, West Virginia- 1918'

"Helen! Helen Varner! Pay attention!" the teacher demands, as she speaks to Helen, who is staring out the window caught up in a daydream. A sudden chill overtakes Helen, a strange feeling of joy and emptiness. "What am I feeling?" muses Helen.

"Are we disturbing you Missy, or do you think you might give some thought to the question?" continues the stern teacher. Helen pulls herself out of the strange daydream and focuses on her surroundings. "Oh, how I hate this dreary classroom," Helen thinks to herself. "I refuse to stay here and throw my life away," she laments. The class giggles with glee over the interruption and the annoyance of the teacher. At last, with the disruption over the class returns to its dull drudgery.

Days later, a clock ticks loudly within a small shabby room, a young Helen sits in the shadows on an old worn bench observing the scene around her. "Simple, sparse and boring," Helen mutters to herself, "just like all the other shacks in this valley!" Suddenly, the moaning of a woman in labor interrupts Helen's thoughts.

Helen rises and walks over to the other side of the open room to a big brass bed. She observes her father and a mid-wife prepare to deliver a newborn. In the harsh light of a single bare bulb hanging from the ceiling, Helen's father appears strong and competent, tall and godly, in his white shirt and tie. In Helen's eyes, he's a marvelous healer, well respected in the community and always there to aid those who need medical care. Helen desires to be just like him, healing all the people of the countryside, bringing peace to the weary bodies and minds of people. The squalling of a baby boy startles Helen; frightened and terrified he cries for comfort. "What will his life be like," Helen wonders as she watches her father hand him to the mother. "Will he be strong and successful, or weak and sickly?"

'March of 1932'

Helen's mother, Maude, helps Helen with her suitcases. "I still worry about your going all the way out there," she says as she fusses with the luggage. "It's no place for a young lady!" "Mother, I'll be fine!" protests Helen as she continues to pack all the things she thinks she will need.

At last, Helen stands back and takes a long look at her surroundings to see if she is missing any crucial items. "Is this the last time," she wonders, "is this it?" "I wish Daddy were here Mother, I need him now more than ever," Helen says emotionally.

In that vulnerable moment, Helen feels herself drain of strength, she feels so lost and alone. Maude stops what she is doing and sweeps Helen up in her loving arms as only a mother can do. Helen immerses herself in the comforting fragrance of lilac and starched linens as Maude holds her tight to her bosom. "So many needed Daddy, and then he was gone. We have to continue on, to be strong," her mother whispers. Then she adds, "Helen, pay attention to your visions, you have a very special gift. Don't ever take that for granted."

The long blast of a steam whistle assails the quiet morning, Helen jumps a bit, nervous now as she boards her train. She settles into a comfortable mohair seat. Outside the window, her mother and sisters wave with hankies, tears flowing. Helen waves back with a feeling of excitement and trepidation in her heart. Amid urgent blasts of a whistle, the train starts lurching and tugging as it steams away. The scene soon fades as the train picks up speed across the West Virginia countryside to Chicago.

As Helen stares out at the view, she contemplates her future. She knows full well her hometown of Clarksburg is the kind of place where a person would never venture unless they were born there or worse yet, lost! Well off the beaten path, certainly, the town was a beloved and peaceful hamlet; however, in Helen's mind it was full of unrealized dreams. To Helen, this environment was simply not glamorous or exciting enough for her. Something else was surely waiting, something monumental, and far away from Clarksburg! Recently, Helen had attended Wesleyan College, and the Institute of Art at Chicago. With this exposure, Helen had experienced the exciting world beyond Clarksburg, and she had no intention of staying!

Helen studies her reflection in the glass. She knows she is no slouch, perhaps more so a 'voluptuous vision', at least that's how a former beau described her to practically everyone he knew, despite Helen's objections! One thing Helen knows, she is radiantly beautiful and sexy, and men fall all over her. In her heart, Helen is well aware this alone will open doors for her, aside from her other creative talents. Yes, Helen is determined she will not spend the rest of her life in a backwoods West Virginia town. "Save that fate for those who aren't brave enough to get out," Helen declares to herself.

Helen soon settles into the easy sway of the coach. Gazing out on the hills and dales, her mind wanders back to the last year. She wonders how life could have gone so wrong for her. She had married a young boy she felt was terrific, a local athlete, and later a high school coach. They had lived together for about seven months, but it just wasn't meant to be, they both knew that. Finally, after many arguments and late-night tears, Helen decided she had to get out. She refused to end up like a many of her friends, miserable, and just pretending to be happy.

A conductor makes his way down the aisle, he looks up from his duties to see the most beautiful young woman sitting in front of him. She possesses a certain vulnerability, making her appear even more lovely and fragile. As he approaches he says, "May I have your ticket Miss?" "Certainly," replies Helen with an absentminded smile as she locates it in her handbag and hands it to him. "Well, well, all the way to Reno, Miss? That's a long trip and your being so young and all," he remarks politely.

Instantly, the conductor knows it must be a divorce, that's the reason for the sadness. "People don't go to Reno unless they're getting a divorce," he muses to himself. The man punches Helen's ticket and continues with his duties. In his mind though, he wonders how such a beautiful young lady is not loved and cherished by some lucky young man.

Later, after transferring to the westbound Atchison, Topeka & Santa Fe, at Chicago, Helen finds her way to the busy dining room car. She sits down at a table of refinement, complete with starched white linens. A waiter comes up and takes her order, "Cream of Wheat please, with coffee, black," says Helen politely, "Would you like some toast Miss?" "Yes, that would be nice," says Helen. As he walks away, Helen notices what a considerate man he is; however, she senses a subservient manner in his interaction with her. This saddens her, as she just doesn't believe in non-equality. "He's African-American, yes, but he's no different than the rest of my peers," she muses. Helen hopes this attitude will change in her lifetime. She always goes out of her way to be kind to those who are in different positions in life than she.

Finishing her generous breakfast, Helen retires to the parlor car where she finds a quiet place to sit down. The car is empty, except for six men playing cards in a corner, they look up briefly as Helen settles in a window seat by a small table. The countryside has changed from green and lush, to the wide-open prairies of the Midwest, past lonely farmhouses and cattle, winding on through a world Helen knows only from books. "The vistas are so vast out here," Helen muses, "I love it, I can see forever, and there are no trees and hills to block my views!" The steady lurching of the coach, coupled with the occasional blast of the whistle, proves hypnotic. Helen soon dozes, as her head falls against the glass.

'Dream of Sedona'

'In a verdant clearing, Helen is surrounded by dancing Indians, their chanting foreign to her, yet entrancing. She feels so at peace, so moved by the music—another life it seems. Helen looks around to see the most beautiful gurgling stream adjoined by towering pinnacles of sandstone red rocks, all complemented by giant deciduous trees, their canopies a lush umbrella over it all. The mysterious chanting grows louder and louder, as the surreal dream vaporizes.'

Helen awakes with a jolt. The loud clicking and screeching of the train startles her, as it lurches onto a siding to let a speeding freight pass. As her sleepy eyes take in the scene outside her window, her mind wanders back to her unusual dream. Helen's body feels electrified by the vision, as if it were a real place, somewhere, somehow. "But there couldn't possibly be a place which is so enchanting, so lovely," says Helen with wonder. The feeling fades as Helen picks up her drugstore novel and loses herself in the romantic distraction.

After a while, Helen notices a couple of men in the corner watching her politely; they look away each time she looks up. One is a tall-refined man, somewhat attractive, and very well dressed. Helen gathers her things and leaves the car, on the way out she hears the conductor announce they are pulling into Albuquerque, New Mexico.

As the train rolls to a stop, Helen steps down to the platform, which adjoins the Alvarado Hotel. "30-minutes," announces the conductor in a loud voice, "30-minutes folks!" Helen makes her way through the crowd into the Harvey House dining room and finds a seat at the lunch counter. As she orders a sandwich and coffee, she notices the man from the train step into the cafeteria. Quietly, he takes a seat near a window. Helen senses he is interested in her; he keeps glancing over as Helen quietly finishes her lunch.

Finally, after finishing a last sip of coffee, Helen rises and walks outside and back to The Chief. She pauses and reaches in her handbag to find her pack of cigarettes, as she searches for her lighter she hears a man's voice behind her. "Would you like a light Miss?" Helen turns around to find the voice belongs to the well-dressed man from the parlor car.

"Why yes, thank you," says Helen gracefully as the man's gold-plated lighter flashes in the sunlight. Helen leans forward, lowers her eyes, lights her cigarette, and inhales. After a moment she exhales, the blue smoke circles around them. Helen smiles, "I don't think we've met?" she says demurely.

The man bows slightly saying, "Cornelius Vanderbilt, Miss." "I'm pleased to meet you Mr. Vanderbilt," Helen says politely, "my name's Helen Varner." Helen observes the man, "A Vanderbilt, oh, she knew the name, everyone did. The Vanderbilt Biltmore Mansion was south of where she grew up. Wonder how this one's related?" she ponders. "Wonderful weather, don't you think?" he says interrupting her thoughts. "Why yes," Helen replies, looking around at Albuquerque, "quite lovely." They continue to chat for the remainder of the stop. Finally, they hear 'All-A-Board' and move toward the train with the other passengers. As they enter the coach, Cornelius asks Helen if he might join her later in the lounge car. "Why thank you," says Helen. "How about we meet in 30 minutes?" "Splendid!" Vanderbilt replies as he slips away.

Helen returns to her compartment to freshen up. Strangely, she's attracted to this older man, this strong mysterious stranger. Helen stands in front of the mirror and assesses her appearance. Quickly, she adjusts herself, brushes her tousled hair and refreshes her makeup, reapplying 'Raspberry Red' to her lips. Helen changes from a traveling suit, she had designed herself, to more suitable evening attire. Low cut, the smart frock enhances her ample breasts. Bending over, Helen quickly slips into a pair of silver heels. As she leaves the tiny space, she grabs a wrap and beaded handbag.

Helen makes her way forward through the gently lurching train. As she enters the lounge car, she looks around to see many elegantly dressed men and women visiting. Many of the men take notice as Helen gracefully makes her way over to where Vanderbilt awaits. Cornelius rises and helps Helen settle into an upholstered chair. "What would you like?" he says politely. "A ginger ale," Helen replies. Cornelius turns around and snaps his fingers; an attendant immediately comes over. "The lady will have a ginger ale, and I will have the same," he states briskly. "Yes sir Mr. Vanderbilt," says the waiter. Vanderbilt turns back to Helen and smiles warmly, "Won't it be nice when prohibition is repealed, and we can order drinks again?" Helen nods in agreement, "Yes, won't it," she replies. Soon they're both relaxed, talking about their lives and travels. "Please, call me Neil," Cornelius says at one point, preferring his nickname.

Within an hour, the two rise and make their way to the dining car. As they enter, a porter immediately comes over to assist them. "Good evening, please, right this way Mr. Vanderbilt." At the mention of the Vanderbilt name the other diners turn and smile, watching Helen and Neil as if they were royalty. After they are seated, the maître d' inquires, "I hope this will be suitable Mr. Vanderbilt." "Yes, yes, it's fine," Neil says offhandedly, "What do you recommend this evening?"

Later, after a delectable dinner, Helen touches the corner of her linen napkin to her mouth. "I think," she says with a smile, "it's time for me to retire." "May I walk you to your sleeper car?" Neil questions, as he stands up and helps Helen with her chair.

At the door to her compartment, Neil reaches out and takes Helen's hand. "I hope I can spend more time with you," he says gently, as his lips kiss the back of her hand. "I would like that," Helen says quietly, "very much so!" she adds blushing. Neil continues to look her in the eye, "Perhaps, you could join me in the morning for breakfast, at, let's say 8 A.M.?" "That would be lovely," Helen replies, as she steps out of the corridor into her cabin. With a racing heart, she shuts the door behind her.

As Helen drifts off to sleep, her mind contemplates the remnants of another person's life. 'Here was a man, one of the most eligible bachelors in America, son of Cornelius Vanderbilt III, the 'Brigadier General' as they call him, and his mother, socialite Grace Graham Wilson Vanderbilt, a couple considered the reigning leaders of New York high society. Helen had once read that Cornelius Jr. was a renegade in regard to his pedigree. Oh yes, and his great grandfather was the Commodore, the family's founder; however, Cornelius marched to the beat of his own drummer. He had attended the finest schools, traveled Europe extensively, and grew up at 640 Fifth Avenue, one of the finest addresses in the country. Inheritance, very generous, and a mother and father, who it appears always paid his expenses and doted on him.

According to the society columns, Cornelius loved beautiful women, and had already been married twice, the last wife named Mary Weir Logan. Neil was 32, and Helen 22, it seems Cornelius was quite out of her league, or was he? Helen prided herself as being a fashionable young lady, a bit worldly with finesse' and class—not a blue blood mind you, but from a comfortable background, and always able to blend in flawlessly at any level of society.'

It was after 3 A.M. before Helen finally drops off to sleep, her dreams filled with the grand life Neil laid at her feet. Eventually, Helen arrives in Reno, a dreary wind-swept town, Cornelius had continued to Los Angeles where he was attending business. Helen quickly files her divorce proceedings and by Tuesday, April 26, her decree is granted.

One day, the phone rings, it's Neil! 'He would be in Reno the next evening and would Helen meet him for dinner?' Helen is ready and waiting when the desk calls to say, 'Mr. Vanderbilt is waiting in the lobby'. She takes the elevator down, and she and Neil walk outside where a chauffeur helps them into a Packard town car, driving them to a quaint restaurant.

The next day, Helen and Vanderbilt travel in the Packard out to Neil's dude ranch, 40 miles north of Reno at Sutcliffe. Vanderbilt had cleverly bought several of these town cars from the White House, at times when they updated their fleet, to use on his guest ranch. Mostly they shuttle passengers to and from the train station to his ranch. Neil's spread was where he did a lot of his writing. On the journey east, he tells Helen about one of his more famous novels called 'RENO', published in 1928. The subject was celebrity divorces and Reno, Nevada, which was the 'divorce capitol' of the United States.

Finally, after a long journey, the big black sedan pulls through the gates of the ranch. Helen notices the name 'Lazy ME' swinging over the entrance. Neil relates the ranch is one of the more famous ones in the area, offering lodging for Reno divorce seekers. The price includes the Reno quick-divorce too! The in-hiding guests of Neil's celebrity get-a-way enjoy a horse to ride, twice-weekly trips to the biggest little city in the world (Reno), and all the cigarettes and liquor they require. The operation is quite similar to the guest ranch featured in 'The Women' (1935).

Chapter 5

A Glittered Life Beckons

'August 1934'

Helen and Cornelius tour Europe—they travel the countryside of England, France, Austria, Switzerland, the Orient, and North Africa. At one point, Neil writes Helen's mother in Clarksburg, West Virginia:

'Dear Mrs. Varner: This is the fifth day of rain. We came to Switzerland to get away from the heat of Paris, which Helen couldn't stand anymore, and this was the result. Helen is now sick of rain and wants to get back to France again! We have zigzagged all over Europe to please her. Next, we shall try Austria! Helen thinks Holland might be better or North Africa! They are only 1,000 miles apart! We are having fun though- Much Love, Neil'

At last, back in the states, the two are staying at Albuquerque, while Helen is sketching, and Neil is writing. At this point, after 3 years of dating, the two decide to get married. They set the event for January 5, 1935; announcing it to no one. They choose Albuquerque, as this is where they first met. Neil is Episcopalian, and since both parties have been married previously, they find no clergy who will perform the ceremony. This disappoints Helen, who has the uneasy feeling that a pall has settled over the event, she remembers her mother's comment about dis-ease and premonitions.

Finally though, she and Neil find a Justice of the Peace, L.M. Tartaglia, at the Bernalillo Courthouse, who graciously performs the nuptials. Tartaglia's sister is a witness, along with a constable, who just happens to be in the office reading a newspaper. On the marriage license, Vanderbilt lists his age as 36 and Helen at 26.

Reporters corner the two downtown for news of the society marriage. One of the questions is whether Cornelius is 'little Gloria Vanderbilt's father?' Neil laughs at this, replying, "Actually, my father is Gloria's uncle, I'm her cousin." The Vanderbilt marriage garners an incredible amount of nation-wide press. Overnight Helen Varner becomes a society celebrity!

The senior Vanderbilts send a telegram congratulating the newlyweds, asking them to come stay at '640' in New York City for an extended visit.

Neil and Helen stay in a suite at the Alvarado Hotel. On their wedding night Vanderbilt pricks Helen with a red rose before making love—a strange fetish he has, something Helen is not prepared for which leaves her uneasy.

Finally, the marriage behind them, the couple leaves for Williams, Arizona and the Grand Canyon, on a preliminary honeymoon. Later, they travel through Boulder City, staying for one night at the Boulder Dam Hotel, then, on to Neil's Ranch at Pyramid Lake. By January 26, the Vanderbilts are staying at the celebrity resort, El Mirador at Palm Springs. Afterwards, they take a train to New York City.

'Spring 1935'

Western Union- 1935, Feb 23,

'Have just been telephoning Neil and we hope so much you and Neil will come to us next Tuesday evening and stay as long as you can. We want so much to have you make us a visit and hope you can arrange to come then.

Love Affectionately, Grace Vanderbilt

Six Forty Fifth Avenue'

A glossy maroon 1913 Rolls Royce Brewster town car pulls up to an imposing 4-story mansion on 5th Avenue in Manhattan. A matching footman attired in Vanderbilt-maroon briskly walks to the door of the motorcar as it glides to a stop. Cornelius Vanderbilt steps out, "Welcome Mr. Vanderbilt," the footman says stiffly as he helps Helen and Neil out of the limo. He ushers the couple to the front door where a butler steps up and takes their coats. "Your mother is in the drawing room Mr. Vanderbilt," the butler states crisply, "please, right this way." The three continue into a large two-story gold leaf and tapestry-hung receiving room.

Neil's mother is sitting on a sofa, while his father sits in an overstuffed chair. The father gets up and walks over to them, shakes Neil's hand and says, "Welcome home son." He then turns to Helen and says, "I'm Neil's father, welcome to New York dear, and thank you for coming to see us." Helen smiles warmly as he reaches out for her hand, which he brushes with a kiss. The three proceed over to where Neil's mother Grace is sitting. Mrs. Vanderbilt reaches out to Helen and greets her formally, "How do you do dear, I am so pleased to have you here." She pats the sofa cushion next to her saying, "Please, please, now sit down and tell me all about yourself."

While the two visit, Neil and his father sit on the other side of the grand salon. The butler wheels a sterling silver bar cart over to them and prepares cocktails. After a moment, he wheels it over to Helen and asks her what she would like. "A martini please," says Helen. After handing Helen her drink, he stands back formally and addresses Grace, "When would you like dinner served, Madam?"

Several dozen guests sit around a massive baroque dinner table, formally set, murmuring quietly among themselves. Gracing the gilded scene, six servants stand formally at the side of the room to serve the courses and attend the guests. Helen and Neil sit at the side of Neil's father, with Grace, at the head of the table.

After dinner, and before dessert, the elder Vanderbilt turns to Helen and tells her what a beautiful young lady she is, and that he hopes she and Neil will be very happy. "I want you to have this," he says as he pulls a long black velvet Cartier case out of his breast pocket and hands it to Helen. Gingerly, Helen opens the case, which reveals a stunning gold and platinum watch, heavily encrusted with diamonds. Mr. Vanderbilt says, "May I?" as he reaches over Helen, removes the watch and attaches it to Helen's extended arm. "There my darling, now you're officially a 'Vanderbilt Wife', I had this made especially for you." Helen, overcome with the old man's gesture, leans over with misty eyes and kisses him softly on the cheek. "Thank you," she says with emotion. "It's absolutely exquisite!" Neil adds, "Thank you father, what a thoughtful gift." He smiles at Helen with pride.

Meanwhile, Grace, who never misses a thing at her dinner table, sees this display and quickly summons her husband over to sit by her with the snap of her finger. Within moments, Grace has her husband engaged with her other guests.

'March 4, 1935'

Neil and Helen are at the Shoreham Hotel in Washington D.C., having just visited 90-cities in two months on Vanderbilt's lecture tour. Helen takes the train home to see her mother for a brief visit. Within weeks, she and Neil connect at Hollywood, where Vanderbilt's 'A Woman of Washington' is in its third week of film production.

'March 22, 1935'

The Vanderbilts are staying at the Miami Biltmore Hotel and luxuriate in the sun at the adjoining Roney Plaza Cabana Sun Club, having come down by train from New York City for a 10-day late winter vacation.

'June 1935'

Neil and Helen, and her family from West Virginia, tour the Warner Bros. 'Dr. Socrates' movie set at Hollywood. The group enjoys lunch with Ann Dvorak and Paul Muni, the stars of the production.

'June 22, 1935'

As V.I.P. guests, Neil and Helen attend the Annual Commodore's Boat Inspection of the Lake Arrowhead Yacht Club and Annual Water Parade. Later that evening, the Vanderbilts attend a dinner and dance at the North Shore Tavern. Neil and Helen are staying at their home on the lake.

'July 26, 1935'

Los Angeles newspapers report, 'Mr. and Mrs. Cornelius Vanderbilt, Jr. are staying at the Grand Hotel in Santa Monica where they are spending their time entertaining, sun-tanning, and dipping in the Pacific. When not out west, the two divvy their time between Nevada and New York.'

By August 1, Neil and Helen close their home at Lake Arrowhead and head east for New York City on the all-Pullman Atchison, Topeka & Santa Fe Chief.

'October 1935'

On a balmy Saturday evening, the Vanderbilts dine at the Lake Arrowhead Lodge. After finishing dinner, Neil excuses himself and leaves Helen sitting alone for some time. Finally, Helen gets up from the table seeking Neil, wondering where in the world he disappeared. At last, Helen finds him in a shadowed alcove, locked in an embrace with a beautiful young woman. Helen quietly slips back to their table before Neil can spot her. As she finishes her coffee, painfully, she remembers the other times she has caught Neil with different women.

Since Helen met Neil in 1932, she was well aware of his amorous wooing of women, but she thought his behavior would change once they were married.

Neil interrupts her thoughts as he returns to the table; his attitude is nonchalant and detached. "I wondered where you had disappeared to for so long," Helen states casually without looking at him. "Oh, I was talking to a business associate," replies Neil as he looks longingly across the room at the blond-haired beauty he had just been embracing. After a moment, Helen responds, her voice tense with emotion. "I saw you with her, please take me home Neil." Without a word, Neil snaps his finger for the waiter, asks for the bill, signs it, and he and Helen walk over to the entrance. Neil asks the coat-check girl for Helen's mink stole and helps Helen slip it on. The two walk out into the warm night where Neil helps Helen into his 1930 custom-made Packard 740 roadster. They drive home in stony silence along the lake reflected in moonlight. Finally, they reach the long driveway to their mansion, Neil pulls in and parks at the rear by the carriage house.

Late the next afternoon, Helen Vanderbilt sits on a brocade sofa at the center of a large drawing room framed by dark Edwardian wood panels. Beside Helen is a large open box with a full-length mink coat spilling out, adjoined by chocolates and roses. Neil, holding a low-ball bourbon, leans on a grand piano in front of massive floor-to-ceiling windows framing Lake Arrowhead. Neil's demeanor is of extreme exasperation—while Helen's, on the other hand, is of anger and annoyance. Helen curtly snaps at Neil, "I will not have you running around the country with other women, then attempting to buy back my affections with furs and roses! You promised me our marriage would be better than that!"

Neil looks down at the rich red and green Turkish carpet, and then up at Helen. He speaks coldly, "Helen, I said I'm sorry, the girl meant nothing to me, I love you, our marriage is sound." With that, Helen looks at him with distain. "*Sound*, you mean after what, at least seven women? How many more do I have to read about in the society columns and hear about from my friends?" Helen pauses as she reaches for a cigarette; the room is heavy with silence. She lights it, pauses, and then exhales. With a sigh she says, "I want out Neil, you can have your women, but you can't have me."

It's evident this comment enrages Cornelius who angrily retorts, "You want out? Who the hell do you think you are? You, my pretty, are a Vanderbilt wife! You *have* no rights! I decide what you'll put up with and what you won't!" Helen ignores this chauvinistic statement as she continues coolly, "Neil, we both agreed if this marriage didn't work, after three years of a great friendship, we would call it quits. I want out and that's that!" After a moment, Helen continues emotionally, "You're a womanizer, Neil! You've embarrassed me for the last time and I simply won't have it!"

With this last comment, Cornelius strides over to Helen in four short steps, he grabs her, pulls her up like a rag doll and strikes her hard across the face, while screaming, "Nobody leaves me, nobody! I'll decide when to cut you loose Baby!" Helen is horrified and completely unprepared for this violent reaction. She knows Neil has a quick temper, and realizes, too late, she handled this all wrong. She stares back at him while she holds her hand to her red cheek. Helen's anger rises, "How dare you strike me," she exclaims through her tears. "I'll ruin you Neil, I'm not one of your cheap floozies!"

At this retort, Neil grabs Helen by the wrist. With clenched teeth, he drags her up three flights of stairs as Helen desperately struggles to get loose. At the end of a long hallway, he flings open a heavy-paneled door with his free hand, and then throws Helen in with the other. Helen lands in a heap in the darkened room. Cornelius screams at her as he slams the door, "Nobody leaves me, nobody!" Helen hears the metallic sound of a key turning, then heavy steps descending the stairs.

Helen peers around in the shadows, all alone, locked in a tower with nothing but gloom to witness her soft whimpering. Hours later, Helen again hears the lock turn, she looks up with trepidation as their English-maid Geneva enters with a tray of food. "Mr. Vanderbilt asked me to bring this up Ma'am. Is there anything else I can get for you?" she says in her heavy accent as she sets the tray down. "Yes, actually there is," says Helen desperately. "You can get me out of here! I want you to call a friend for me in Los Angeles." Geneva protests, "Oh Ma'am, I just can't, I dare not get involved, I'm sure Mr. Vanderbilt will let you out soon, and be very sorry indeed! He'd surely fire me if I'd release you, surely he would!" Geneva backs out of the room, shuts the door and locks it.

Later, after Vanderbilt leaves the mansion for dinner, Geneva, in a moment of deep empathy, sneaks back up to the locked room. After slipping in, she asks Helen, "Who should I call Ma'am?" Helen starts crying and hugs the young girl. "Thank you, oh thank you Geneva," she whispers emotionally.

In the kitchen of the mansion, Geneva dials a big black telephone, the words "Beverly Hills Hotel" spills from the receiver. Geneva asks for "Mrs. Garnett Gardiner". After a pause we hear only parts of the conversation, "Yes, this is Garnett, he did what? My Lord, that beast! Why of course I'll help!"

The girl explains Garnett need come up tomorrow afternoon when Cornelius leaves for the yacht club, drive around to the rear of the mansion and enter through the service entrance. The door will be unlocked, "Oh, and the door key? It will be hanging next to the servant bells, tag says turret room." Geneva abruptly hangs up.

That night, an exhausted Helen rests on a fainting coach in her dark tower room with a silk fringe blanket pulled up to her chin. Suddenly, she awakens with a start! She hears a sound, as her eyes adjust to the darkness; she makes out a form standing over her. Silhouetted in defused light spilling in from the open doorway, Helen is terrified to see its Neil, crouching just inches from her face. With a wild look and bulging eyes, his breath is hot on her cheek as he stares down at her. Helen is too terrified to move! She looks at him fearfully, "Is this it," she thinks frantically, "is he going to kill me?" Then, as quickly as he appears, he's gone. The door shuts, the key turns, and Helen is alone again, trembling in her prison of shadows.

The next day, late in the afternoon, Garnett arrives at Lake Arrowhead with a male friend in a Lincoln coupe. They negotiate the winding lake drive until they get within sight of the stone mansion. Pulling off at a scenic viewpoint, they watch the house from afar. Within a short time, they see a big Packard convertible pull out of the long driveway and continue past them toward town. "Well, that takes care of Neil," says Garnett to her friend, "let's continue now." The man guides the car out onto the road and turns through the gates of the Tudor chateau, continuing around back to the service entrance, where they both exit the coupe.

The two quickly scurry through the rear door. On a hook, below six servant bells, Garnett grabs a key. They hurry through the kitchen, out into a large dining room and up the main staircase. At the third level, they see a door at the end of a long corridor. Garnett knocks gently and calls out, "Helen, darling, are you there?" They both hear a muffled voice from behind the heavy paneled door and the words, "Yes Garnett, it's me, please, please hurry!" Helen urges, "Do you have the key?" Garnett quickly fumbles with the key and turns the lock. When she pushes the massive door open, Helen practically falls out into their arms. "Thank God, Garnett, I thought I would never get out. I am so happy you didn't leave for Shanghai yet!" Garnett soothingly puts her arm around Helen and comforts her. "Come on dear, we have to get out of here, *right now*!"

The three start back to the main staircase, but Helen thinks better of it saying, "No, come on this way, down the servant's staircase, it leads straight to the kitchen." Once downstairs, Helen says, "Please, wait a moment while I gather a few personal items and my two dogs." Helen leaves the two in the kitchen and exits to the dining area, soon after she returns with a Great Dane and a police dog. "There, there," she coos as she comforts the excited dogs who had been contained. "Helen dear, please, let's do hurry, he could come back any moment," Garnett pleas urgently. At last, Helen says, "I'm ready."

They all exit through the rear of the chateau and over to Helen's car which is parked at the carriage house. Helen herds her dogs into her 1934 Chrysler coupe, where they settle on the red-leather seats. Garnett and her companion continue to their automobile parked nearby. The sun is orange as it plays through the trees, reflecting on the lake behind the house. Suddenly Helen cries out, "Oh my, I forgot my purse Garnett, I'll only be a moment! You two go ahead and start back down the mountain, I'll follow you in a minute!" Garnett hesitates, but with a worried look she says, "Well, O.K., but Helen please hurry. We'll meet you at the hotel later." Helen replies, "Of course Garnett, and thank you so much for rescuing me, I'll be fine now, I have my dogs to protect me."

With that, Helen disappears into the dark mansion, and Garnett's Lincoln speeds off down the driveway and back toward the valley. Helen gathers her purse and a few more items, taking longer than expected. Finally though, she makes her way back out to her Chrysler. Helen starts the engine and quickly backs out of the carriage house. She puts the car in gear, releases the clutch, and pulls around the house and out on to the lake drive. The sun has set and its dark.

As Helen drives toward town, she nervously watches behind and in front of her automobile for other cars, she relaxes a bit when she sees no one on the road. Suddenly though, right before she passes a turn toward town, a large automobile with big headlamps turns her way and starts toward her. Helen's heart freezes as she watches the car come closer and closer. "It just couldn't be," she says to herself nervously as the car passes on her left. She watches her rearview mirror as the big car slows and makes a wide turn in the road and starts to follow her in a cloud of dust. "It's him," says Helen fearfully. "I thought he would be gone all evening!"

Helen stomps on the accelerator and the car leaps forward; however, it's obvious Helen's Chrysler is no match for Neil's powerful Packard, which quickly gains on her from behind. In a moment, the big car is on her tail with engine throbbing. Helen begins to drop down the canyon road, careening around several hairpin turns. Gripped with fear and shaking, Helen is nearly blinded by the Packard's oversized headlamps, which flood her car from behind. Helen cries out frantically to her dogs, "I can't see the road darlings!" Her dogs whimper anxiously as Helen flies around a hairpin corner, too fast, and the coupe skids toward an embankment in a cloud of gravel and dust. The car nearly careens off the road and over a cliff before the tires suddenly grip and the car edges back on the highway. But, it's too late! Neil's powerful car edges around Helen and forces her back off the pavement. Helen slams her foot hard on the brake, the coupe skids in the soft dirt, sliding to a stop in a cloud of dust.

Neil jumps out of his idling Packard, quickly, he walks back to Helen's car. Helen, finding herself trapped, is unable to back up or go forward because of the cliff. Quickly, she rolls the driver's window up tight and locks both doors. Neil, who has reached the driver's side of the car, yells through the glass, his face contorted in rage, "Where do you think you're going Helen? Open this door right now! I'm taking you back home!" Helen is frozen, too scared to utter a word; however, her blood runs cold as she notices a tire iron in Neil's clenched fist! "He's going to kill me!" Helen thinks with terror. Neil raises the tire iron, ready to smash the window, when suddenly, Helen's dogs jump over her and lunge at him. Helen slides back on the bench seat. "He may smash the window, but my dogs will surely kill him!" she says under her breath. In a mad frenzy, the dogs, teeth bared, claw at the glass with malice, viciously growling and barking at the threat! Neil, with a look of fear on his face, suddenly, leaps back onto the highway, almost falling over backwards.

At that moment, another car appears from around the bend and approaches from behind. Neil looks back at the car, and then at Helen and the snarling dogs, his eyes wild. He yells, "This isn't over, you're still my wife, I'll never give you a divorce! You'll get nothing from me, nothing!" With that threat, he tucks the tire iron under his sport jacket and walks briskly back to his automobile. Neil jumps in and throws the Packard in gear, the powerful auto leaps forward spraying Helen's coupe with gravel and dirt. The huge motorcar spins in a circle back on to the highway, just missing the oncoming sedan, which slows, as it pulls up beside Helen. Neil's Packard roars back up the canyon in a cloud of dust.

A woman rolls down the passenger window and calls out to Helen, "Goodness gracious Miss! Do you need help? What in the world is going on here?" Helen gingerly rolls the window down as she watches her rear-view mirror reflecting Neil's Packard racing back to Lake

Arrowhead. Petrified with fright she addresses the kindly woman saying, "I'm fine now, uh, really I am, I'll be O.K." Then, Helen adds in a shaky voice, "Please go on, really, I'm fine. Thank you for stopping to help!" With a trembling voice Helen adds, "You saved my life, God Bless You!"

The woman looks at Helen with compassion, then to her left at the male driver and back to Helen again. Slowly, the car pulls away as the two mutter to each other and look back. Helen watches the taillights disappear leaving her in inky darkness. The dark mountain swallows Helen up but for her dim dash lights and yellow headlights. At last, Helen begins to relax, her chest heaves, as tears roll down her face. She collapses and begins to sob uncontrollably, her breath coming in short gasps.

It seems like an eternity before Helen feels strong enough to continue. Finally, with her left foot, she depresses the clutch and puts the car in gear. Slowly, she pulls back on the road toward the safety of Los Angeles and The Beverly Hills Hotel where Garnett is waiting. Helen's red tail markers disappear into the dark void of the isolated canyon.

After Helen leaves Vanderbilt, they never live together or speak again, except through telegrams and attorneys, for five long years. True to Cornelius' word, he refuses to grant Helen a divorce. Rather, he insists on a reconciliation of sorts, never once considering Helen's plea to set her free. Helen is his prisoner.

'November 7, 1935'

Newspapers report a rift in the Vanderbilt marriage. Surprisingly, within a day, Neil Vanderbilt's attorneys, Max D. Steuer and Samuel Platt, confirm the rumor. The story spreads nationwide.

A newsreel re-plays shipside film footage captured in August of 1934 showing First Class Passengers boarding the transatlantic ocean liner M.V. Britannic. The camera zooms in on Cornelius Vanderbilt, Jr., and his fashionably dressed companion, Helen V. Varner. Confetti rains down on the couple as they proceed up the gangplank smiling and waving to friends on the dock. An announcer narrates the film:

"News-Flash! New York City society scion and his lovely West Virginia bride are already contemplating divorce, after let's see, just 11 months! Goodness gracious, what gives? It seems the two lovebirds, who met in 1932, were just as happy as clams, until, that is, they got hitched! Yet, Mrs. Vanderbilt, who is currently holed up at her mother's 3-story Clarksburg West Virginia home has denied reports any divorce action is planned by her or her husband. Really, Mrs. Vanderbilt? Further reports state Mrs. Vanderbilt says she has just returned from a weekend at Washington D.C. where Mr. Vanderbilt is said to be gathering material for a new book project."

Additional film footage shows Vanderbilt Mansion, 640 Fifth Avenue at New York City, with the following narration:

"Reporters camped outside of the cavernous Vanderbilt Mansion at '640' experienced an icy reception when the be-jeweled 'Queen of New York Society' exited with no other than her solo-son Cornelius Vanderbilt, Jr. When asked about the absence of the 'Mrs.' and about a separa-

tion Mr. Vanderbilt responded impatiently, 'No comment'. Whilst, his foreboding mother shook a bejeweled finger at the assembled press and crisply retorted, 'Have you no shame? We're late for the theatre! Now go on, get out of my way, you hooligans!' Shame? What's the shame in a bit of high-society scandal, I say? Rumors of Vanderbilt Jr., his many tarts and oh too many wives are the talk of New York City! Vanderbilt footmen, or should we say henchmen, quickly parted the way for the passing duo, from mansion to Rolls Royce!"

Chapter 6

Shanghai: Shimmering Mirage of Mystery

'1936'

From 1932 to 1935, Helen and Cornelius Vanderbilt socialized all over the world. The Vanderbilt name opened doors, and American royalty mixed with the age-old titles of Europe.

In late 1935, after Helen escapes from Neil, she returns to the Orient, finding comfort in the elite international commune of Shanghai—an exotic locale then known as 'the Paris of the East'. Heady with glamour and exciting people, from artists to royalty, opportunists to the idle rich, Shanghai is the expression of decadence, wonder, and liberation. Mrs. Cornelius Vanderbilt, Jr. is a perfect fit! A bonus to this decision is Helen's employ with Pond's Cold Cream Company, who request she travel to their new Shanghai manufacturing distribution division as a representative. Helen had become associated with

Pond's in 1935 as a magazine cover girl. Her image circulated world-wide, making her recognizable everywhere she went. Helen continues this association with Pond's well into the late 1940's.

The enticing fragrances of gardenia and jasmine waft over Shanghai Harbor to San Francisco, wrapping around another kindred spirit named Garnett Butler. Born in Chadron, Nebraska this beautiful young woman is much more than a farm girl; her destiny rather, lay in the presence of royalty. After her family relocates to Portland, Oregon, Garnett attends Oregon State College, known today as Oregon State University at Corvallis. Unfortunately though, due to the Great Depression, Garnett is unable to complete her education and leaves before graduation. From Corvallis she returns to Portland, and then to San Francisco finding a job with Northern Pacific Railway. This position awakens her inner desire to travel; however, the vistas Garnett seeks are not to be seen from a Pullman car. The 'City by the Bay' with its oriental influence, ignites in Garnett a desire to experience the mystic orient, an exotic locale where a group of friends has already relocated.

Thus, in the summer of '32, the 22-year-old Garnett books passage for Shanghai, traveling with her Nebraska-born college friend Marjorie Popple. Marjorie is already a resident of Shanghai, having married there in 1930 to Eugene A. Richards. As Garnett's ship steams out of San Francisco Bay, Garnett gazes back on her familiar world, excited, yet full of trepidation in regard to her new path. The steamer's heading is the commercial port of the Yangtze region—the gem of the orient via Hawaii.

After weeks at sea, Garnett's steamer docks at the frenetic harbor city of Shanghai. Garnett has but $200 in her handbag, stalwart and brave, somehow, she knows she will survive. She's grateful for her friends who welcome her with open arms. After settling in, and in discussing her prospects, they encourage her to familiarize herself with the city and visit the American Consulate for a possible employment.

Within days, Garnett finds her way through twisting streets filled with rickshaws, vendors, and intoxicating aromas she can't identify. Finally, she arrives at the Consulate, housed in the Kalee Hotel, which overlooks the waterfront at 248-250 Jiangxi Road. When asked what skills she possesses, all she can offer is typing. One asset though, not on the table, is that Garnett has presence and is radiantly beautiful. Fortunately, in this case, with little to sustain her in this foreign land, the officiate, with a quick look up and down of the glamorous Garnett, exclaims, "You're hired!"

From this point on, Garnett's path truly unfolds! With her embassy connections, she immerses herself in Shanghai society and is included in social gatherings of the very finest residents. Within 6 weeks, the entrancing Garnett receives six marriage proposals. Out of these beaus, a charming Canadian society doctor from Ontario, Canada, named William H. Gardiner captures her heart.

Soon after, Garnett at 23, and the doctor at 45, travel to Hawaii and marry at the Royal Hawaiian at Waikiki. By December 8, they steam for Shanghai via Japan. Once they arrive, they settle into a grand apartment in the old American Settlement on the harbor.

In regard to Garnett's life in Shanghai, Helen Vanderbilt would later state, 'The man was rich as sin. Their home was filled with ivory, jade, and pearls.' Later in life, Garnett herself spoke of the experience, "Life was wonderful. We had a 14-room penthouse and a houseboat. Everybody had a car and a chauffeur—to say nothing of the good and faithful houseboys, cooks, and Amahs. If you were at one of the clubs, swimming or playing cards, you'd call the cook and say, we're going to be 12 for dinner, and, then you'd go home at 8 p.m., and there would be dinner! Life was so easy and fascinating." Twenty-Three-year-old Garnett was about as far away from Nebraska and Oregon as a country girl could possibly venture!

During this time frame, Garnett is introduced to socialite Helen Vanderbilt. Both women, glamorous and lovely, have a legion of men at their feet and a myriad of dazzling parties to attend. Helen and Garnett soon find they have much in common, often even, they share outfits, passing themselves off as sisters; life is glamorous and exotic. Other girlfriends in Garnett's circle are Mary Star, Trudi Davis, and Marlys Josephine Chatel (a housemate from the earliest Shanghai days). With her new financial independence, Garnett steams back and forth to the States whenever she desires to see family at Portland, or shop at San Francisco and Los Angeles.

Unfortunately, by the late 1930's, the Yangtze region becomes politically unstable, with rumors of war. Mrs. Vanderbilt returns to the safety of the States, followed by other expatriate pals. Garnett, a more permanent resident, coupled with her physician husband, becomes ensnared by the Japanese occupation that is in full swing by 1941.

Like sisters, living uncannily similar lives, Garnett is now imprisoned too; however, her jailer is not a possessive husband, but rather the Japanese Imperial Army.

Under house arrest for seven long months, and with limited provisions to sustain themselves, Garnett and her intimates subsist on cracked wheat. Caught up in the cloak and dagger of the occupation, Dr. Gardiner slips out of their flat each day on covert missions, endeavors never revealed; however, his silence and secrecy protect Garnett's life.

Garnett's pleas for liberation do little but cause wringing of hands in the States. Helen Vanderbilt, nor any other person of influence, is able to secure her freedom. Finally though, amid political tensions and fear of permanent imprisonment, a deal is put forth by the United States Government offering exchange of a Japanese spy for one of Gardiner's patients—a diplomat named J.B. Powell.

John Benjamin Powell was a well-known columnist, serving as managing editor of the Weekly China Review, managing director of the China Press, and correspondent for the Manchester Guardian, London Daily Herald, and Chicago Tribune. During the early 1940's, Powell proves no friend to the Japanese government, which imprisons him from 1941-1942. Obviously, this man could not become a political pawn of the Japanese regime.

Powell's health suffered greatly at the hands of his captors. With his shoes confiscated, his feet froze, and he lost both to gangrene. His weight, reduced from 165 to 75 pounds, the result of starvation and cruelty. Just prior to his liberation, he was transferred from Bridge House Prison to Shanghai General Hospital and placed under Dr. Gardiner's care for 3 months. To insure Powell's physical health during his voyage back to the states, Dr. Gardiner is assigned to accompany him during passage. This serves a lucky break for Bill and Garnett—-their fate surely ominous if not for their release.

On June 29, 1942, Garnett stands on the deck of the repatriation ship S.S. Conte Verde as it departs the mystical mecca of Shanghai, now no more than a barbed wire-enshrouded containment camp. Through her tears, Garnett knows they will not be returning anytime soon. As she watches the hubbub of the waterfront, she realizes her destiny is not with these people—she is from a different world. In a letter posted to her mother she states, "The Paris of the East has deteriorated from a fascinating thriving city into a dreary dismal and virtual concentration camp." Later, the passengers transfer to the M.S. Gripsholm for the remainder of the voyage home and sail past the Statue of Liberty on August 25.

Little does Garnett realize, her heavy heart will soon be mourning the end of her marriage as well, a marriage which is more so a product of the exotic Orient than the west. Coupled with her escape from the orient, Garnett and William reach an impasse and decide to divorce. This separation stems from William's desire to have no children; a treasure Garnett simply cannot forego. Consequently, the war soon dictates Bill return to his homeland of Canada.

Powell dies by 1947, at 60 years old. Up until the end though, he's an international spokesperson and staunch denouncer of the Japanese brutality of World War II, this, a man who suffered great war-time atrocities, and one who remained devoted to the liberation and humanity of his fellow man.

After reaching New York City, Garnett travels out west and settles in Los Angeles. Initially, Garnett spends a majority of her time on the lecture circuit, speaking about her experience in Shanghai. Her life is about to change though, as often in life, when one door closes, another is flung wide open!

Within a year, Garnett meets the dashing and attractive Baron Constantine (Steno) de Stackelberg at a Washington D.C. luncheon. Surprisingly though, Garnett retells a different story of how she met Steno to business associate Carol Kender. She states she was in route to a speaking engagement, 'chewing gum like a teenager,' which always helps her relax in between her taxing schedule of lectures. As she stepped out of the taxicab, Garnett states she literally bumped into the Baron and 'it was love at first sight!' Certainly, this is a cherished memory for a woman who had seen her share of anguish in the world, and no doubt, Garnett is due a little bliss!

Garnett and the Baron are married August 9, 1945, the beginning of a royal fairytale romance for them both. During this time, the Baron is involved with state work in Washington. In my interview with the Baroness she related, "Steno knew Jack Frye long before I came on the scene." How they met is unknown, but the Baron was to become an employee of Transcontinental & Western Air, Inc., and as well, a consultant of sorts to Jack Frye and the executive office. Later still, Steno offered his considerable foreign diplomatic experience as an official consultant to TWA on International and Economic Affairs.

Helen, like Garnett, was forever touched by her experience in Shanghai as evidenced by a treasured book she always kept close-at-hand entitled, 'Rickshaw Boy' by Lao She, written about life in Shanghai, published in 1937.

'November 1937'

On one of her trips back to the states, Helen accompanies her sister Mildred to Reno who is seeking a divorce. They are staying in a fine hotel; for Reno, that's a stretch! While sitting in the lobby chatting, Helen is startled by a porter announcing, "Paging, Mrs. Cornelius Vanderbilt, Jr., Paging, Mrs. Cornelius Vanderbilt, Jr." Before Helen can respond, a beautiful finely dressed woman gets up and walks over to the front desk and states with pride, "Why, I'm Mrs. Cornelius Vanderbilt, Jr." Helen and her sister both look at each other, flabbergasted! Who is this beautiful young woman supposedly now married to Neil?

For some time, Helen had tried to get some kind of a settlement or divorce out of Vanderbilt; however, he was always out of reach of her attorneys, traveling around Europe somewhere. Quickly, Helen devises a plan. She composes a telegram in which she states, "Funny thing, both your wives just happen to be in the same hotel at the same time, isn't that interesting?" She sends the telegram to the mansion of Vanderbilt's stuffy mother at '640' on Fifth Avenue.

Within a couple days, Helen's long-awaited monetary settlement, which Vanderbilt had often reneged on, came through! Vanderbilt, married 7 times over his lifetime, was notorious for leaving his wives penniless and destitute.

Chapter 7

Soul Mates

'July 1938'

High up in a Manhattan high-rise, Jack Frye is the V.I.P. guest at a cocktail party. Helen Vanderbilt, who is 'oft invited to parties for her sparkling wit and personality, attends as well.

Helen watches Jack from across the room. She is very impressed with this charming well-dressed man who towers over the women who have him helplessly cornered at the bar. Suddenly, Jack catches Helen's gaze, he breaks away and strolls over. Stopping in front of Helen, he looks her straight in the eye, he smiles, illuminating the dimly lit room. In looking up at him, Helen feels herself go weak from head to toe. "No wonder he was cornered by those women," she thinks, "what a charismatic man!" Jack greets her, "May I sit down?" Helen replies, "Why, of course, you're Jack Frye, aren't you?" Jack replies, "Yes, darling, one and the same. And you're Helen Vanderbilt, aren't you?" Helen just smiles, unable to utter a word. She pulls a cigarette out of a diamond-encrusted gold case. Jack quickly pulls out his gold lighter. As Helen leans in for a light, she notices the lighter has an airliner etched on it. Helen settles back on the sofa drawing in on her cigarette, she looks Jack up and down as she exhales. "Now, please darling, do sit down," Helen says smiling graciously.

For the next 4 hours, Helen and Jack are inseparable. Helen's heart beats wildly each time Jack leans in close, leaving her lightheaded. "What's wrong with me?" she questions herself. "I have never felt this kind of attraction for any man before." They talk about everything, their unhappy marriages, and, in guarded tones, they speak of finding the perfect partner, someone who can truly share life's path. Helen realizes, in short order, Jack is not shallow, but deeply reflective—a spiritual man, a free spirit, and very well read.

Later, in the wee hours of the morning Helen watches the first rays of the sun as it rises over Central Park from her hotel suite. She sits down at a desk and drafts a letter to Jack. She offers him advice as to how Transcontinental & Western Air can improve their advertising and service, this in reflection of their conversation the previous night. With this move on Helen's part, she makes an impression on Jack who has never met a woman who took an interest in his business. Indeed, Jack is so impressed he actually implements Helen's suggestions.

Jack and Helen date for the next 2 years, before and after Jack's divorce from his beautiful Parisian-wife Jean LaCoste, on September 9, 1939. Finally, Jack is free to move on.

'December 1940'

Reporters at Hollywood and Tucson hound Helen Vanderbilt for news of an impending wedding. Helen relates the only reason for her visit to these cities is to see old friends. She confirms to reporters that she and Vanderbilt were indeed divorced on December 18, 1940, at Carson City, Nevada.

Reporters soon discover only with the help of Jack Frye's powerful attorneys was Helen able to break free of Neil; whereas, Neil's crafty attorneys were successful in sealing the divorce proceeding permanently, to protect Neil from any scandal hidden within.

Interestingly, at the time of the divorce, Helen was set to publish a 'not so flattering book' about her time with Vanderbilt. However, Jack used his influence with Helen to stop the publication, this to protect Helen from further pain and to protect TWA from any scandal in regard to Jack's intended marriage to Mrs. Vanderbilt.

Miraculously, Neil emerges unscathed, not because of any concession toward him, but rather because of Helen's marriage to Frye and his desire to protect her and his beloved airline.

'Christmas Eve 1940'

Jack Frye orders his personal Lockheed Electra Jr. NC18137 ready for a west-coast trip and clears his desk for Christmas vacation. Even though Jack denies his intent to marry Mrs. Vanderbilt, consensus is this is the reason for the trip west. Reporters jump on the story at Kansas City, starting with the Kansas City Star, and out west at

Los Angeles. Late in the day, the TWA president lifts off for Tucson-Phoenix; however, he only makes it far as El Paso, grounded by strong headwinds.

Incidentally, Jack Frye, as president of Standard Air Lines, developed the El Paso Airport in 1928, when his company pioneered passenger service coast-to-coast. With a familiar feeling, Jack secures his TWA executive plane on the tarmac and checks into a downtown hotel. This flight transports Frye only, no co-pilot.

'Christmas Day 1940'

Frye, while waiting for weather to improve enough to fly out again, finds himself cornered by reporters at the airport who question him about his supposed intention to marry the beautiful socialite Mrs. Vanderbilt. Frye responds with 'no comment' but shares an 8x10 glossy of Mrs. Vanderbilt he retrieves from his briefcase. Frye states, 'I'm on my way to Tucson, and from there, to Los Angeles on TWA business.' He further states, 'I'm due to return to Kansas City via Houston after the first of the year.'

Shortly before noon, with twin engines at full power, the newsmen standby as Frye's private Lockheed lifts off into the western sky for Tucson. Within minutes, reporters wire west coast affiliates of an expected arrival around noon.

Later, at about 1 P.M., the brilliant, polished to a mirror TWA Lockheed circles over Tucson, dropping down for a perfect landing in the warm winter sun amid dozens of Saguaro.

Mrs. Vanderbilt is waiting at the airport and strolls out to greet Frye as he steps out of the plane. Reporters are hot on the trail of the couple and confront them as Frye proceeds to secure the Electra Jr. Reporters query the two celebrities about an impending marriage, but Jack and Helen are evasive. Instead, Mrs. Vanderbilt tells reporters of plans to open a millinery shop at Beverly Hills, with Frye as her business advisor. The 36-year-old Frye comments, 'the flight from El Paso was rough, I'm in Arizona to get over a bad cold and enjoy some sunshine.' Reporters later relate, 'Mrs. Vanderbilt is an expert designer of women's clothing and was dressed in light green slacks with beige sport coat offset by chic dark-sunglasses. Mrs. Vanderbilt had just arrived from Los Angeles, previous to Frye.'

Several newspapers print in error that the couple depart by auto for Phoenix. This, after Mrs. Vanderbilt revealed they would be visiting a Clarksburg friend (Mrs. Anita Smith) who was staying at the fashionable Camelback Inn at Scottsdale; however, even though the couple leaves the Tucson airport by car, they are merely going to lunch, and return late in the day, departing in Frye's plane for Sky Harbor at Phoenix.

Indeed, Phoenix reporters later interview Mrs. Vanderbilt as she steps down from Frye's Lockheed at Phoenix. By evening's end, the two celebrities are booked at the Scottsdale Camelback Inn in separate suites.

Chapter 8

Married to TWA

'January 1, 1941'

The Arizonan western-style Frye wedding takes place at Scottsdale, Arizona against the red cliffs of Echo Canyon with a wedding party of 11 people. Helen Vanderbilt is dressed in a buckskin skirt with fringe jacket and wedding corsage of Ocotillo blossoms. The members of the wedding party ride horses to the ceremony, all dressed in costumes of western regalia. Everyone is booked at the Scottsdale Camelback Inn, which adjoins the beautiful Echo Canyon preserve.

The incomplete guest list is as follows: TWA Director Ralph S. Euler as Best Man, and his wife, from Sewickley, Pennsylvania. Matron of Honor is Mrs. Anita L. Smith, a dear friend of Helen and her mother's. Others are TWA Director Paul L. Hibbard, and his wife, from Westwood, California, and it is thought, Donald Frye. Justice of the Peace, Paul V. McCaw performs the ceremony.

The wedding breakfast is a hearty sunrise fare, which includes bacon and eggs cooked over a crackling campfire. Mrs. Frye herself is the host, not only helping to cook breakfast but graciously serving her wedding guests as well.

On January 4, the Fryes leave Scottsdale westbound for Los Angeles in Jack's Lockheed, after which, they check into the Beverly Wilshire. Within days they continue on to Palm Springs where they lodge at the El Mirador, this the initial stage of their honeymoon. Unfortunately though, Jack has to return to the east coast, as his job with Transcontinental & Western Air is 24/7.

By January 10, the TWA Lockheed twin circles over the White House and touches down at Washington National. Jack, dressed in a herringbone suit helps Helen deplane as their luggage is loaded in a limousine. The black sedan drives the happy couple through the streets of Washington to the posh Mayflower Hotel. In an interview in the Frye hotel suite, Helen, wearing a stunning mink jacket with large square shoulders chats with reporters. They marvel over her unique hat, a Helen Frye original designed out of copper wire framing with silver daisies and stitched out of silver radio antennae wire. Encompassing the hat is a large black velvet bow. Laughter erupts in the room when Jack quips, "Likely as not, somebody will tune in and get a radio program." He looks over at Helen and winks.

After Jack finishes his business at the nation's capital, the two depart for New York City on a Transcontinental & Western commercial flight. On the evening of January 12, 1941, the DC-3, with Jack and Helen as V.I.P. passengers, sets down at LaGuardia Field. The airliner, with clearance markers glowing and landing lights illuminating the tarmac, taxis up to the company's passenger terminal.

Once the engines cease, reporters rush the plane as the cabin door swings open. Within minutes, the magnanimous president of TWA and his socialite wife, Helen Vanderbilt, exit the cabin and descend the TWA stairs waving to the crowd amid a dozen flashes of cameras. At the bottom of the ramp, Jack, dressed in a herringbone topcoat over his suit, holds one of Helen's furs. Helen, wearing a winter coat with large mink collar and wearing black gloves, heels, and a broad velvet hat, holds a white fox fur jacket, leather purse, and day-planner. Tired and at the end of a long day, the two smile graciously as they field questions from anxious reporters about their recent marriage.

Helen burbles of her new husband, "He's really what a woman dreams for, the most wonderful man I have ever met. I guess the romance really developed from my criticism of TWA's advertising. I said, 'they should portray the romance and adventure of flying instead of only focusing on comfort and speed.' So, Jack gave my theory a test, and it proved out." Then with a laugh, Helen adds, "At least we're married, and the advertising is being changed!"

The Fryes are media darlings, not only because they are so young, with Helen at 32, and Jack at 36, but because Jack is such a success! This aviator is the youngest airline president in the world, and the only one to hold a commercial transport license. Jack can fly his own airliners full of passengers, at any time, having started his first commercial airline, Standard, at just 23 years old!

By January 26, Helen and Jack are at the Hotel Ambassador, at New York City. Society reporters engage the two while they enjoy drinks with friends at the hotel's popular lounge.

The next day, Jack and Helen tour his new palatial office on the third story of the stunning art deco Airlines Terminal Building at Park Avenue and 42nd Street, across from Grand Central Terminal. Jack tells Helen TWA moved into the facility the previous year. As she steps into the magnificent suite, Helen is struck by the prominent crimson-leather desk and chair, complemented by a matching crimson leather divan, comfortable armchairs and a huge world globe. "Wow!" exclaims Helen. "What an office!" Jack tells her, "The red leather is the exact same hue of the lettering on all my planes. I also have the same leather in my automobiles—it's called TWA-RED."

'February 1941'

The Frye honeymoon is 'oft delayed due to Jack's business with TWA and his involvement with the ensuing war effort; however, despite this, finally Jack and Helen board Jack's private Lockheed and head south for the destinations of Louisiana, Florida, Cuba, and the

Caribbean. One lost photo shows the honeymooning couple stand-ing in front of the Lockheed on a sandy beach, with a resort hotel in the background, surrounded by a ribbon of palm trees. This was the Caribbean end of the Lockheed honeymoon.

In the early months of 1941, whenever Jack and Helen are out west, Jack sets aside a few days for him and Helen to canvas the Western United States by air to find the perfect ranch property. Jack Frye comes from an historic cattle ranching family who owns a large por-tion of the Texas panhandle. What he is seeking is a large enough acreage to sustain a cattle ranch, coupled with an ample water supply. Following all the waterways with the Lockheed, Jack and Helen scour the ground from over-flights of New Mexico and Arizona, hoping to discover the perfect southwestern ranching property.

On one particular trip, Jack's silver Lockheed drops down from Flagstaff south, navigating a picturesque rust-hued canyon with a ribbon of water running through the center. At the bottom of the chasm, the Lockheed soars out over an open valley of red rock spires. The sparsely populated region, displayed below the soaring Lock-heed, is remote and rugged, so much so, that rarely has it seen air traf-fic. Ranchers rush out of their homesteads to look up, shading their eyes with their hands as they watch the silver TWA airliner bank and circle through the tight canyons.

Helen, stylishly dressed in slacks and dark shades, gazes out below, waving and smiling in wonderment at the scene. Typically, Jack is dressed in a suit, with a cigar at the corner of his mouth. He expertly sweeps and banks around towers of crimson, the ground below un-folding like a fairytale of red rock pinnacles. Suddenly, a picturesque valley appears outside the starboard window, with a flowing creek at its heart. As the plane plows through low clouds, corkscrewed around red-hued spires, Helen cries out passionately, "Look, look down there Jack, this is it! This is where I want to live!"

Spread out beneath the plane, a picturesque ranch appears, hugging a creek, which snakes through a red rock valley peppered with cottonwood trees. Jack looks out the port window, as he banks sharply, exclaiming, "Helen, I think we've found it, at last our Shangri-La!" He circles several times trying to identify the area. Finally though, with an eye to the fuel gauge, Jack tells Helen they have to start back, but he will find out where they are and look into it when they reach Los Angeles. Helen is disappointed there is nowhere to set down; yet amazed she and Jack can search for real estate in Northern Arizona by day and be back at the coast for dinner by nightfall.

The plane drones off into the western sunset, the massive twin Pratt and Whitney engines slowly fade away, as the rugged country below returns to silence after the noisy intrusion.

After a flight with speeds of well over 200 M.P.H., and in less than 2 hours, Jack sets the Lockheed down at Los Angeles. After unloading the plane, the couple takes a limo to the Beverly Wilshire where they freshen up and talk about their exciting discovery over a quiet dinner in their suite. Jack pours over Transcontinental & Western Air navigation charts, yet despite hours of searching, he finds no reference to the region they spotted from the air, let alone a nearby airstrip. The red rock valley does not show on any of his up-to-date TWA navigation charts!

'Interview- Ambassador Hotel- Beverly Hills Hat Shop'

'March 14, 1941'

After returning east for a month Jack and Helen are once again back at Los Angeles, this time staying at the Ambassador, instead of the Beverly Wilshire. As is typical, Jack is there on TWA business, but Helen is promoting her new millinery shop that has recently opened in Beverly Hills.

Helen's hat shop is a joint venture between herself and Mrs. Mark T. McKee, with Jack Frye backing the enterprise financially. Mrs. Mark McKee of Pasadena, is also known as Evelyn McKee, married to wealthy airline executive Mark T. McKee, longtime 30-year board member with Pan American Airways, among other executive positions.

Helen, a fashion designer since high school, interviewed and photographed in the Frye suite at the Ambassador, displays over two dozen unique hats—all Helen Frye creations! Many of her hats were designed prior to the opening of her shop, at her studio in South Pasadena, at 259 Monterey Road. This, the location of the mansion she resided at before she married Jack Frye.

The March 14, 1941 interview with photos ran in the Los Angeles Times. Helen is described by Times Fashion Editor Sylvia Weaver, as an auburn-haired, blue-eyed beauty, dressed in a smart 'tailleur' of beige gabardine, with a bright green silk blouse and slacks, all highlighted by a beige straw hat of red and green with high crown and wide brim. Helen tells Sylvia she feels a lady's hat 'should frame the face, not deter from it'. Further she states Jack Frye pre-approves her hats before she wears them, certainly a courteous concession by this very independent and modern woman, who Sylvia describes as the 'picture of chic, and an aviator and flyer herself'!

Helen indeed appears to be a pilot, a fact that surfaced in another interview with her former husband Cornelius Vanderbilt, Jr. in the 1950's. Helen, likely trained with Jack Frye, or her former hometown pal Tommy Smith, who was an accomplished aviator himself. It is not likely Helen kept her piloting skills current after the mid-1940's, and an F.A.A. license has never been located as issued to Helen.

Sylvia describes Helen's creations as 'daring and original'. One of Helen's creations resembles a mock birthday cake, in cream fabric, with a full spray on top to simulate candles. "I get ideas for hats all the time," Helen explains. "When Jack and I were in Florida recently on our honeymoon, I wanted something to keep the sun out of my eyes. So, I cut up a newspaper and folded it like a little boy's soldier hat, and presto, I had a bonnet which folds into nothing, for packing, yet unfolds into a very attractive off-the-face-hat; I'm having it patented now. Jack encourages me in designing. I tie scarves around my head in a circle halo on top of my hair, letting three corners hang down in back, which gives a new line." Mrs. Frye continues, "A man wants to look at a lady's face. If he can't see her eyes, he complains. What's the use of hiding your eyes, your hairline, under a lot of flowers or straws or ribbons? I'm having a hat made now of Philippine grass which I saw on a piece of furniture—and of course, you've seen my hat made out of copper chicken wire and antennae, haven't you?" Mrs. Frye lays out bolts of exotic fabrics and materials utilized in her designs, cleverly obtained from her travels around the world.

As an ardent sportswoman, Helen has traveled every corner of the United States, receiving her fashion ideas from the country's styles-at-large, and as well, the women she meets. In the past, she traveled with her dogs in her automobile, from region to region, often alone. The former Mrs. Vanderbilt also traveled extensively by steamer, back and forth across the Atlantic, throughout Europe and the Orient—two regions that no doubt have influenced her fashion creations, just as the orient-influenced art-deco trend has swept across the world, influencing fashion and décor.

In her travels with her husband TWA president Frye, the two recently returned from Florida and the Caribbean. On business, they have traveled extensively on the east coast and throughout the mesas of the southwest. No region, Helen states, has the 'California sport style'. A trend she admires for its smart appearance, simplicity, and vibrant array of colored fabrics.

Mrs. Frye conveys to Sylvia that she feels Los Angeles will someday replace Paris as the fashion center of the world, especially in regard to the Hollywood studio factory of clothing styles, which have greatly influenced current trends and clothing designs nationwide. At the time of the article, Helen Frye was designing a complete 'air wardrobe'—an ensemble of smart and practical outfits for the modern woman to wear who travels on airplanes extensively.

A last Helen Frye quote from the article: "My shop? Oh, yes, I am part owner of a hat shop; but, my fashion career comes second, definitely second, to my marriage. Why should I bother about selling hats when I'm happily married for the first time in my life?"

'March 27, 1941'

Jack and Helen are at Chicago on TWA business. Helen spends the afternoon visiting her old alma mater, 'The Art Institute of Chicago'. Chicago Tribune reporter June Provines encounters the former Mrs. Vanderbilt strolling the hallowed halls taking notes on murals. Helen utilizes this opportunity to view new additions to the collection and reconnect with old friends. In her mind, she is amazed at how her life has changed since she attended this prestigious institution as a young woman, 10-years prior.

'June 1941'

On one of their trips out west to Los Angeles, Jack clears his schedule for several days, planning a surprise air trip for Helen. Not telling her where they are going, he flies the Lockheed out to Prescott, Arizona where he lands at the primitive airstrip fringed by tall fields of grass. Jack taxis off the runway, parking in the tall grass as deer look up curiously from their grazing. After Jack and Helen deplane, they rent an old car and drive over the mountain to Cottonwood. Jack leaves Helen at the car, while he seeks a realtor who can show him a ranch he has found for sale. Jack doesn't find the realtor, but instead his secretary, who directs him to Baldwin's Crossing (now Red Rock Crossing) where her boss Andrew Baldwin agrees to meet them near Sedona.

Once the group connects, Andy has the Fryes follow him over to the old Armijo Ranch, which is for sale and owned by a banker, Andrew Blackmore from Los Angeles. The ranch is one of several the Fryes had overflown in the valley on their earlier exploration air trip that spring.

Jack and Helen spend an hour or so looking over the property and buildings when Jack suddenly turns to Helen and says, "Helen, I'm buying this entire spread just for you honey!" Overwhelmed by Jack's generous gesture, Helen starts to cry. Nobody had ever offered her such a gift before. The realtor discusses terms and water rights, etc. with Jack, while Helen wanders the rustic old Armijo homestead.

Late in the afternoon, Jack asks Andy to wait at the farmhouse, while he and Helen walk the property alone. They end up at the creek where they both strip and skinny-dip in the cooling waters, a respite from the dusty day. A day, Helen would later tell friends was 'beastly hot'! Finally, refreshed, the newlyweds walk back up to the Armijo ranch house and Jack and Andy finalize the deal. Jack instructs Andy to send all paperwork to himself in care of Transcontinental & Western Air, Inc. at Kansas City.

After this initial purchase, Jack proceeds with his plan to develop a large cattle ranch, gradually buying up whatever parcels he can obtain in the adjoining valley. One of these purchases is the neighboring Schuerman Ranch, to the north, with 'Willow House'. The deal closes in December of 1941. Jack mentions this in letter as displayed below:

'November 5, 1941

We have also purchased the Schuerman property across the river from the site and should get delivery on it about December 1. We may want to spend a few hundred dollars on the house there to try to remodel it to use until our house is built and then lease it out. Jack Frye'

The 'site' Jack mentions is where he and Helen desire to build a new home, and the house he wants to remodel was the Willow House at the ranch.

In the ensuing years, with purchase of additional parcels, and U.S. Forest Service land trades with other Arizona Frye ranches, Jack and Helen accumulate about 700 acres in the red rock loop area, this outside of property owned near Cornville, Arizona, close by. Helen christens their initial purchase, 'Deer-Lick Ranch', for the natural salt licks on the property, and the second parcel, 'Smoke Trail Ranch', for the ancient Indian trails worn into the cliffs above Oak Creek.

Conjointly with the Sedona acquisitions, were two other ranches in Northern Arizona: a 22,000-acre parcel east of Flagstaff, and a 4,500-acre parcel north of Williams, both slated for summer grazing. Jack and Helen name these new ranches respectively, the 'Sunshine Ranch' and the 'Spring Valley Ranch'. Interestingly by 1948, newspapers print the Fryes own over 50,000 acres of ranch property in Arizona, along with a sizeable ranch near Wheeler in the Texas panhandle. The additional acreage has never been located.

The Frye marriage is 'in the air an equal amount of time it's on the ground'. Because Jack is head of TWA, he flies constantly in his private plane for business meetings back and forth across the country, more than not these trips include Helen, who sits at his side in the co-pilot seat. All other flights are by TWA airliner, where Jack occasionally acts as captain; however, because his time is so valuable, more so he remains in the cabin pouring through crucial TWA business. Helen keeps busy as well, graciously assisting Hostesses assigned to commercial flights. By 1942, the Fryes are constantly flying between Kansas City and Washington D.C., the latter, where Jack establishes a second operations center for TWA due to the war.

The Fryes maintain a home at Merriam, Kansas, a suburb of Kansas City. This 5-acre estate, with swimming pond is of the French-country design with three levels and parking underneath the house. The comfortable home with four bedrooms, three baths, office-bar, and guesthouse, is a showplace of entertaining for celebrities and V.I.P.'s, to include Senator Truman, Howard Hughes, and the Lindberghs. Jack maintains a staff of four, to include butler, cook, chauffeur-groundskeeper, and a housekeeper.

During World War II, Jack, considered one of the nation's most powerful corporate leaders, enjoys unfettered access to the Oval Office, working closely with Presidents Franklin D. Roosevelt, and later, Harry S. Truman. Jack's military rank during the war was Lieutenant Commander U.S.N.R., this, until 1952, at his discharge.

'August 10, 1941'

Jack arrives at Albuquerque, N.M. in his personal Lockheed 12A for a conference at Eagle Nest. Anytime Jack lands at a TWA airport, or anywhere around the country, he always takes time to walk around and greet all his employees, most remarkably though, he greets each one by name! Shortly after taking care of TWA business, Jack has a TWA courtesy car transport him to the local Hilton. Jack is at Albuquerque to oversee Eagle Nest Flight Center at Kirtland Air Force Base, an operation he developed for the specific purpose of training U.S.A.A.F. personnel on heavy transport equipment. By Tuesday, August 12, Frye is winging his way on west to Los Angeles.

Eventually, Jack appoints Chief Pilot and Vice President of TWA, Otis Bryan (a former Army pilot) to head the Albuquerque school that soon becomes associated with many other 'heavy' flight schools around the nation. These training efforts greatly aid our military advancements in the Pacific and European theatres. Up until this juncture, the Army Air Force has no experience with large multi-engine equipment. It's Frye's involvement and development of this training center (christened the 'Jack Frye Training School') that greatly aids the war effort overseas. TWA pilots are recruited to train Army pilots on TWA planes surrendered for the war effort to transport troops and personnel during the war. As connected with this effort, on December 24, 1941, and in a direct connection with Eagle Nest, Jack signs into effect the Inter-Continental Division of TWA, or (ICD).

'October 18, 1941'

A silver TWA Lockheed 12 touches down at Santa Fe's Continental Airport, so named for scheduled north-south Continental Airlines service. After the engines wind down, Jack and Helen exit the plane and step into a waiting courtesy car. The driver turns around and asks Jack where they will be staying. "La Fonda," Jack responds, as the auto speeds away. Helen murmurs, "I am so excited Jack to meet Mr. Meem and discuss our new house at the ranch!" "Yes Helen," Jack answers, "I'm also anxious to get the project underway and John Gaw Meem is the most prominent architect in the Southwest. He's the perfect choice for our new Sedona pueblo home."

Later, Jack and Helen are at Meem's office with his secretary and assistant discussing their Sedona home. Finally, Jack suggests, "John, I'd like to fly you over tomorrow to see the building site if you're available. I feel in order for you to get the proper feeling of what Helen and I desire, seeing Sedona from the air is just what's required. What do you say?" "Well," replies John, "that'd be an experience no doubt, I've never flown much but it would give us the overview for the mockups. Yes, I think it's a great idea!" "O.K." Jack replies, "Let's say you meet Helen and me at the airport, tomorrow morning, around 8:00 A.M."

'October 19, 1941'

On Sunday morning, Jack descends over Sedona, navigating in and around the picturesque Red Rocks until he reaches his creek-side property. Out of the starboard windows, as Jack follows the creek, he points out the boundaries of Deer-Lick and the recently purchased former Schuerman Ranch.

After another pass, he and Helen point out the building site of their proposed home. John nods and smiles as Helen and Jack describe their dream house: "On the edge of the cliff as it drops down to the creek," says Helen as she shouts over the rumbling din of the engines, "will be the grand living room, and in the rear the pool and terraces!"

Finally, the air-tour over, Jack banks to the northwest, and climbs up and out, over Sedona. Adjusting the throttles, Jack increases the air-speed to about 200 M.P.H., within an hour and a half, the Lockheed twin is on approach to Continental Airport at Santa Fe. After landing, Jack and Helen can only stay for an hour, as Jack must be back at Kansas City Monday morning. Bidding John farewell, they take off again, settling into a long evening flight, eastbound for Kansas City.

On October 30, John Gaw Meem writes in letter to the Fryes describing the day. "My adventure of two Sundays ago still seems quite incredible to me and the vision of the site as we approached it from the air is more like a dream than realty." Writing further and quite eloquently, Mr. Meem continues, "My partner, Mr. Zehner, tells me that my delay in sending the sketches to you is due to my desire to create a genuine 'Oak Creek Canyon Architecture'. As a matter of fact, he is not very far from the truth because I feel very strongly that no established or period architecture quite belongs - whether straight Pueblo or straight modern. My solution, as you will see, lies somewhere between these extremes and is an attempt to express as simply as possible your requirements with stone and adobe available at the site."

In an interview with John's daughter Nancy Meem Wirth she recalls the air-trip out to Arizona with Jack and Helen was not so ideal for her father who suffered from vertigo. It seems after Jack did some loop-de-loop like maneuvers in the Lockheed her father was quite overcome.

'October 21, 1941'

At Los Angeles, a TWA airliner full of passengers sits at the TWA gate awaiting clearance to depart. Restless passengers anxious to make their schedules soon learn the plane is being held for no other than screen legend Bette Davis who is making an emergency trip back east.

Finally, after 30 minutes, a Warner Bros. limousine pulls up to the gate. TWA officials rush over, as a chauffeur helps Bette Davis and two traveling companions exit the vehicle.

Accompanying Davis is her good friend, Helene Byers, and Bette's business manager, Lester Linsk. Airline officials quickly escort the Davis party onboard the waiting DC-3. As the air stairs are pulled, the engines are started, and the airliner makes its way out to the runway where it's cleared for takeoff, eastbound for Kansas City.

Early that afternoon, Davis, notified her husband was gravely ill back east, rushed off the movie set of 'The Man Who Came to Dinner' to catch the waiting airliner. Former airline pilot Arthur Farnsworth was in a hospital at Minneapolis, stricken with double pneumonia; his condition so grave recovery seemed unlikely.

Once in the air, Davis is able to relax and visit with her fellow passengers, but still, she is tense and nervous in regard to her mission; a trip ill-timed and soon to be fraught with poor weather. As the DC-3 begins its approach to Kansas City, the pilot announces, 'all flights are canceled east of the Mississippi due to heavy fog'. Collective groans erupt from the cabin as many passengers have already missed their connections and are disheartened at yet another delay. Finally, at dark, the plane taxis up to the terminal at Kansas City Municipal.

Once on the ground, the news of Bette Davis' dilemma reaches the offices of Jack Frye. Jack meets with the actress and graciously offers his own plane for her flight north. Fortunately, Jack's private transport is not restricted by commercial traffic weather restrictions. "Once my plane is ready, you can board and continue to Minneapolis, likely tonight," Jack informs Bette confidently. Jack orders his Lockheed twin ready for the trip north, telling the ground crew there will be one V.I.P. passenger, two guests, and two pilots. Because Jack's schedule is so tight, he's unable to fly the plane himself though, especially in regard to the fact that he and Helen are taking the plane west, October 23, the next day.

Jack picks up the phone and calls his right-hand man, TWA Executive Vice-President Paul Richter. Jack asks Paul if he has the time to fly Bette up to Minneapolis. Paul agrees, and TWA Captain Leonard Hylton is assigned as co-pilot. Unfortunately for Bette, weather continues to dog any outbound departure. Finally, it's decided the Davis party should stay the night, and if conditions are favorable, everyone can depart in the morning.

Dressed in a smart suit and tie, Paul greets Bette Davis at the plane, where reporters photograph the two as they visit early the next morning. Bette is fashionably dressed in tailored suit, hair held in a snood, and holding an alligator handbag. At last, by 8:00 A.M., the Lockheed Electra Jr. lifts off, ascending through ominous skies, northbound to Minneapolis amid a jumble of grounded commercial airliners.

After being in flight for a little over an hour, Paul receives radio notification by TWA that Minneapolis is below limits and has closed. He quickly makes a decision to divert to Rochester. Paul steps back to the cabin to relay the news to Bette, advising her he has arranged for a limousine to pick her and her party up once they land. He also informs her the distance will be 90 miles from Rochester airport to the Abbott Hospital. Exhausted by the trip and the many delays, Bette thanks Paul graciously for all his efforts.

After landing, Bette and her party depart at 10:30 A.M., whisked away by hired car, northbound through heavy fog, whereas the TWA Lockheed departs southbound for Kansas City. Paul and Leonard arrive within an hour, whilst Bette unites with her husband by noon.

Farnsworth soon rallies, and Bette is on her way back to the studio the next evening on a scheduled commercial airliner. Unfortunately though, for Farnsworth, although offered a temporary reprieve, he is unable to escape the reaper, and dies mysteriously, just two years later at Hollywood, on August 25, 1943.

Even though TWA was known as the 'Airline to the Stars' and certainly they offered legendary First-Class service from Hollywood to N.Y.C., it's highly unlikely Jack Frye held a fully loaded TWA plane at the gate for a half hour, even for a famous celebrity like Bette Davis. Frye's acumen in regard to schedule can be traced back to the late 1920's when Frye flew his Standard Air Lines schedules so tight you could set your watch by his overflights, thus his nickname: 'On-The-Dot-Frye'. Later, as head of TWA, whenever any of his pilots complained they could not meet their schedules, Frye responded by showing up at any given airport unannounced where he would relieve the pilot and take over the flight with passengers. Then, he would proceed to fly the schedule, to the minute, thus proving his point!

The success of early airline service was all about delivering passengers and freight according to strict schedules. Any pilot who could not or would not adhere to this critical requirement by Frye was promptly sacked; if you worked for Frye you were the best, if you weren't, you worked for another airline or not at all. Frye was a consummate pilot with as much or more experience than many of the men who flew for him. He knew planes and he knew the traveling public. This is what made him a successful airline mogul.

As to who held the flight, likely we need look no further then aviator-playboy Howard Hughes, a man who showed no regard for the inconvenience of TWA or their loyal passengers. Howard's romantic alliance with Bette Davis, previous to this incident, was well known publicly, and therein lies our answer. There is nothing within TWA that occurred without Frye's knowledge and little escaped Hughes either.

Interesting to note, Davis and Farnsworth were married in Rimrock, Arizona at the ranch of Davis intimate and starlet Jane Bryan-Dart, just one day apart from the Frye marriage at Scottsdale. As a matter of fact, Jack and Helen's ranch at Sedona was just a few air miles from the Bryan spread at Rimrock. Could this be why Jack insisted on having Bette flown to Minneapolis on his own private TWA transport or was it more so a phone call from Howard Hughes? It appears we will never know for sure.

The Lockheed's radials had barely cooled before Jack and Helen de-part west to Los Angeles, via Sedona, the next day. Jack's two execu-tive planes, the Lockheed 12A (1940-1945) and the larger Lockheed Lodestar 18 (1945-1947) are constantly in the air, from Kansas City to Washington D.C., and back and forth to the west coast, as associ-ated with Jack's expert management of TWA.

'October 23, 1941'

Jack and Helen depart Kansas City for Albuquerque on Jack's 12A. They land after dark and take a taxi to the Hilton Hotel downtown.

'October 24, 1941'

The next morning, before Jack and Helen depart Albuquerque, Jack encounters old friend Timothy Riordan from Flagstaff. Jack asks him to join him and Helen in flight to Arizona in the Lockheed.

Frye first met Riordan November 22, 1927, when he took Riordan and his wife for their first air-flight over Prescott, Arizona in a brand new 8-passenger Standard Air Lines Fokker airliner. Jack made six promo flights that day, with guests, even to the destinations of early Jerome. As an honorary guest of the Arizona Industrial Congress meeting, Jack was lodging at the famous Prescott Arizona Hassayam-pa Hotel.

After a pleasant flight west, Riordan is deplaned at Koch Field (now a housing development). Jack and Helen take off again south for the

Frye Airstrip at Cornville Road and 89A near Sedona. The current airport at Flagstaff (Pulliam) was not developed yet, instead, Koch Field was Flagstaff's main airport at the time.

Documentation of this flight turned up later as filed in the Riordan Mansion State Park archives at Flagstaff:

'Jack Frye, TWA President, and his wife, picked me up at Albuquerque, N.M., October 24, 1941, at 10-10 a.m., and dropped me at Koch Field, Doney Park, Flagstaff, at 11:45 a.m., same day- Great Treat! (Signed) T. A. R. (Timothy A. Riordan)'

So, how was the flight that Friday afternoon in Jack's Lockheed 12A? Calculating flight miles from Albuquerque to Flagstaff, at 286 miles, the time in the air was about 1 hour, 35 minutes. The Lockheed twin, at cruise, attained 210 M.P.H. (averaged) with dual 450 H.P. Pratt and Whitney R-985 power plants. Without a doubt, the Lockheed 12A was one of the all-time most sophisticated and fastest executive prop planes ever designed, even by today's standards!

'October 25, 1941'

As covered by local media, Frye's private landing strip and airport near Sedona, is dedicated on this warm October day. Christened the 'Verde Valley Airport', this event is attended by 200 officials and locals. Verde Valley residents are most excited to attend so they can hear the valley's newest and most well-connected resident, Jack Frye as guest speaker, and meet his glamorous wife, Helen Varner Vander-bilt Frye.

Jack Frye is not only one of the best pilots in the nation, but as well a national aviation celebrity featured in national newspapers and media copy regularly. Speaking before the crowd Jack expounds on the future of Verde Valley aviation and TWA with enthusiasm. After-wards, Jack generously transports local aviation officials on flights over the airport in his 'private Lockheed plane' as a newspaper writer coins it. These promo flights are reminiscent of Jack's visit to Prescott in 1927, 14 years earlier.

Jack always shares his accomplishments, so it was only logical for him to open his private airstrip to public use, and the Army, for a training field. Sedona, Arizona had yet to develop an airport, so any landing field nearby was a boon for the community which had to come and go from Clemenceau (Cottonwood), Sky Harbor-TWA (Phoenix), Koch Field (Flagstaff), and the Transcontinental & Western Air, Inc. full service terminal at (Winslow). Many times, the Fryes, when trav-eling by TWA airliner, had ranch hands pick them up at Winslow, after a westbound or eastbound flight.

Western Union Telegram(s):

'1941, Nov 29,'

TO JOHN GAW MEEM

SUBJECT TO WEATHER WE HOPE TO ARRIVE SANTA FE LATE THIS AFTERNOON IF ITS CONVENIENT WOULD

LIKE TO SEE YOU DURING EVENING. KIND REGARDS, JACK FRYE

TO JACK FRYE

AM FLYING TODAY TO DENVER WITH MRS MEEM WHO IS ILL BUT ARRANGE TO HAVE MEMBERS OF MY STAFF MEET WITH YOU TONIGHT PLEASE WIRE, REGARDS JOHN GAW MEEM

'1941, DEC 1'

TO JOHN GAW MEEM

RETELL OUR DEPARTURE FROM KANSAS CITY DELAYED SO WILL BE UNABLE TO STOP TONIGHT. WILL TRY TO MAKE IT ON RETURN THURSDAY. REGARDS, JACK FRYE

'1942, July 28'

MAIL CARE DEER LICK RANCH- SEDONA, ARIZ.

MY HOUSEKEEPER AND SECRETARY DRIVING TO RANCH SHOULD ARRIVE FRIDAY EVENING OR SATUR-DAY. DO NOT BOTHER TO CLEAN HOUSE BUT PLEASE TURN ON REFRIGERATOR AND HAVE STOVE FILLED.

MR. FRYE AND I AND BUTLER EXPECT TO ARRIVE SOON AFTER. BEST REGARDS, HELEN FRYE

There's no way to know exactly which house at the ranch Helen was referring to with this telegram, as there were two ranch dwellings the Fryes resided at in the early years. One was the larger Armijo ranch house, included in the first property purchase, coupled with the (now demolished) ranch manager residence nearby. The second was the Willow House on the Schuerman parcel, which Jack purchased shortly after in December of 1941. The Armijo ranch house and the Willow House were extensively remodeled and brought up to the standards the Fryes required.

There was no phone service at the ranch in the early years, so Jack and Helen communicated by telegram with ranch managers (the above communiqué was received by Roy Kurtz, an early ranch foreman.) The housekeeper and butler were borrowed from the Frye estate on Foster Street at Kansas City. The secretary was likely a personal secretary who worked privately for the Fryes (Helen and Jack both had home secretaries).

On this stopover, the Fryes open the ranch to guests from Hollywood and Washington. In a clearing down by the creek, a party unfolds honoring a very special friend. Under the shade of Cottonwood trees is a mock Hollywood Western movie set with trail rides and all manner of western activities. That evening, under the brilliant stars of the virgin Arizona sky, sitting around a bonfire, guests are entranced as Marlene Dietrich serenades in her sultry song.

Previously, at a party in Beverly Hills, Helen, as always, was wearing one of her fabulous hats. Another guest, Marlene Dietrich joined Helen to chat. After introductions, Marlene exclaimed in her sultry voice, "Darling, where did you buy that lovely hat?" To which Helen replied, "I designed it myself!" Marlene then said, "Please, Helen dear, won't you design hats for me?" Helen, thereafter, graciously agreed to supply Marlene with smart stylish hats, launching a life-long friendship. Later, even, she designed clothing outfits for Marlene, specifically, slack suits. We all know Marlene Dietrich was a trendsetter in regard to slacks. Could it be that Helen herself helped contribute to this Marlene signature look? Helen even delivered an entire Helen Frye Design to Marlene in Beverly Hills at one time. Marlene had the outfit fitted by her favorite Hollywood seamstress, before she wore it.

'Fall of 1942'

A Stork Club house photographer captures Jack and Helen seated at a table huddled in closely with columnist James Westbrook 'Pegler' at New York City. The club, packed with uniformed officers on leave, is a popular hangout during the war.

Within weeks, back at Los Angeles, a long black Lincoln limousine negotiates the narrow winding streets of Hollywood as Jack and Helen snuggle together and visit in the back. The car turns, pulling up to an old mansion. Jack steps out and goes in while Helen waits in the car and adjusts her makeup. Within minutes, Jack and a tall man, accompanied by a young Hollywood starlet, exit the house. The chauffeur helps them all into the back of the limousine where Howard Hughes greets Helen warmly as the car rolls away from the curb and down to the Ambassador Hotel Cocoanut Grove Club.

When the four-some enter the busy club, the maître d' quickly walks away from the patrons he's attending. Briskly he approaches the group, "Good evening Mr. Hughes, same table?" he questions. "Yes," replies Howard as the group is ushered past busy round tops. The din of the room quiets, as people look up and stare, several whisper, "Why that's Howard Hughes!" After being seated, they all order drinks and dinner, Helen visits with the starlit about clothing trends while Howard and Jack talk about 'how TWA will dominate the world at the end of the war with the Connie'.

'November 4, 1942'

At 1:45 A.M., Jack and Helen are fast asleep at their Kansas City home. In the master bedroom, Jack thrashes about violently as if he is having a troubled dream. Helen awakens with a start, "What in the world?" she thinks as she looks over at Jack covered with sweat. With mumbled words Jack exclaims, "No, No, please don't!" An ear-deafening bang of a gunshot rings out as Jack bolts up in bed. Looking at Helen with wild eyes he exclaims, "Did you hear that Helen?" Helen says, "No darling, it was just a bad dream." Obviously concerned, Helen comforts him, "Its O.K. sweetie," she says as she rubs his shoulder gently. However, Jack is not to be placated. "Something terrible has happened Helen, something awful," he says with anguish. Just then, the phone on the bedside stand rings.

Several hours before dawn, Jack's Lockheed twin sweeps down the runway at Kansas City Municipal Airport, lifting off with just Jack and Helen in the cockpit and no passengers. As they climb out over sleeping Kansas City, the landing lights flash out, and the plane settles in at cruise altitude with a heading for Dallas. For hours, the two fly in silence over desolate ranch land without a word. Helen reaches over, gently, she takes Jack's hand in hers. By the reflection of the instrument lights, she studies his face, she notices his eyes are moist; his jaw set hard, his teeth clinched. Helen's eyes fill with tears, she knows she can make no attempt at conciliation, no words can help, the next few days will be some of the darkest of Jack's life and all she can do is stand by, nothing in his past has prepared him for this trial.

By dawn, Jack's TWA Lockheed sets down at Dallas, after Jack secures the plane; he and Helen take a car downtown. Jack leaves Helen at their hotel while he goes to the coroner's office. Jack bites his lip as the body is uncovered, with great resolve, he suppresses tears and his voice shakes as he identifies the body as his little brother Don. Leaving the stark, sterile room Jack wonders how this could have happened. How could Don let a broken marriage lead him down such a dark path? He knew Don and his second wife Claire had separated, but he never knew Don was suicidal. Jack did know though, Don was a hopeless romantic and when he was involved he was lost in the throes of the relationship.

Don and Claire had gone out to dinner the night before, really more so an opportunity for Don to beg for a reconciliation, but Claire would have none of it. Don returned to his downtown hotel, wrote out his suicide note, pulled a .32 automatic from a dresser drawer, and called Claire. When she answered, he knew she had not softened; she was surly and didn't even want to stay on the phone. He told her he had something he wanted to read to her. When he finished, again, she just brushed him off; she wanted no part of him. It was then Claire heard an explosion and called the police.

When the Dallas police arrived at the downtown Hotel Whitmore, they find a .32 in one hand and the suicide note in the other. Donald Patrick Frye was dead, just a few weeks short of his 35th birthday.

Jack visits the police department next, he collects Don's personal effects; when he sees the gun, he turns to the sergeant and says, "Destroy it." "Yes sir, Mr. Frye," the officer says, "by the way sir, I am so sorry, I knew Don," quietly he continues, "he was a good man." "Thank you, yes, he was a 'great' man," Jack says quietly as he leaves.

From his hotel, Jack calls Claire, he tells her he and Helen will fly her up to Wheeler for the funeral. Before a group of stunned mourners, the story of Don's life unfolds, related in part by former teacher of Don and close family friend, Judge R.H. Forrester.

'Donald Patrick Frye, born in 1906, was a leader and pioneer in the field of aviation, and founder-director of the copyrighted system of schools which bear his name. His company, Frye Aircraft School of Aviation, trains thousands of students nationwide to support the war effort.

At the young age of 10, Don was building model airplanes with his brother Jack who is now head of TWA. Heading out to California with his brother in 1922, Jack soon taught Don to fly, at which he became an expert aviator. Don moved in with his brother Jack and his wife Debbie, along with their sister Sunny, out near Jack's airfield on Western Avenue. He soon found work at his brother's aviation concern and became one of the 'flyers of Burdett Field'.

At just 16, Don was said to be the youngest licensed pilot on the west coast, he also held a transport pilots license. Famous aviation mechanic Walt Hamilton taught Don to repair planes, and Don attended all the weekend airshows with him and fellow aviator Paul Richter. Don was a flying member of the famed Holmoky Flying Circus, he wowed audiences flying stunts in clipped-winged Spads and Nieuports.

At 24, Donald Frye had already served 2 years in the U.S. Army Air Corps and was engaged as a flying instructor for the Guatemala Air Service. After this stint, he returned to the states, finding employ in almost every department of the Douglas Aircraft Company at Santa Monica. Later, he took a position as Personnel Manager for Consolidated Aircraft Company at San Diego. While serving in this capacity for five years, he became aware of the critical shortage of trained aircraft workers. Knowing the needs and requirements of nationwide aircraft manufacturers, Donald Frye organized the Frye Aircraft Company, with the assistance of his brother Jack. His mission statement was to help American men and women get basic training in aircraft production for the war effort, to include airliners slated for commercial service.'

After the funeral, Jack and Helen, Jack's father and his stepmother Laura, Sunny, and immediate family members and close friends gather outside the Frye Ranch house. Seated at picnic tables the family attempts to eat some of the food provided by neighbors and friends, but, as can be expected, no one is hungry. The family is still reeling from the tragedy and a shadow descends like a pall over the afternoon.

Sunny sits next to Jack and Helen on one side of the table, while Claire sits on the other. Sunny especially, is overwhelmed with grief at Don's demise, a tragedy she feels is absolutely unthinkable. Sunny can't help but give Claire looks of loathing and disgust, after all, she was there, 'Why didn't she stop this horrific tragedy from unfolding? Why did she act the way she did and practically encourage Don, goad him on?'

Finally, Claire notices Sunny's manner and inquires, "Do you have something to say to me?" Sunny responds icily, "Not now, maybe later." This comment serves to aggravate Claire who responds in a scornful manner, "Don hated you, Sunny!" Before Claire can utter another word, a stunned Sunny rises and throws her drink in Claire's face. "How dare you!" Sunny retorts, her voice shaking with rage, "I worshipped Don, we never had a cross word. But you, well, I know full-well how rocky your marriage was and how cruel you were to Don!"

Jack then rises, he reaches out to Sunny and with a strong arm, he embraces her saying, "It's O.K. Sunny, please, let's just try to get through this unscathed." Sunny looks up at Jack's face, his eyes betray his pain and anguish; she collapses into his arms in tears. Helen watches all this, her eyes misty, her husband and sister-in-law crying in embrace, finally she says gently, "Don't you all have any religion that can help you through all this?" Sunny, still feeling contrary snaps back, "Not like you, we don't!" The day is unraveling fast and all anyone yearns for is retreating to their respective corners of comfort, back at their own homes.

Sunny, Jack, and Don were very close, they lost their mother Nellie, on June 11, 1912, an event that bonded them together from that point on. Practically orphaned, they were not raised so much by their father, but more so by their beloved grandparents, Henry and Lula. Finally, at a young age Jack and Don moved out to California and Sunny was soon to follow.

Claire, caught in the fallout of the tragedy, seemingly, is blamed for her inability to reconcile with a troubled man, a man she couldn't connect with, a man she couldn't reach. Subsequently, without malice, the family never speaks to her again, blinded by their own pain and loss.

Suicide is a devastating event; the person struggling in darkness certainly can't be blamed, yet certainly they are not the only victim, as it never ends with this one event. Collateral damage is widespread, the scar never heals, and those left behind become the walking wounded for years to come.

At last, the nightmare over, Jack and Helen fly back to Kansas City, the dark event behind them. Jack desperately seeks answers, respite and salvation. He yearns for his brother to call and say, "I'm fine Jack; it was all just a bad dream."

'November 20, 1942'

Jack and Helen leave the ranch in their smart Pontiac convertible with red leather interior, the exact same hue as the lettering on Jack's TWA planes. Helen turns to Jack, as they pull away to the west, "I hope Howard likes our ranch, Jack. I think it'll do him good to get away from Los Angeles." Jack replies, "We'll get in some fishing, riding, and relaxing. It will be fun Helen! You'll see."

After a twenty-minute drive south toward Cottonwood, the crimson red Pontiac pulls off 89A in a cloud of dust, pulling onto the Frye airstrip. Jack parks next to his TWA Lockheed twin. Within moments, he and Helen hear a plane and see it come into view. Howard's twin-engine plane circles around and drops down to the packed dirt runway. The plane taxis over to Jack's Lockheed where the engines shut down. The cabin door swings open and Howard steps out, turning to help his passengers, two beautiful Hollywood starlets.

Helen and Jack walk up to greet the flight party, while Howard reaches out to shake Jack's hand. While looking around Howard says, "So, this is your secret get-a-way, huh Jack?" "Not quite," Jack answers, "just the airstrip and grazing acreage. Wait until you see my ranch near town." Helen steps over and reaches out to Howard saying, "Thank you for coming out, Howard. I hope we can show you a good time." Howard looks Helen up and down and says, "I'm sure you will Helen, I'm sure you will!" Helen greets the girls graciously, while Jack and Howard secure the plane, off-loading the luggage to the Pontiac.

With Howard and his bevies in the back, and Helen and Jack in the front, the red coupe speeds across the desert toward the red rocks of Sedona. Finally, Jack swings down into Deer-Lick Ranch. Stunning red rock spires, juniper, and cottonwood trees adjoin the red dirt road as the convertible drops down to Oak Creek. As Jack approaches a shallow ford, he turns and says, "Howard, I'll drop you off at your quarters, cross the creek, where you can freshen up, the girls are staying over with us near the Willow House. I'll send my pilot Robby to get you in an hour, if you need anything, just ask him, O.K.?" "Sure Jack, that's great. What a stunning spread you have here, all these red rock monoliths are unbelievable!"

Several days later, Helen, Jack, Howard, Robby, and the girls, are relaxing at a flagstone sitting area near the Willow House. The guests, comfortably seated on handcrafted sapling chaise lounges with adjoining side tables, are enjoying the warm Indian summer afternoon. Resting on a multi-colored leather footstool is a fringed silk throw with 'J.F.' monogrammed on the corner.

Helen is serving drinks and hors d'oeuvres, while Jack is tending to a half-dozen thick steaks on a smoking grill. One of the drinks being served is Moscow Mules in copper mugs, which originate from the 'Cock and Bull' Restaurant & Pub at West Hollywood.

Thirty-four-year-old Helen is stunning in a two-piece teal Hawaiian-style after-swim wrap she designed herself. Her face is made up perfectly, nails ruby red, her shoulder-length auburn hair piled up high in a peek-a-boo turban with curls escaping the top front in a pompadour, all highlighted by large gold hoop ear-rings and a gold charm bracelet. On her feet, ruby red painted nails peek out of red-leather pumps (high-steps) with straps around the ankles.

Helen walks over and asks Jack if he needs any help with the steaks. "No, no, Helen, thanks, I'm fine. But, I have to say," he looks Helen up and down, "you look stunning darling," then he whispers, "I love you." "Thanks sweetie," Helen says as she swishes away. She turns and throws a kiss over her shoulder. Jack smiles back lovingly.

After lunch, the group freshens up and regroups on the patio. Helen has changed into cream slacks and a lime green halter-top, skin tight. As they all visit on the patio, her diamond and ruby bracelet sparkles in the sunlight, coupled with her charm bracelet, which flashes, as she gestures with her hands up at the nearby cliff showing her guests where she and Jack plan to build their ranch home.

Jack is dressed in his typical 1940's Arizona-casual, tailored silk shirt and cravat, covered by a western style shirt-jacket, western cut boiled wool trousers, and polished cowboy boots. He and Helen are smoking; Jack has a lit cigar at his side.

The late afternoon sun is warm and soothing, as Jack visits with Howard and Robby. "I want to turn this acreage into a working-ranch, not just a scenic get-a-way, but more so like the spread I grew up on in Texas. I'm trying to obtain an interesting breed of cattle I've found to run here. A good friend Dick Kleberg owns the King Ranch in Texas, they're engaged in an experimental program breeding Santa Gertrudis cattle. The Santa Gertrudis is a cross of the Afrikaner, Brahma, and shorthorn cattle. The Afrikaner originates in Southern Africa and is well suited for high temperatures; whereas the Santa Gertrudis are very large animals adapted for hot climates. They require little water and are capable of foraging the desert scrubland for food."

Jack pauses as Howard comments, "That's very interesting Jack, and a nice diversion from aviation. I hope you'll be successful." Jack smiles as he continues, "The breed is considered rather docile and friendly under normal circumstances, but a major disadvantage is they have to be handled with very large horses. If they are sick and need doctoring, they can go through a barn wall. It'll be a challenge, but I have good people out here, and Helen and I think it will work."

Robby, who grew up on a ranch comments, "I would love to see them Jack. I sure hope I'm out here sometime when you have it all pulled together!" Jack smiles and continues, "I flew Congressman Kleberg down to Texas recently from Washington to join some friends and me on a hunting expedition. While down there I tried to cajole Dick to sell me some of his Santa Gertrudis, but he said the King Ranch was not ready to sell yet. I was very impressed with the operation at the King Ranch, and needless to say, I was very disappointed."

With that, Jack rises, "What do you say Howard, you join Robby and me down at the creek and we can get in some fishing?" Howard smiles, "I would love that!" Jack turns to Helen, "Helen, do you and the girls want to come down with us, or stay up here?" The women all murmur between each other and agree to stay up at the Willow House. Jack disappears into the barn and comes out with three fishing poles. The men start down a path, which hugs the creek.

Jack and Howard follow the creek path to an area of Oak Creek where Jack likes to fish, while Robby follows closely behind. When Jack and Howard reach an area, where the trail is right above the creek, by 6 feet or so, Robby is trailing at about 15 feet. Robby can't help but overhear Jack and Howard visit, Howard is talking about women 'and how he has his choice of any beauty who crosses his path'. As Howard continues in his matter-of-fact manner, what Robby hears next flabbergasts him. Howard pauses a moment, turns to

Jack and in a sincere tone says, "You know Jack, I've been going to ask you something ever since I arrived. How 'bout you let me sleep with Helen tonight?" Robby's mouth falls open as he watches Howard wait for Jack's answer. At first, he thinks he surely misunderstands what Howard just said; however, what happens next confirms the question.

As Robby watches, Jack stops cold, utters nary a word, spins around and clocks Howard so hard, he falls over backwards into the creek with a large splash! Robby is stunned and frozen in his tracks. Here is the richest man in the country, and Jack just knocked him silly!

Meanwhile, Howard is thrashing around in the creek, sputtering in about four feet of water. Jack stands above, looking down at Howard, his face crimson with anger. Finally, he turns to Robby with the order, "Get that S.O.B. out of the creek and off my property. Drive him back to the airfield!" Robby jumps to attention. He pushes through the brush down to the water where he wades in and helps the soaked Howard stand up. The two struggle back up the embankment to the trail, with Howard looking all of a drowned rat.

Jack walks briskly back to the Willow House. When he reaches it, he informs Helen and the girls, "Howard's leaving! If you two gals want to leave with him, you can, but you are welcome to stay a few more days with Helen and me, we can fly you back to Hollywood." Jack then walks into the house and slams the door behind him. Helen looks over at the girls, her face aghast. She says quietly, "Excuse me girls, I'll be right back. What in the world could have happened?" Helen enters the Willow House and shuts the door behind her. The girls look at each other with their eyes wide, they whisper in hushed tone.

Howard and Robby do not walk back up the path to the Willow House; instead, they circle around to the ranch Jeep and leave in a cloud of red dust. Robby drives Howard to the Deer-Lick bunkhouse-guesthouse where he retrieves his gear. Then the two drive out to the airstrip in silence to Howard's plane, where Robby drops Howard off. "Have a safe trip back to L.A.," Robby says awkwardly. Howard mumbles, "Thanks," as he throws his gear in the plane and shuts the door behind him.

Back in Los Angeles at his Hancock Park mansion, Howard is sitting at a desk with a note and envelope in front of him. He writes:

'Jack, I could not be more remorseful as to my behavior last weekend at your ranch. The manner in which I disrespected Helen was unforgivable, but yet, I ask you just that, to please forgive me. I have no excuse for my un-gentleman like behavior, except to say, I had had one too many drinks. Your defense of Helen's honor was admirable. Regards, Howard'

'December 28, 1942'

Jack and Helen had invited Jack's father and his stepmother Laura up for Christmas to their home in Kansas City. At the end of their stay, Jack and his private TWA pilot, Robby fly the couple back to Texas. On the morning of the flight, the Lockheed twin is iced-over, so Robby has it pulled into a hangar, sprayed with hot water, and dried off. The engines are started at 11:40 A.M.; departure though is delayed until 12:45 P.M. With a ceiling of 1500 feet flight conditions are poor; the plane flies south and lands by 2:59 P.M. at Twitty, Texas. Time on the ground is just twelve minutes; Jack must get back to his office. The Lockheed 12A lifts off again at 3:11 P.M., and by

5:28 P.M. the plane sets down at K.C. (Twitty is the nearest landing strip to the Frye Ranch at Wheeler, Texas.)

Western Union Telegram

'1942 Dec 31'

John Gaw Meem, Architect

WE HOPE YOU CAN MEET US AT CONTINENTAL AIRPORT ELEVEN O'CLOCK TOMORROW MORNING FOR AN HOUR. REGARDS, JACK FRYE

Jack and Helen arrive in Santa Fe and meet with John Meem to discuss the Sedona house. Meem invites the Fryes for dinner at his home on Sunday evening, January 3, unfortunately though, Helen is exhausted and collapses. After she recovers Jack helps her back to La Fonda.

Wardman Park Hotel (stationary)

Connecticut Avenue and Woodley Road

Washington D.C.

January 19, 1943

Dear Mr. Meem:

Am enclosing your memorandum with a few changes and explanations - - sorry I didn't have a typewriter but hope you can make-out what I've done.

I am very keen about the model - - however, on the complete house I have many more ideas than what is shown - - but we can take this up after the first part is started.

Tell Mrs. Meem I am sorry for having been such a stupid guest. Her luncheon was so delicious, your house so enchanting, and all the children such darlings - - I felt very badly at having acted so.

We finally decided it was because I'd blown fixing dope on my sketch the night before, was a little dopey from it, and my system drained of oxygen, just couldn't take the Santa Fe altitude on top of it all.

With kindest regards,

Helen Frye

'Spring of 1943'

Helen and Jack are at the Shoreham Hotel in Washington D.C. at a swanky party with senators and politicians. Helen is sitting at a round top and Jack is across the room visiting with a colorful looking 55-year old man dressed in western duds and boots. The men walk over to Helen, and Jack says, "Dick, this is my beautiful wife Helen, and Helen, this is Congressman Kleberg. "Well, well," says Congress Kleberg, "this is a mighty special treat. You, my dear, are 'bout as pretty as a Texas sunrise!" "Why, thank you Congressman, I sure hope that Texas has lovely sunrises," responds Helen with a smile. "The most 'beautified' in the country my dear. Would you like to dance? And please, sweetheart, call me Dick."

Jack stands back as the two move toward the dance floor amid the strings of Glenn Miller's 'Moonlight Serenade'. Helen is the first to speak as she looks up at Dick, "I understand you had a poker game going with Jack." The Congressman replies, "Yes, the boys and I managed to get a game together, but we were short one player." He pauses, and then continues, "Now I know a pretty little filly like you would never stoop to playing a sinful game of poker with us good 'ole boys, but I'll be damned if we didn't have a big 'ole southern gal step up who turned out to be one mean player. Why, I just wonder if she's some notorious card shark from a Mississippi gambling boat?" Helen laughs merrily at this saying, "I take it she took you to the cleaners?" "Why yes, ma'am, she did. If it was money we was a gambling for, I could have paid her off in truckloads." Helen was intrigued, "Well, Dick, what in the world were you playing for, or should I ask?" Dick replies, "Oh no, Mrs. Frye, it wasn't anything untoward. No, no, my dear, it was for nylons." Helen starts laughing heartily, "Oh my Lord, nylons? Now, I thought you were a smart Texas boy, how'd you fall for that? Since the war started, nylons are as hard to be had as diamonds!" "Well, Helen, I do admit I know more about cattle than ladies apparel. Why, do you know I can't find a pair of lady's stockings anywhere on the east coast?"

Helen leans in and says, "I'll tell you what Dick, I think I can help you." "Really?" says Dick. "Yes, you see, my Jack anticipated the shortage, as he works closely with the war department, so he purchased about 100 pairs for me so I wouldn't run short." "Goodness gracious Helen, your Jack sure knows how to make his little filly happy," Dick replies with a grin. Helen continues, "Well Dick, if your card-shark pal can use my size, I'll let you have as many as you need to satisfy your debt." "Oh my, Helen, you'd do that for an 'ole Texas boy like me?" "Of course I would darling. I'll never wear all those stockings anyway," Helen replies with a warm smile. At that Dick says, "Well, now that I am off the hook, I think that calls for a drink. Would you join me my dear?"

Later, Helen is at her and Jack's suite in the posh Shoreham Hotel. The phone rings, Helen walks over and picks it up. "Hello," says Helen cheerfully. "Helen dear, this is Dick Kleberg in Texas. I wanted to ring you and thank you for your gracious offer of the nylons." Dick hesitates, as he continues, "But, unfortunately, you being so petite, well, my poker pal was not able to wear the nylons you offered." "Oh, I am sorry Dick. Hmmm, let me see, I may have a solution for you, hang on a minute." Helen sets the phone down and walks over to a phonebook. She looks up a number and walks back to the phone. "Dick?" says Helen. "Yes, I'm still here," replies Dick. "Write this phone number down dear, it's for a prominent department store here in Washington D.C., they're holding a large supply of nylons for their best customers. All you have to do is tell the owner Jack and Helen Frye sent you in, I'll even call and let him know he will be hearing from you. Now, since you are back in Texas, you just call Jack and he'll fly you up here to get them in our private plane."

Dick is extremely grateful. "Well, golly Helen, I'm, well, I can't believe it. Here you have rescued me, not once, but twice! How can I ever repay you my dear?" Helen responds, "Don't give it a thought Dick, just promise me you will have dinner with Jack and me the next time you're in Washington."

Within 2 weeks, Jack and Helen are in their New York City suite at the Hotel Ambassador, on Park Avenue, when they receive a telegram stating:

'SANTA GERTRUDIS AND AFRIKANDER TO ARRIVE FLAGSTAFF –STOP- PADDED BOX CAR –STOP- PREPARE RANCH FOR DELIVERY -STOP- FOREVER GRATEFUL, DICK KLEBERG'

'April 10, 1943- Kansas City, Missouri'

In a letter to her architect at Santa Fe, Helen tries to help John Gaw Meem understand the level of home she and Jack desire be built at Sedona.

Dear Mr. Meem-

We were very enthused about your sketches, and if they aren't exactly on the right track, they at least give us something of a foundation to work on. Yes, we are very anxious to go ahead with the three rooms of the Deer-lick house. We do understand these government hold-ups, in fact, we more than have our share of the same thing.

First of all, I want to say that I don't believe you have the right picture in mind of the kind of home we want in Arizona. We have had, and I suppose will always have, all the formal life we can digest away from Arizona. You probably are like a lot of our friends who can't believe that Jack and I really go in for ranch work ourselves. We not only do it, but love it with a passion. We are never there that we don't spend all our time working the same as the ranch hands. That is, we irrigate, dig ditches, drive the tractor and trucks, help with the harvest, work with the animals, doctor and wrestle with the hogs. We seldom wear anything but work clothes and boots. We are always tired, dirty and hungry on coming to the house in the evenings and usually too tired to clean up before we eat. The red dust we drag in is fierce. I want a house that will not embarrass us. It must be beautiful, but rugged enough to take it and it must offer loads and loads of comfort. You see, we are down-to-earth, close to nature people and the house must be part of that life.

The exterior must be Hopi, like your first sketch, and which I thought you understood. Jack is part Indian, and besides this fact, Hopi seems to me to fit the cliff. The large windows I know are not true to the Hopi style, but they looked all right in our sketch- the only thing is, we want <u>more</u> window. Particularly, <u>wider,</u> or so the outside is as much open as you dare make it. After we saw the El Paso Air Terminal (Hopi) Building, made of stone instead of adobe, we were sure we would like it. While that building is of a very ordinary stone and a cheap job, still it has an appeal that we like. I think in the red stone and with your artistic hand, we'll have exactly what we desire.

The front door I think need not be a fancy affair, but a heavy weather-worn door of plain two-by-twelves, with heavy latch.

The bar-b-que looks like it will require a separate chimney from the range; if we have the old-fashioned range Jack intends to build himself, it won't be the kind to have windows behind it. I keep thinking that the same chimney should serve both.

The fire-place in the living room is too modern, delicate, fancy and too much like the three we have here in Kansas City. We like the pool arrangement and tunnel very, very, much, but want the fire-place to be longer and larger. We like the rectangular or oblong pattern. We want a mantel or mantels and the whole thing must be heavy, massive and bearing a sense of balance. The bookcase doesn't have to be, but the dog-bed-wood-box does have to be. I think we want something of a combined Indian-Spanish idea for the fireplace. There was something we liked about one of the small sketches. This I am returning with other sketches marked in red pencil suggestions. I haven't anything definite in my mind or I would try to send you a drawing to work from. If you would send me several of your ideas on Spanish-Indian design, probably we could arrive at something. Don't bother to draw them up in detail. I can tell exactly what it will be from just a few basic lines—and you can detail them after we decide.

We loved the ceiling of the view-room. It gave me an idea for the fire-place for that room. Now, I don't want a monstrosity, but what could you do with a crooked old tree on each side of the fire-place, set several inches in relief of the stone around it, and having twisted limbs effecting the mantels. Leave a center space for the head of a small deer with horns. There is a walnut tree here in my patio that I am tempted to cut down for this purpose.

We do want one door between the view-room and living room. We like the indented one. However, I feel I would like it indented from both sides. This would not make it as deep as you have it shown now.

The stair-case looks much narrower than I expected, and I want more drama to the entrance. I want it to be an object of great interest in itself. The steps can be of flat rock or hewn wood timbers.

The book-cases I don't like (in back of living room). There is something skimpy about them. I have suggested on the sketch that they have a beam across the top and run clear to the edge of walls. I drew in the picture we plan to hang there with measurements. I thought maybe a single row of *book-shelf under it would help. Considering the dust, do you think the last two bottom rows should be drawers instead of book-shelves?*

(In letter to Meem- October 27, 1947- Helen reveals: In my original plan I had a bookcase on each side of the space for a painting (opposite wall of the fireplace in the main living room) that I believe you talked me out of using. Where are the books going to go for the living room? My husband buys every book that is published I think. Of course, I don't keep all of them, but there should be space for them in the living room even though we use the piece of furniture that boarders the back of the divans for such—I don't think it's enough.)

I thought the ceiling of the stair-case should be the same as the entrance from the front door. I am sure I would like wider planking above the beams of the dining room— and even wider beams.

Will the floor of the living room and the dining room be hard enough to take spurs? I don't want to put a lot of expensive hard wood floors in the house; nor do I want the same that requires great daily care to keep it looking well. I am not one to appreciate fancy wood floors. Flat stone rock appeals to me here, and so does heavy, stained planks.

The kitchen I designed for the easy cooking of a meal, keeping an eye on the front door and serving food on the veranda where the bar-b-que is located. I fully realize this is not arranged for the old-fashioned one I want. Still, it has to have both characteristics. Please see what you can suggest. I cook, but rarely do the dishes. I believe you may have done dishes in your time—hence the sink. We think we ought to have two sinks in the kitchen. Also, we want to put a small sink with cold water piped to it from the cold storage in the center of the wine and liquor cabinet in the dining room. It must be so that it is covered except when using it. I don't know what asbestos cement flooring is, but will this be easy on the feet? I think whoever does this house work is sure to end up with feet trouble, the house will be so spread out. Did I tell you we like the floor plan for the view-room?

Oh yes, the privacy you mentioned concerning the open tunnel fire-place might be taken care of temporarily with a metal shutter or screen. After we have the bedroom and office added, we will not be concerned with privacy, but there is the possibility of perhaps wanting just to heat the view-room.

By the way, don't forget our huge, old logging wheels. We want to use these somewhere, perhaps a gate entrance, but if you have any other ideas, let us know. They are heavy, made of iron and oak, the axle coming to about my shoulders.

After writing this letter, I am convinced that architects with home builders like us must have plenty of headaches.

I believe Mr. Frye spoke to you before about your charges, but I hope that we are not getting in too deep with all these studies.

Most sincerely,

Helen V. Frye

'June 28, 1943'

Dear Mr. Meem:

Your office wrote you'd be back from the East the first of June - - and I've been watching every mail to see if there isn't something from you and what you thought of the drawings I marked up with corrections and the long letter on our ideas of the ranch house.

I have at last succeeded catching myself a "papoose" or rather the promise of one - - I got off to a bad start but am feeling better and as soon as the doctor says it's safe to travel I am going down to the ranch for the summer where I can get plenty of Arizona sunshine.

I'd like nothing better than to have our baby born in the new ranch house - - Do you think we have a chance?

With Best Regards,

Helen Frye

However, by July 15, 1943, Helen wrote again from Washington D.C., "The doctors are not sure that I will carry through with the baby, so maybe there is not so much hurry after all."

'September 30, 1943'

TRANSCONTINENTAL & WESTERN AIR, INC.

OFFICE OF THE PRESIDENT

Dear Mr. Riordan-

Mr. and Mrs. Frye are in Washington. I know they will be delighted to receive your interesting letter of September 27, which I am forwarding to them.

Knowing how very busy Mr. Frye always is when he is in the East and that Helen is spending all her time trying to find a place to live, I thought I would write this note so you would understand if some time elapses before they have a chance to write you.

Sincerely,

Meriam L. Furse

Secretary to Mr. Frye

'January 14, 1944'

Jack and Helen are staying at the celebrity get-a-way Deep Well Guest Ranch near Palm Springs, tomorrow they are off to Los Angeles.

Letter to Timothy Riordan at Flagstaff-

Our Christmas cards are just catching up with us. Thanks for your kind thoughtfulness. Your beautiful bottle of Scotch and a handsome pair of chaps that Jack had made for me in Flag are all the Christmas we have had yet.

You see, this war and our traveling around first completely upsets all holidays and social life. Hell, won't it be fun when we all get back to work and leave all our packages to unwrap- let me guess- about "Ground Hog Day?"

We are due back in L.A. soon, maybe tomorrow. We were so busy the few days that we were at the ranch that I didn't get to call you folks. Maybe by the time I do you will be there, too. I certainly hope so because I want to make a date with you to take you out for dinner and a show. I can't depend upon Jack when he is in town doing anything except his work. But I don't think he will mind seeing such a good friend as you going out with me.

Should you not be in L.A. when we get there, Jack says that he's hoping to come back to our ranch next week. I'll contact you because you might like to fly back to California with us then.

Thanks again for your lovely Christmas spirit, 'spirits' we need them both.

Hope to see you soon.

Sincere Regards,

Helen V. Frye

Helen is still under the weather from her pregnancy last summer, after which she tragically lost a child with a miscarriage on her third trimester; unfortunately, Helen lost three of Jack's children in this manner, always on the third month. With the unfathomable anguish only a woman can experience, this last pregnancy broke Helen's heart; she never discussed it or spoke of it again. Fate had decreed she and Jack were not to have children.

By February 7, Jack and Helen are out in Albuquerque on TWA business. They take this opportunity to fly up to Continental Airport at Santa Fe so they can consult with their architect John Gaw Meem. While there, Helen tours art museums and purchases two high-dollar paintings from local artist Foster Jewell. The titles are 'As In A Dream', which Helen finds displayed near the Plaza, and the second, 'Symphony In December', which Helen views at the artist's studio at 834 El Caminito Street (just off Canyon Road). The Santa Fe New Mexican reports this transaction is the most important of the winter art season, citing, "Mrs. Frye whose husband is president of TWA, lives in Washington D.C. and has a ranch in Arizona."

With hardly time to unload the paintings at Washington D.C., the Lockheed is fueled for an outbound emergency flight to Wheeler, Texas to retrieve Jack's father who is deathly ill, along with Jack's stepmother Laura. After landing at Twitty, Texas the Lockheed 12A takes off almost immediately for Albuquerque. The Fryes connect with a waiting ambulance that rushes the stricken Dr. William Frye where he undergoes an emergency gall bladder operation at St. Joseph's Hospital by Dr. Lovelace (of Lovelace Clinic).

Jack favors Lovelace at Albuquerque for all his medical needs, to include as an official flight-physical clinic for TWA pilots for many years. Jack had a long-standing association with both the senior Lovelace, and his son Dr. William Randolph Lovelace II (Randy). By February 21, Jack and Helen are again back at Washington D.C.

Chapter 9

The Camelot Years of TWA

In early 1944, a Buick convertible pulls up a long drive to an imposing looking Arlington colonial mansion, resting on a knoll overlooking Washington D.C. A man and woman approach the Buick as it rolls to a stop. An impeccably attired Helen Frye steps out, fashionably dressed in an elegant tailored suit, matching open-toed pumps, crowned by a huge 1940's-style hat. "So, this is it?" says Helen, "quite impressive!" A leasing agent steps up and holds out her hand, "Welcome Mrs. Frye, yes, this is the Doubleday Mansion. It sits on the highest promenade in the area, with lovely views of the White House and the capitol. There are 30 rooms and about 70 acres. Please, do come this way, and we'll show you around!"

Helen strolls through the dusty rooms of the mansion; occasionally, she appreciatively caresses a piece of exquisite woodwork with her violet-hued glove. Carefully, she sizes it up for Jack and TWA, comparing it to all the other homes she has toured in the area. She surveys the gardens, and even finds a charming location for a pool. Finally, after an hour, she turns to the agent and says, "This is it, I think it will do splendidly. It is just picturesque, and what views, absolutely divine!" As the male secretary takes notes in a leather binder, Helen says, "Please send all paperwork to TWA, the address is '1740 G Street N.W., Washington D.C.' I'll make arrangements for my decorator and house staff to come out for a tour."

'March 1944'

One evening, Jack and Helen are at the mansion, which is in a state of renovation. The doorbell rings, Helen sets down her decorator magazine, rises, and answers it. Opening the door, she greets a beautiful young girl and a tall, distinguished man, both African-American. "You must be the Browns," says Helen graciously. "Please, please do come in." Helen leads them into the drawing room. Jack rises and greets them, "How do you do?" he says. The petite young girl introduces them both, "This is my husband Aubrey, and I'm Evangeline," she says. "Please, sit down," says Jack warmly.

Jack quickly explains the responsibilities of the staff at the mansion and what would be required if the two were hired. He also states he expects total loyalty from his staff—this includes privacy, as in not divulging his or Helen's whereabouts to reporters, or any details of their guests. "There will be a lot of V.I.P.'s staying out here," he concludes.

Helen asks Evangeline what her prior experience is, and who her previous employers were? Evangeline explains her past positions and hands Helen a stack of references. Helen goes over to an overstuffed chair, adjoined by a lamp, and carefully reads the letters. Finally, she turns to Jack and says, "Well, what do you think dear?" Jack replies, "It's totally up to you Helen, the house is your concern." Helen turns back to Evangeline and Aubrey, she pauses a moment, "Well, you are certainly very personable, and definitely well-recommended, but," she hesitates, "I can't help but think you are too young, at 22, to handle the enormous responsibility which will placed on you as chef and manager of the household." Helen looks over at Jack, he gives her a look of, 'I'm staying out of this'.

At last, Evangeline speaks up, "I'll tell you what Mr. and Mrs. Frye, I guarantee I can handle this house with ease, and my husband can represent you as chauffeur and houseman with confidence. I just ask for one favor." "And what would that be?" says Helen cautiously. "Please, let me go in the kitchen and prepare dinner for you and Mr. Frye, totally on me, mind you, just to show you I can handle the culinary side of the house." "Well, I see no reason why not," says Helen, "I'll show you the way, please be advised though, the cupboards are poorly stocked at the moment." Once in the large kitchen, Evangeline rolls up her sleeves and pitches in.

Within a short time, Evangeline returns to the drawing room, "Dinner is served. I found no table in the dining room, so I set it up at the kitchen table." Jack and Helen follow her into the kitchen, where they find a beautiful dinner laid out. "My Lord," says Helen, obviously impressed. "How did you manage this spread with nothing to work with?" Jack and Helen sit down to dinner as the Browns excuse themselves. After dinner, Helen and Jack go back into the drawing room where the Browns are waiting. Jack says, "You're hired, you start tomorrow!" With misty eyes, Evangeline reaches out and shakes both their hands, as does Aubrey. "Thank you, oh thank you, you won't be disappointed!" says Evangeline joyfully!

Helen interviews various other staff members to assist Evangeline and Aubrey, and the Browns become Helen and Jack's most treasured help and extended family at the Washington estate. Soon the house is a-buzz with renovations, which Transcontinental & Western Air finances. Helen and Evangeline travel across the east coast buying up fine period furniture, tapestries, and antiques for the historic colonial mansion. When Helen and her decorator finish the house, it is stunning, and can easily receive the highest officials of the country. The Fryes rename the estate Hillcrest Farm; however, in Washington, the estate is still identified as the Doubleday Mansion.

Many parties are held at the mansion, attended by the Who's Who of Washington D.C., members of the League of Nations, the corporate world, and personal friends of the Fryes, many of the same are guests at the house. The mansion is setup to serve as a strategic power-center at Washington, so TWA can assist in the war effort, and obtain the overseas routes for airline passenger service after the war.

At one point, Jack has Evangeline flown down to old Mexico, so she can master the preparation of Texas Chili, his all-time favorite. Chili, so hot, that after each bite, one needs two sips of beer! Evangeline prepares the chili in mason jars, so Jack can have it in the cockpit and share with his friends. Meanwhile, Howard Hughes, a frequent guest with his own suite of rooms, takes a shining to Evangeline, and she and Helen learn how to cook his steaks just the way he likes them. Reporters hound the Browns for news of Howard and the Fryes just like Jack had predicted, but the Browns are stalwart protectors of the privacy of the Doubleday Mansion, never divulging any personal information. Mrs. Brown slams the front door shut many times against the relentless intrusion of reporters trying to breech the mansion's perimeters looking for Hughes and Jack Frye.

'April 17, 1944'

Witness to the Constellation Celebration, as mentioned earlier, is a color movie of Jack and Helen at the event, with Helen dressed in a three-quarter length baby-blue tailored suit, full-length fur coat and heels. The film displays Helen walking past Jack and Hughes, up the polished aluminum-boarding ramp to the new Constellation airliner for one of many preview flights. Jack follows within moments. The wonder of this scene is when Jack reaches the top of the stairs,

Helen and he embrace and kiss, while Helen holds a purse with her leathered-gloved hand.

Recently, in viewing this old color movie from April 17, 1944, I couldn't help but be awestruck by the real-life moving images of Jack and Helen Frye. Most startling though, and a real asset for early TWA, was that the two celebrities were so young and vibrant. Both Helen and Jack lend an element of pure class to the airline.

Jack was just 40, and Helen just 35, whereas Howard Hughes was only 39. TWA, with the exception of the board, was not operated by old men, as was typical of such large corporations, but rather at the time, was notated as being managed by the youngest airline head in the world (Frye).

Amazingly, when Jack helped found Transcontinental & Western Air, Inc., he was just 26-years-old! However, he had already been a flight school owner and pilot from 1923, at just 19 years old! The film displays a look of pride and accomplishment evident on everyone's face!

The seeding of TWA was with dreams, dedication, and hard work—an era never repeated, certainly not without the dedication of Jack Frye, truly—'the Camelot Years'.

'April 19, 1944'

At the Statler Hotel, now the Capitol Hilton in Washington D.C., Jack and Helen Frye host a party for 1500 guests in the Presidential Dining Room, this to commemorate the record flight of the Constellation just days earlier, the world's largest land-based transport.

Howard Hughes attends too, and contrary to popular rumor of the day, which states Howard never shakes hands out of fear of germs, he stands by graciously beside Jack and Helen and proudly shakes nearly 1000 of them! This promo, hosted by the Fryes and Transcontinental & Western Air, celebrates the future of TWA, a grand introduction to Trans-World air travel via the futuristic Constellation airliner, an event all but forgotten today!

'A Weekend Adventure, New Wardrobe, 21 Club, Poker'

Senator Harry Truman was a passenger on Jack's Lockheed Electra Jr., several times over. Most the trips were hunting and fishing and not 'official', therefore it is difficult to document them. Jack Frye was one of the most influential men in the Democratic Party in the 1940's and it is not at all surprising Harry and Jack became friends, let alone the fact, they both hailed from the same region of the country in regard to business (Missouri). As a mover and shaker within the hierarchy of the party, if you needed a favor or wanted something done, you picked up the phone and called Jack Frye.

In July of 1944, Truman became the nominee for Vice-President of the United States. Jack was enlisted to fly Truman and other Democratic V.I.P.'s to New York City for Truman's vice-presidential 'make-over'.

"Would you like some more eggs, Mr. Frye?" Evangeline says as she removes Jack's plate and pours him some more coffee. "No, thank you Evangeline, I have to get going." Helen says, "Jack, I hope you have a good time up there, but sounds more like business first, and a lot of waiting around." Jack says, "Yes darling, it will be a long week-end, but we have to insure Truman is groomed for the presidency, especially since Roosevelt may not finish his term due to his illness. However, we will get some card games in while we are there." "Well, just make sure you and Bob enjoy yourselves," Helen replies. Jack pushes his chair back, walks over, kisses Helen on the lips, and leaves the room saying, "I love you Helen." Jack grabs his briefcase with sport jacket and leaves the mansion. He steps into the back of a limousine, "To the airport Aubrey. I had hoped I could swing by the office, but we're out of time." "Yes sir, Mr. Frye." The limo pulls away from the mansion and disappears down the drive.

Jack arrives at Washington National just as Bob Hannegan steps out of a long black sedan. "Well Bob, I see you were able to get away," Jack says with a grin as he greets Bob with a handshake and slap on the shoulder. "Yes," Bob replies, "I feel I have to be there for this one. By the way, the girls are getting together while we are gone. Irma mentioned she and Helen are doing lunch." "That's great Bob! We might as well go ahead and board," Jack states as he and Bob walk over to Jack's 12A parked on the tarmac. As Bob steps inside, Jack turns and confers with a TWA ground crewman in white overalls with a red TWA embossed on the back. "The plane is serviced and ready to go Mr. Frye. Is there anything else we can do for you?" "No Chester, just make sure you load the luggage as it arrives." "Yes sir, Mr. Frye," replies the young man.

Another limousine arrives, after it glides to a stop, the chauffeur exits and opens the back door. Senator Harry Truman and Edwin Pauley step out, while Jack and Bob exit the Lockheed and walk over to greet them. Jack shows Truman around the plane, as Pauley and Hannegan step inside. Finally, the TWA co-pilot arrives. He stows his luggage, follows Truman and Frye into the plane, he shuts and secures the cabin door behind them.

Jack makes sure everyone is comfortable, then, he makes his way to the cockpit stepping over the wing bulkhead. He sits down in the left seat, while the co-pilot settles into the right seat. After the radials fire one by one, Chester pulls the wheel chocks and the plane taxies out on to the runaway. Jack powers up the engines and the plane pulls away as the twin tail lifts with the prop wash. The tail-dragger, now level, quickly accelerates down the runway and is off the ground in a flash.

Jack banks sharply toward New York, with the Doubleday Mansion and federal buildings spread out below the cabin windows. Hannegan, Pauley, and Truman visit in the cabin while watching the panorama below. After the 12A reaches cruise altitude, Jack asks Harry if he would like to join him in the cockpit. Truman rises and makes his way up to the right seat as the co-pilot retreats to the cabin. Jack explains to Harry the fundamentals of operation and points out various landmarks below. Finally, after fifteen minutes, Jack and Harry join the others in the rear after the co-pilot takes control of the Lockheed. On approach to New York City, Jack again takes the helm, he announces they will be landing at LaGuardia in about thirty minutes.

True to his word, Jack sweeps in over Manhattan and lands at LaGuardia within twenty-nine minutes. The Lockheed taxies to a private area near the TWA terminal, where a Cadillac Series 75 limousine is waiting; the men step into the car while the driver loads the luggage. Finally, the black Cadillac glides away toward the Sherry-Netherland, at 5th Avenue and 59th Street. After the limo reaches its destination, the bell staff escorts the V.I.P.'s to the tower of the residential hotel where Pauley keeps a 3-bedroom suite. Hannegan, Pauley, and Frye occupy this floor, while Truman is booked into a suite on the floor directly below. Pauley and a friend own most the bonds for the building and maintain the suite for the duration of the war. The lavish Sherry-Netherland consists of 24-stories (a base of 10-stories crowned by a 14-story gothic tower) all overlooking Central Park.

While in Manhattan, Pauley refreshes Truman's style of dress and appearance, with the aid of his personal tailor and shirt-maker. One might wonder why Truman needed wardrobe advice in light of the fact that he was once a haberdasher by trade. Simply put, the Democratic Party was grooming the future vice-president in a more conservative manner befitting the White House, rather than the typical flashy Senator Truman style.

In between the 'make-over' fittings, the men play cards, a pastime relished by Frye and Truman. The preferred game is poker, but they also play games, which Truman personally invents.

Before the group flies back to Washington, Pauley treats Truman to 21 Club, which is near his clothier. Truman enjoys the diversion, as he had never been to the restaurant before and didn't know it was once a speakeasy.

As testament to the poker antics of Truman and Frye is a comment by Jack's sister, Sunny Frye Thomas. Sunny attended the dedication of the new TWA Jack Frye Training Center at Kansas City, April 26, 1962, at which former president Harry Truman was the Speaker of Honor. During the ceremony, Truman nudged Sunny saying, "I liked Jack, because he'd let me win at poker!" Truman had been acquainted with Sunny years earlier when he was entertained at the Frye estate in Kansas City. He also played cards with Jack at Hillcrest Farm (the Doubleday Mansion) at Washington. In comment, after Jack's death, Truman said of his friend, "He had imagination, which damn few businessmen have!"

In conjunction with this, Jack and Helen are also close friends with Robert E. Hannegan, and his wife Irma. Robert is a democratic powerhouse and Chairman of the Democratic National Committee (1944-1947). He also serves as Commissioner of the Internal Revenue (1943-1944), and Postmaster General (1945-1947). Indeed, he is the Postmaster General referred to in the famous Christmas film, 'Miracle on 34th Street' (1947), with Maureen O'Hara and John Payne.

'July 10, 1944'

In letter, Helen describes life at the Doubleday Mansion at Washington-

'We have had the League of Nations represented here this week and all of them, you understand, are in direct line of business and most of it post-war planning. Col. Shoop—who was the first man out on the invasion on 'D' day, flying a P-38, and the first man back to report- was here for a dinner of hot dogs cooked over the barbecue at the pool late one evening.

His tales are very exciting and interesting and I guess he is very lucky to be back here now, although he will return soon. He says those bombs- the robot ones- are really terrible. This fellow was test pilot for the Constellation and was on the trip coming across.

We have had during the past week people from France, Holland, Arabia, China, South America, New Zealand, Egypt, Canada, Scotland, and Africa. There's no use explaining to you why my husband hasn't any time to go visiting. I am more thankful every day for the swimming pool; otherwise, he would be doing like he did the last three years—working in the hotel and office all the time. Now, he often takes his people to the pool and they can keep cool, bodily as well as mentally, while they work on their plans.

Last night at midnight, you would have probably gotten a kick out of seeing him and another man, like two porpoises in the pool, just leisurely moving about under a big moon. It looked like pleasure but when you got close enough to hear them they were working on very serious business.'

'July 24, 1944'

Jack and Helen host the marriage of close friends, movie star Julie Bishop, and flight test pilot Lieutenant Colonel Clarence A. Shoop, at their Arlington mansion. Attended by military brass and Hollywood celebrities, the gala is a lovely event, which spills out on the lawns overlooking the Potomac, catered by Evangeline Brown.

'September 29, 1944'

The Fryes are back at the Deep Well Guest Ranch at Palm Springs for a little R&R. After flying on to Los Angeles, they return to Washington within a week.

'October 1944'

La Posada Hotel- Winslow

Dear Mr. Riordan-

So sorry you weren't able to attend our dinner party but do hope this finds you on the mend and able to be up and around very soon-

Helen V. Frye

'November 4, 1944'

Late in the evening, at the Frye mansion in Washington, Jack and Helen are asleep in their second-story master bedroom suite. In the defused twilight of the large room, all of the sudden the phone on the nightstand starts ringing. Jack, in a sleepy stupor, reaches over to answer it, "Hello?" Helen sits up slightly and watches Jack as he says, "This 'IS' grave." Continuing to listen, Jack swings out of bed and rests his feet on the floor, suddenly; he's wide awake and focused. "The plane crashed, inverted, after losing a wing? Jesus! How many passengers and crew died? What time?" Finally, after a pause, Jack says, "Yes, get him out there tonight. I want to know exactly how this could have happened. And as soon as Bartles gets up there, have him call me right away!" After another pause, Jack says, "Yes, goodbye."

Slowly, Jack replaces the receiver. Helen reaches over to comfort him, resting her hand on his back and rubbing it gently. Jack slowly slumps down as he sits deep in thought. He reaches over, finds Helen's hand, and squeezes it. "These accidents are the hardest part of running an airline Helen," he pauses, then says softly, "the safety of every crew member and passenger rests on my shoulders." Helen responds soothingly, "Yes, I know dear, I know."

Suddenly, a sound is heard, a thumping on the stairs, and a tapping on wood floors. The sound gets louder and louder as it enters the room—the pitter-patter of dog's feet. A large form approaches from the doorway, across the room, and around the bed to where Jack is sitting. The dog pauses in front of Jack, resting its muzzle on his lap, then it whimpers softly.

Jack looks up with surprise as the animal starts licking his hand and face. He reaches up and strokes the dog's head saying gently, "There, there old girl, how you'd know I needed a friend, now, more than ever?" Helen watches the scene with surprise; finally, she finds her voice, "I can't believe it! Sonja's been trained to never come upstairs, and she never has, just like you desire, however, after a plane crash, she knows you need her and here she is in the middle of the night! It's like she's psychic, I just can't believe it!"

As Jack rubs Sonja's ears, the German Shepard climbs up on his lap, her rear feet resting on the floor. Jack says softly to Helen, "I think I failed Sonja by restricting her from our private quarters and the cockpit. From now on she's welcome up here, and when I fly she can sit in the cockpit between us Helen, just like she always wanted to! What an intuitive dog!" Jack reaches down and rubs Sonja's ears, "Thanks, old girl."

In the late 1930's, as Mrs. Cornelius Vanderbilt Jr., Helen was shopping on 5th Avenue in New York City when she noticed unsavory people beating a German Shepherd police dog in an alley. Without an ounce of fear, this glamorous socialite walked up to the dog, grabbed the leash, and walked away, to the amazement of the abusers! Sonja, as Helen named the rescue, became Helen's loving companion for the remainder of the dog's life. This experience galvanized Helen and opened her eyes to the plight of unwanted pets. Later, this humanity resulted in Helen co-founding the Sedona Humane Society. Previously, with no Sedona facilities, Helen and other founding members housed the cast-aside pets of Sedona in their own homes, at their own expense.

'December 2, 3, 1944'

Jack and Helen host the Grand Canyon wedding of coppery-blond 27-year-old movie star, Faye Emerson, and 34-year old Colonel Elliott Roosevelt (President Franklin Delano Roosevelt's son), with Jack serving as best man and paying all expenses. Jack and Elliott, and Helen and Faye, are all close friends, as is Howard Hughes' publicity manager, Johnny Meyer, also in attendance. Meyer had introduced Faye and Elliott, the previous year, at his Beverly Hills home, September of 1943.

On the morning of Saturday, December 2, Howard Hughes dispatches one of his planes, a WACO bi-plane, tail number NC15706, to retrieve F.D.R.'s granddaughter, Ruth Chandler Roosevelt at Santa Barbara, delivering her to Hughes Field at Culver City. Little Ruth will serve as maid of honor at her father's wedding. Chandler's father Elliott, and his fiancé Faye, join the 10-year old Chandler at the airport. Ms. Emerson, under contract to Warner Bros., had worked late the previous day on the film 'Danger Signal'—this tight schedule a concession for Faye and the only way Warner Bros. would release her for the wedding-honeymoon and trip to the White House, thought to be some ten days in production delays.

Jack and Helen greet the passengers at Hughes Field where they proceed to board Jack's Lockheed 12A. Previously, Jack had retrofitted his executive transport by removing the first two passenger seats and installing two auxiliary forty-eight-gallon fuel tanks. This increased the fuel load to 296 gallons (from 200) resulting in a safe six-hours flight, enabling Frye to fly non-stop from Kansas City to Washington D.C., or Kansas City to Winslow Arizona, or even his Sedona Ranch airfield near Cornville. Unfortunately, this reduced cabin capacity from six to four passengers, with two pilots.

Historically, there is confusion as to which two TWA Lockheed twins Jack utilized on this wedding flight, further, this is the first time the press mentions Jack's private plane as a Lockheed 'Lodestar'. Up to this juncture, from 1940, the executive TWA plane utilized by Frye was always his 1937 Lockheed 12A, Electra Jr.

By December of 1944, though, Jack secured another executive transport, this, a two-year old former U.S.A.A.F. Lockheed Lodestar 18, C56D, C/N 2170, registration number NC33604, TWA fleet number 241. This plane served Frye capaciously, with a passenger load of fourteen, and crew of three. Luxuriously refitted by TWA for executive service, the mini-airliner carried a TWA Hostess (flight attendant) with added bonus of a restroom or 'Blue Room' as pilots nicknamed it. The Lodestar and the Electra Jr. were both sophisticated swift transports of their day and had the dual purpose of executive transports for Frye, as well as TWA flight research labs; the infamy of both these planes became 'as associated with Jack Frye and TWA' for the rest of their lives.

Because of passenger load notated in copy of the day, we will assume the plane used December 2 was the Lockheed 12A. At 1:30 P.M. Jack ushers his guests onboard, to include Elliott (in the right co-pilot seat), and Faye and Chandler in the cabin. Jack boards two additional wedding guests, Hollywood actress, Mrs. Clarence A. Shoop (Julie Bishop), and matron of honor, Mrs. Joseph B. Livengood.

The captain, of course, is TWA president Jack Frye, the airlines most tenured and experienced pilot. Certainly, 36-year-old Frye is well qualified to transport the president's son and granddaughter. With a full load of passengers and fuel, the dual-450 H.P. twin engines throb powerfully as the Lockheed taxis out on the runway. By 1:55 P.M. the silver plane lifts out of Culver City, banks over Hollywood, and climbs out toward the Mojave Desert and on to Valle Airport, about thirty miles south of the Grand Canyon. This small airport is quite familiar to Jack and Helen, as they own the Spring Valley Ranch nearby, north of Williams, Arizona. Within three hours, and by 5:00 P.M., the gleaming Lockheed circles, amid snow flurries, touching down gently at Valle Airport. A limousine awaits the inbound flight, and after offloading passengers and luggage, the wedding party is whisked to the South Rim of the Grand Canyon, arriving after 7:00 P.M.

The initial Frye transport is but one of three wedding-guest planes to depart from California this day, to include a fourth plane full of reporters, which sets down at Blythe, California, due to icing and snow flurries. The men quickly hire a car and continue over hazardous roads, missing the wedding, but catching up with the Roosevelts the next afternoon for press photos.

The third plane is forced to land at Kingman Airport, with passengers Lieutenant Colonel Clarence Shoop, Lieutenant Colonels David Brooks and John Hoover. Subsequently, these stranded military officers are unable to attend the wedding. The TWA 12A, with Jack in command, is the only plane to arrive at its intended destination, navigating through treacherous flight conditions.

Helen Frye is on a second plane that makes an emergency landing at the primitive location of Ashfork Arizona, dictated by blizzard-like flight conditions. This dirt-pack airstrip provides a rather rough and tense landing for the small plane, which settles and slides through accumulating snowdrifts. Once on the ground, Helen and her cabinmates, John Meyer and Janet Thomas, walk four miles in a freezing snowstorm before a United States Secret Service agent finally spots them and transports them on to Valle Airport and the Grand Canyon.

Meanwhile, Jack waits anxiously for Helen to arrive at the Valle Airport while he has the 12A fueled and serviced. After she arrives by auto, he and Helen board the Lockheed and take off for their Sedona Ranch, landing at the Cornville airstrip after dark. After driving over to the ranch and retrieving clothing, riding tack, and saddles, etc. for wedding activities at the Grand Canyon, the Fryes instruct their ranch hands to prepare for the Roosevelt party. At last, with landing lights illuminating the dirt-pack runway of the Frye airstrip, the Lockheed lifts off north to the Grand Canyon, climbing up over Williams and dropping into Valle Airport through freezing temperatures. Jack and Helen deplane and take a hired car to the Grand Canyon, checking into the eighty-room, log and rock constructed El Tovar Lodge, by 11:00 P.M.

The next morning, at 9:20 A.M., Jack serves as best man, and Johnny Meyer gives away the bride at the glass-enclosed Yavapai Observation Station overlooking the Grand Canyon. After which, the guests attend a champagne breakfast at El Tovar lodge, one mile away. Despite the difficulty in reaching this isolated area of Arizona, Faye

Emerson later commented on the 8-minute ceremony, "Well, at least we had a white wedding!" Adding, "It was a good thing there was something white about it, because this was my second marriage and I was not allowed to wear white myself." It was Roosevelt's third. Faye also told the press the event was, "Probably the most beautiful wedding there ever was!" Lastly, the new Mrs. Roosevelt told the press, "I'm a loyal Democrat you know!" That's a relief, as everyone else in the wedding party was too, to include, her in-laws at the White House!

After the wedding, Jack and Helen depart for the Sedona Ranch on the 12A, having invited Elliott and Faye to come down later, after they depart the Grand Canyon. On December 6, Jack and Helen drive up to Flagstaff, where they meet Elliott and Faye at Hotel Monte Vista. Jack treats everyone to dinner, including local friends, Mr. and Mrs. Hugh Victor Watson, making a party of six. The group leaves for Sedona, but it's much too late, and the roads are icy, so the party stops for the night at Mayhew Lodge in Oak Creek Canyon. The next day, two cars continue to the Frye Ranch, followed by a third, with a Secret Service detail. Once at the ranch, the Roosevelts spend the rest of their honeymoon at the Willow House. By the weekend, Jack is in the air again with Elliott and Faye, with destination of Hughes Field, at Culver City.

Petty opposing political pundits try to direct attention on aircraft fuel consumed for this event, as reflected by wartime rationing, but this is for naught and found to be just so much Republican ankle biting. In an interview on December 23, at Washington, we learn the following: 'TWA President Jack Frye says he gave Col. Roosevelt only one plane, not three, for his wedding party. The other two were rented by the press associations to cover the wedding story.' Frye further states 'he has known Elliott a long time, admired what he did in the war, and so turned over a two-engine Lockheed 12, about eight-years old, which he uses for observation purposes and for trying out various gadgets. The plane, he says, was not pulled out of service.'

Within days, Faye and Elliott fly east to the White House to meet the President and the First Lady. The wedding event is on Jack Frye. Indeed, Jack picks up the entire tab at well over $850.00. The weekend stay is not charged to TWA, as media sources infer; but rather Howard Hughes reimburses Frye for all expenses incurred.

'December 20, 1944'

Helen entertains gal-pals Faye Emerson Roosevelt and Garnett Gardiner, soon to be the Baroness Stackelberg, at the Mayflower Hotel Lounge, in Washington, for a martini lunch. The Fryes had flown home for the holidays to their Arlington Doubleday Mansion from the west. Faye Emerson Roosevelt was meeting the First Family for the first time. Many dignitaries and celebrities interrupt the luncheon, all of them anxious to meet Elliott Roosevelt's new wife, to include, Senator Albert Benjamin 'Happy' Chandler.

The Washington Post runs an article with photo of Helen and Faye in front of three martini glasses. Garnett is not in the shot as she stands up so Faye and Helen can be in the photograph at the small round table together. Mrs. Roosevelt, with a perfect complexion and blond hair held in a chignon, wears a light-blue wool suit with taupe felt beret cocked low over her right brow, framed by a full-length mink coat. Mrs. Frye sports a wide-brimmed straw-colored hat, with wide ribbon around the crown, cream tailored suit bordered by embroidered trim and uplifted padded shoulders, accented by ruby-red lipstick and matching red nails.

'January 1945'

Jack is relaxing at his richly appointed executive office at 1740 G Street N.W., Washington D.C., just off Pennsylvania Avenue, two blocks from the White House. In front of his massive paneled desk, Helen relaxes in a burgundy leather-tufted club chair, dressed in seamed-stockings, her legs crossed elegantly. The long desk is befitting a president with blotter and pen set, three telephones, a large polished oak intercom with a dozen switches, and a Dictaphone at the end. A large chrome model of a TWA Constellation sits at the front center, with light spraying out the bottom onto a crystal ashtray with a lit cigar. Displayed on the wall behind Jack's desk is a dramatic 46' by 56' near life-size portrait of Helen in a rust buckskin skirt and top, laying on a Native American patterned formal sofa with backdrop of Cathedral Rock.

Helen is dressed in the latest style and fabric. Her indigo-blue brushed wool suit with matching gold soutache braided jacket is offset by matching suede pumps, an outfit which enhances her sapphire-blue eyes. A chic two-foot-wide black velvet hat with indigo blue ribbon rests off Helen's brow accenting her softly curled auburn hair. In her right hand, Mrs. Frye elegantly holds a cigarette, with glistening diamond and ruby ring, aside deep ruby-red painted nails. Helen's left hand rests in her lap, graced by an 18K basket-weave wedding band she and Jack both share, she holds her gold-jeweled cigarette case.

Jack and Helen quietly talk together about their new home plans at Sedona, when the intercom buzzes intrusively. The voice of Jack's executive assistant Mary P. Battle fills the room, "I'm sorry to interrupt you and your wife Mr. Frye, but Miss Harriet Appelwick is here. Should I ask her to come back after you have lunch?" Jack reaches over and presses one of the switches, "No Mary, please send her in." "Right away, Mr. Frye," responds Mrs. Battle.

In a moment, a wood-paneled door opens, Mary shows Harriet in, while introducing her to Jack and Helen. Jack stands up as he reaches out in greeting saying, "Good morning Miss Appelwick, won't you please sit down?"

The attractive, smartly dressed 22-year old woman sits down in front of Jack in a leather chair adjoining Helen. "So, Harriet, you'd like to fill the position of TWA's 'V.I.P. Hostess?'" Jack questions. Continuing he says, "My staff has assured me you come highly recommended and are of the utmost professional manner and ability. "Yes sir," replies Harriet confidently. "I do feel I'm qualified, and I would very much like the opportunity to serve TWA and its in-flight V.I.P. guests."

Jack looks over at Helen inquisitively; his face reflects a desire for her opinion. Helen returns the glance, nods to Harriet with a warm smile, and looks back at Jack, saying nothing. Jack continues confidently, "This position goes far and beyond normal Hostess duties. You would be required to entertain my passengers and clients in the air, and at times on the ground. Additionally, you would be required to be available 24/7, with no excuses or delays mind you, totally at the whim of my schedule and flights, which can change on a moment's notice. Your placement on my plane is to represent TWA and myself, and to complement Helen who often entertains our guests in flight. My plane is an extension of my executive office; I conduct the same manner of business in the air as I do on the ground at Kansas City or here at Washington, and often with a secretary. You will also be required at times to staff my plane for our largest stockholder

Howard Hughes who occasionally utilizes my private Lockheed on business."

Jack pauses and studies Harriet before he continues, "I often pilot commercial airliners on scheduled or charter flights from Los Angeles to Kansas City, New York, or Washington. Helen, again, often entertains the passengers. During these flights, you may be required to assist her and the other onboard Hostesses." Jack pauses for Harriet's response.

Harriet replies, "Being a fully-trained TWA Hostess, Mr. Frye, I feel I can confidently handle all duties assigned to me." She continues, "I would devote myself to the position competently!" Jack smiles warmly and replies, "Just what I want to hear!" He looks at Helen, "What do you think about our lovely Hostess, dear?" Helen looks at Harriet and smiles, as she turns back to Jack she says, "I think she's just darling Jack, I have no doubt she would fill the position perfectly." Jack turns back to Harriet, "Are you hungry, Harriet? Helen and I are on our way to lunch and we would love for you to join us, we can talk further there."

Soon after, Jack, Helen, and Harriet are finishing their lunch at the Mayflower Hotel Lounge. Jack signs the check, then stands up and reaches his hand out to Harriet. "I would like to welcome you as my new private Hostess, Miss Appelwick. Please report to Mrs. Battle for all further details. We will be leaving for Los Angeles tomorrow afternoon, I expect you to be at Washington National one hour early. Harriet smiles warmly and replies graciously, "Thank you, Mr. Frye! I'm honored beyond words and I look forward to staffing your flights!" Jack turns to Helen and says, "I have to get back to the office honey, I'll see you this evening." Helen and Harriet rise, Helen reaches out to Harriet and the two hug briefly. Helen graciously says,

"I just know we're going to have such fun together darling and be the best of friends too! I can't wait to show you our ranch in Arizona!"

'Unknown Date'

Pacing back and forth in his Washington mansion drawing room, Jack is fuming with cigar in hand. Helen is sitting in a floral cream and crimson winged-back chair, smoking a cigarette. "I'm so weary of all this Helen, again Howard is nowhere to be found and we have that meeting scheduled tomorrow. No one can know he is so irresponsible, and he has to be there. I've got to find him!" Helen replies, "Well darling, I wish I could help, but I haven't heard anything of him for a week." Jack quickly walks over to the phone and dials a number, when it connects we hear him say, "Get a recovery team together, take my Lodestar, I don't care if you have to pull a pilot off the flight line, find him! And make sure no one talks about this!" Exasperated and frustrated Jack hangs up.

Jack's brilliantly polished Lodestar flies low over an obscure desert plateau. After several passes, the pilots spot a brilliant flash of silver on the horizon. The Lockheed circles for a low pass as the pilots peer out to see a wrecked plane with a lanky man slumped on the ground beside it. After circling once, the Lodestar descends and lands on the hard-pack desert. Before the powerful engines fade to idle, four men jump out, and quickly help the dazed man into the plane. Within minutes, the Lodestar powers up and lifts off in a cloud of dust. The throbbing din of the radial engines fade out as the plane disappears north over the horizon.

Later, after landing at Washington National, the Lodestar taxis up to a waiting nondescript black sedan. The crew ushers Howard Hughes into the car, which glides away, headed to the Frye Mansion. When the sedan arrives at the Frye estate, it navigates around cars and limos parked along the long drive. The black car pulls around to the servant's entrance and stops, the men help Howard into the kitchen under the cloak of a large blanket.

Jack is waiting when Howard comes in. He walks over to him and says, "You gave us quite a scare Howard, are you O.K.?" Howard, obviously dazed, mumbles softly, "I think so Jack, thanks for finding me." Jack reaches out and pats him on the shoulder, "Sure Howard, sure, now we have to get you ready for that meeting, the men are already seated." Jack turns to Evangeline stating briskly, "Can you help get Howard cleaned up and dressed for the meeting?" Evangeline quickly replies, "Of course Mr. Frye, of course." Gently, she leads the dazed Howard over to the sink. She helps him out of his torn clothes, down to his boxers. At this point, she runs water on a washcloth and slowly starts cleaning the grease and mud off his scratched-up body, gingerly, she dabs at several areas of dried blood.

Meanwhile, there's a soft knock on a door leading into the mansion's kitchen. Jack walks over, opens it slightly, and says softly, "Come on in Helen." "I found this suit in Howard's room, I'll hang it over here for you Evangeline," Helen says. She then steps back to a corner window and lights a cigarette. Helen observes Howard warily, as she blows the smoke across the room.

At last, Howard is cleaned up, and Evangeline helps him dress. Spiffed up and looking like an executive, Jack leads Howard out of the kitchen to the drawing room where about twenty government officials and corporate executives are waiting. As they enter, the men politely acknowledge Jack and Howard; yet, none of them is wise to the fact that Howard was recently missing in yet another plane accident, and was just found, hours before.

'Spring of 1945'

Previously, in 1943, Jack and Helen, always short on help at the ranch, interviewed a young man named Al Nuanez as a ranch-foreman. The interview was fruitless however, as Al conveyed to Jack he wanted to serve his country first, then he might consider an offer.

Unfortunately though, within 15 months, Al is injured and shipped back to the States on a troop carrier. In the mid-Atlantic, he receives official notification he is 'hereby officially exempt from active duty'. When Al reaches the States, he's assigned to the Navajo Army Depot, west of Flagstaff, Arizona for the rest of his enlistment.

In early 1945, Jack and Helen Frye again drive up from Sedona, and request Al come to the Frye Ranch and take over the ranch-foreman position. Al states he is unable to accept the position, as his hands are tied, until he is eventually discharged. Jack and Helen are disappointed, as qualified ranch hands are extremely difficult to come by. Most able-bodied local men are serving overseas for the duration of the war.

After several weeks, Helen Frye drives up from Sedona and meets with Al again. She invites him to dinner at the Willow House that evening, saying she wants to discuss some good news. As promised, over dinner, Helen says with a smile, "Jack just called from Washington D.C. and cleared the way for you to get out of that job! Take our pickup truck home and bring your things down here to the ranch tomorrow."

Al is flabbergasted and says, "I'll believe it when the Captain informs me, Mrs. Frye." He thanks Helen for dinner and drives back up the canyon to the Army base at Bellemont Arizona. When Al pulls into the Army Depot, he is ordered to report to the Captain's office immediately.

"I thought I had a court martial or something," Al later said. "The Captain saluted me and said congratulations! For what? I responded. I just received a note from Jack Frye, you are to go work for him, he replied. I signed on the dotted line and it was official. I was released from the Army! The Captain congratulated me on bettering myself and I moved down to the Frye Ranch where they handed me a shovel!"

Jack Frye was a powerful man, his arm had a long reach, to include connections with the U.S. Military, and the Office of the President of the United States.

'April 3, 1945'

Dear Mr. Meem:

Mr. Frye and I will be stopping over night the 19th of this month with a party of guests at the La Fonda Hotel, and we are hoping to be able to see you on the day of the 20th.

If this is not going to be convenient for you, would you please let us know as soon as possible.

Sincerely,

Helen V. Frye

(Unfortunately, this trip never materialized due to Jack's ever-changing schedule with TWA.)

TRANSCONTINENTAL & WESTERN AIR, INC.

1740 G Street, N.W.

Washington 6, D.C.

OFFICE OF THE PRESIDENT

April 24, 1945

Dear Mr. Meem:

Mrs. Frye had planned on stopping in Santa Fe on her way west, but at the last minute, had to go directly through to the ranch.

She asked that I forward to you a photo static copy of the first floor plan of the house. She will contact you or see you before returning east.

Sincerely,

Mary P. Battle

Staff Assistant (Jack Frye Personal Assistant)

'April 18, 1945'

Jack and Helen join Howard Hughes' associate, Johnny Meyer at Miami for fishing and relaxation. Jack is in town on business and he and Helen fly out again by April 19.

Soon after, Jack and Helen host a flight to Florida, with 14 guests, on their private Lodestar. All passengers are high-level White House Democrats associated with the Roosevelt, now Truman Administration.

Late afternoon, at Washington National Airport, a black Cadillac Fleetwood is parked next to Jack's TWA Lockheed Lodestar. Aubrey, the Frye chauffeur, unloads luggage and hands it to a Transcontinental & Western Air ground crew member, who secures it in the forward hold under the cockpit. All the Lockheed exterior doors are open, with ground support equipment and heater battery pack attached to the fuselage.

Helen and her private TWA Hostess Harriet Appelwick have boarded the airliner and are readying the luxurious cabin for passengers. There's a knock at the open cabin door, Helen steps over, as Aubrey hands in trays of hors d'oeuvres and appetizers. "Here you are Mrs. Frye," Aubrey says, "Evangeline says just keep them cold till they're served." "Oh my, thank you Aubrey, they look scrumptious as usual, Evangeline has surely outdone herself!" Helen hands the tray off to Harriet and turns back to Aubrey saying, "You can go back to the house now Aubrey, thank you." "Yes, Mrs. Frye, good evening, and have a safe trip."

As the Cadillac limo glides away, Helen starts plumping pillows, she pauses at the bar checking to see how well it is stocked for the flight. She turns to Harriet and sighs, "We certainly need more bourbon and whiskey, and maybe another vodka for the girls." Harriet smiles and says, "I should say so Helen, I'll take care of it!" They both laugh.

On the tarmac, another car pulls up, the headlights flash the interior of the cabin as the car swings around. Helen stops what she's doing and steps out of the cabin entry as passengers exit a Lincoln limo. The guests include Irma Hannegan, wife of Robert E. Hannegan (United States Postmaster General and Democratic Party National Chairman), followed by Kathryn Murphy Nunan, wife of Joseph D. Nunan Jr., (Commissioner of the Internal Revenue). Other smartly dressed women follow. The passengers gather around the limo as a chauffeur starts unloading luggage from the trunk.

Helen greets them all graciously. Irma says cheerfully, "It's so nice to see you again Helen, this trip will be so much fun! By the way the boys are coming in another car from the White House." Helen replies with a smile, "Well, we certainly won't get off the ground without my Jack, but this will give us girls time to visit and have a drink." Helen turns to the women, takes Irma by the arm and says, "Come on girls, how about a pre-flight cocktail?" Murmuring and smiling, they all move toward the Lockheed's cabin.

Within 15 minutes, another Lincoln pulls up to the plane, Jack and Bob Hannegan exit. The driver steps around to retrieve luggage out of the trunk, while several other men exit the car, all dressed in tailored suits. Jack leads the men over to the plane where they all board. After he introduces everyone, he and Bob make their way forward. As Jack passes Harriet who is standing at the flight attendant station behind the cockpit, he greets her, and whispers, "Make sure everyone has plenty to drink." "Yes sir, Mr. Frye," Harriet replies with a warm smile.

Jack and Bob enter the cockpit. Bob settles in the co-pilots right seat and Jack in the left seat, as Jack explains the basic operations of the aircraft. The Postmaster General listens with rapt attention as he says excitedly, "This is sure a mighty fancy machine compared to the one we took to Washington last summer with Truman." "Yes Bob, it sure is, I loved the 12, but this 18 is better suited for entertaining clients in the air, and of course, the added convenience of a blue room, you know, a restroom in the rear. Did I ever tell you, that in the early days I used to land at a service station between Phoenix and Tucson, out in the middle of the desert with two outhouses, just so my female passengers could use the bathroom?" "No Jack, I've certainly never heard that one!" Jack smiles at Bob saying wistfully, "Boy, has air travel changed!"

At last, a final car arrives, a Mercury coupe with a man and woman. The passenger, a uniformed TWA captain, steps out and briskly walks around the car to the driver's window as the woman hands him keys. He steps around to the trunk and removes a valise and a small suitcase, then back around to the driver's window. He hands the keys back to his wife, kissing her, he says, "I'll be back in a week darling, take good care of yourself and the children for me." She gives him a hug and says, "Fly safe honey!" He walks up to the nose of the plane and hands his suitcase to the ground crew to load in the forward baggage compartment. The captain then walks around the glistening Lodestar, looking it over carefully and checking off items on a clipboard. Within minutes, he too, disappears into the Lockheed cabin, shuts the door, and settles in the co-pilots seat next to Jack.

Soon the engines turn over, one after another with a rumbled roar, settling into a throbbing idle. With clearance lights glowing, the wheel chocks are pulled, and the plane taxis away. In no time, the sleek TWA Lodestar accelerates down the runway lifting off toward the horizon and south to Florida.

'Summer 1945'

At the Sedona ranch, Jack, Helen, and her mother Maude are walking up the creek path to the Willow House after an afternoon swim. Jack, carrying a movie camera, walks ahead of Helen and Maude as they walk together visiting. Suddenly, Helen sees a snake on the path. "Oh my," says Maude, "it's a rattler and he's huge!" Helen responds excitedly, "Stay right where you are mother, don't come any closer!" Helen walks the short distance to the Willow House and gets her bullwhip. "Now watch this," she says as she starts snapping it at the snake, 'Crack, crack!' "Stop that Helen!" says Maude, "you're making him mighty angry!" Meanwhile, Jack has turned around and is capturing the encounter on film. 'Snap, snap,' each time the snake tries to attack Helen cracks him near his head. Suddenly, Helen's towel falls off and she's totally nude, still having a standoff with the snake! "Helen!" Maude says, "Stop that right now and put your towel back on, really!" Helen responds impatiently, "Oh Mother, you know Jack and I never wear any clothes out here on the ranch. What's the big deal, do you think the snake cares?" Helen continues to dance around, following the snake as it tries to slither away into the brush. Jack is howling with laughter as he captures Helen's antics on film. Exasperated Maude says, "Put that camera down Jack, for goodness' sake! You two are nutty!" Finally, the wayward snake manages to escape. Helen, looking disappointed, grabs her towel and dons it. "Someday Helen, one of those snakes is going to get you, and you won't be so quick to get him first!" says Jack as they all start back up the path. "Well," protests Helen in defense of her actions, "I'm scared to death of those fierce creatures, they give me nightmares!"

'August 1945'

One summer night, Helen and Jack are ready to leave for an elegant ball at the White House. Jack is waiting at the bottom of the mansion's grand staircase as Helen's mother Maude and her two grand-daughters visit in the foyer. Softly echoing throughout the main hall is Glenn Miller's orchestra playing 'Moonlight Serenade' from a '78 spinning on the library phonograph.

Suddenly, a sound descends from the landing above. Jack, Maude, and the girls look up as a glittering vision appears at the top of the grand staircase. Helen, dressed in a stunning ivory form-fitting gown, with matching high-heels and handbag, gracefully descends the staircase like a movie star. The sequins on her dress sparkle like a thousand stars, complemented by her diamond jewelry, all reflected under the mansion's massive crystal chandelier. In her hand, Helen drags a sumptuous white full-length mink coat.

Jack, dressed in a tuxedo, stands at the bottom of the stairs, mesmerized. He watches her every move, as he looks her up and down like a searchlight. Finally, as Helen nears the last step, Jack gallantly reaches out to take her hand. The room is silent with all eyes on the couple. Jack looks up into Helen's sapphire-blue eyes and speaks in a trembling voice filled with passion, "Helen you are an absolute vision, simply stunning, you take my breath away!" As Jack touches Helen's hand to his lips, he whispers the words, "I love you so much darling."

Helen's mother, who is watching from the shadows, holds a hankie to her eye. She whispers to her granddaughter Sheryl, "That's simply the most romantic thing I have ever seen in my life!"

Helen and Jack bid everyone goodbye and are out the door in a flash. Aubrey helps them both into a waiting Cadillac limousine. The family watches as the car glides away, disappearing down the winding drive into the starlit summer night. After the taillights fade, Sisty turns to her sister Sheryl and says, "It's like an enchanted fairytale!" With that, Maude looks down at the two and says, "Yes dear, now come on you two, its way past your bedtime!"

'February 3, 1926 - February 3, 1946'

Jack selects this date to commemorate Standard Air Lines (a predecessor of TWA) and to pay tribute to the two historic airlines, both which he helped found. The 41-year-old president-pilot flashes coast-to-coast at the helm of TWA's 'Star of California' Constellation, one of 36 new Lockheed luxury liners added to the TWA fleet after the close of World War II.

Departing Burbank @ 3:59 A.M., the transport sweeps across the United States nonstop, landing at LaGuardia @ 11:27 A.M., with average speeds of 345 to 350 M.P.H., and peak speed of 375 M.P.H. (per Jack). Conjointly with co-pilot Lee Flanagin, Jack claims two records: 'west-east transcontinental' @ 7 hours 27 minutes, and 'maximum passengers carried to date' @ 52 passengers and crew. The futurist airliner attains five miles per minute and consumes 450 gallons of fuel per hour.

This flight was truly the crowning achievement of Jack's tenure with TWA on many different levels. Not only did Jack envision the Constellation, and nurture its creation, but he also knew the transport would fulfill TWA's destiny of 'round the world' service, resulting in legendary status for the airline. This flight was the stuff of realized dreams and the culmination of a lifetime of aviation milestones for Frye. Never again, would Jack feel so on 'top of the world'. TWA was truly 'The Airline Jack Built', and no man realized this more than Jack or worked as hard as he toward this end.

Little known is the fact that Jack was in so much pain on February 3 with a wrenched back, he could hardly turn around to greet enthusiast photographers in the cockpit after the record flight.

One time, perhaps the same week, Jack was laid up at the Hotel Ambassador in New York City for several days suffering from the same condition. Because the doctor insisted Jack not move, he conducted business with aviation executives from his bed. Normally, Jack worked sixteen-hour days, so this restriction undoubtedly was extremely frustrating for him.

Concerned at Jack's dark mood, Helen left the hotel and canvassed New York City for kittens, and within an hour, she collected a box full. Upon returning to the suite, she found Jack engaged in yet another serious meeting with a group of his staff. Quickly, Helen flung the door open to the bedroom, threw the kittens on the bed, and shut it abruptly. After a moment of silent surprise, she heard Jack and the men burst into laughter as they played with the lovable kittens. Smiling to herself Helen knew she had achieved her objective—she had lightened Jack's bleak day.

'February 5, 1946'

At a media-covered celebration in New York City, Helen christens the first regularly scheduled TWA Constellation airliner to embark on passenger service from LaGuardia to Paris. This event, another TWA first, witnesses Helen in a luxurious leopard skin coat, veil, and leather gloves, looking all the role of a president's wife. Graciously, she christens the magnificent overseas transport with a cloud-gun, marking a milestone in U.S. airline history!

There's an interesting story behind the acquisition of this particular coat. It's a well-known fact that Jack Frye loved to play poker with his friends, it helped him relax from the pressures of running TWA—and he was a damn good poker player at that! Of course, his most famous poker buddy was Harry Truman, among many other prominent business associates. On one of their trips to New York City, Jack and Helen were staying at the Hotel Ambassador where they maintained a suite during the war years. Jack, as usual, was playing a spirited game of poker with his pals. One of these men lost quite a bit of money to Jack, and was unable, for whatever reason, to pay up. The man tells Jack he just bought a new leopard coat for his girlfriend, 'would Jack accept this as payment instead of cash?' Jack Frye was a fair man and after a moment of consideration replied, "Sure, why not?" Later that evening, as Jack returned to his and Helen's suite, he tossed the large gift box on the sofa telling Helen, "Here's a present for you darling!"

No doubt, toward the end of Helen's life, she likely would no longer wear real fur, but in the early years, furs were all the rage and almost a requirement. Helen owned at least three full-length mink coats, mink jackets, several huge mink muffs, stylish mink hat, and a silver fox jacket. These are just the furs I've seen, in photographs of Helen. When Helen tired of a fur, she would give it away to family or friends. Diamonds and furs are a girl's best friend, or so I'm told, and Helen Vanderbilt Frye deserved nothing less in regard to the high-society life she lived.

'May 19, 1946'

On one of their frequent cross-country business trips in the Lodestar, Jack and Helen board passenger Baroness Garnett Stackelberg on a flight from Washington D.C. to Los Angeles. Typically, Miss Appelwick staffs this flight as Hostess. It's possible this trip is the one Garnett related where they stopped at Sedona to see the ranch.

After the plane lands at Los Angeles Municipal Airport, reporters greet the group as they deplane. Jack and Helen are always good copy, and the Baroness is Washington royalty and a D.C. insider. As a matter-of-fact, the Baroness is voted Washington's 'Most Beautiful Woman of the Week' recently by press on the east coast.

'June 1, 1946'

Jack's TWA Lodestar lands at Continental Airport south of Santa Fe. After deplaning, the Fryes and their hostess take a car to La Fonda. The next day, after a meeting with their architect John Gaw Meem, Helen and Jack relax over drinks at La Fonda with their private hostess Harriet Appelwick. As they decide what to have for dinner, Harriet notices a good-looking man observing her from across the room. She whispers to Helen, "I think he's interested in me Helen."

Jack and Helen both look over and observe the young man who is having a drink at the bar. Helen turns to Harriet saying, "Well, sweetie, why don't you go over there and say hello?" Harriet looks at Jack and Helen and responds embarrassingly, "Goodness gracious Helen, I can't just walk up to some strange man and say hello!" Jack laughs heartily, while Helen replies, "Well darling, I certainly can!" Helen rises as Harriet tries to grab her arm pleading, "Don't you dare, please Helen, sit down!"

Approaching the young man, Helen introduces herself and inquires, "Do you want to meet her?" The young man replies with a grin, "You bet I do!" Helen invites him over to their table and introduces him to Harriet and Jack. "Jack, Harriet, this is Frank Pecarich, but he prefers we call him Yanks." Helen turns to Frank and says, "This is my husband Jack, and our private hostess Harriet Appelwick." Jack asks Yanks to sit down, after which the four immediately hit it off. Noticing Yanks is very thin, Jack is concerned, he says, "What would you like for dinner Yanks? We're all having steak and I'm buying, won't you join us son?"

During dinner, Jack talks about TWA and the war, while Yanks asks Harriet about her life as a TWA Hostess and living in Washington. Finally, Yanks starts opening up about the war. He shipped out in August of 1941, soon though, he found himself in the Philippines on the Bataan Peninsula with the Two Hundredth Coast Artillery. Frank pauses a moment, and a shadow passes over his face, then he continues solemnly, "I was 159 pounds when I enlisted but down to 85 pounds when I finally set foot on American soil again. I was held for four years as a prisoner of war. When I was rescued, I was at Osaka POW Camp."

Yanks relates he and his division were captured and forced to walk some eighty miles in the march of Bataan, nothing more than a 'march of death" he says quietly. "The details," Yanks says solemnly, "well, they can't be discussed in front of ladies. I never lost hope, but it was truly the darkest time of my life. All I could think about was my life in Gallup, my family, and all the things I loved about the United States. After our liberation, I and many of the other men felt guilty. 'Why were we allowed to live when so many died in such agony?'" Finally, the young man says no more. He looks down at his plate in silence, his eyes misty and far away.

At this point, Helen and Harriet are both wiping their eyes, Helen reaches out and squeezes Yanks' hand, "No one," Helen says softly, "should ever have to endure such cruelty and inhumane treatment." Jack speaks in a fatherly tone, "I've heard these stories Yanks, and it's hard for me to even comment, except to say, 'thank you'. You and all the other boys who went over there and experienced these untold atrocities are the heart and soul of this great nation! We are all eternally grateful for your contributions toward freedom, not just for our country, but for the world as well." Looking up at Jack, Yanks says, "Thank you Mr. Frye, from you, sir, that's truly an honor."

Helen asks Yanks what he's doing to regain his health and weight. Unsatisfied with his answer, she turns to Jack and says, "Jack darling, why don't we have Yanks flown out to the ranch and let him stay there for some R&R? When we are out there I can cook for him and help him recover." Jack turns to Yanks, "We would be honored to have you at the ranch, you can stay at the Willow House. Helen and I will be in and out, flying back and forth to Washington, we could see you each time we are there. In addition, as far as Helen's cooking, well, you couldn't be in better hands! Just look at how she's fattened me up!" Jack pats his belly.

Yanks, overcome by such a generous offer thanks Jack saying, "I'm certainly honored Mr. Frye. I never dreamed in a million years I would run into you and your beautiful wife, and your lovely stewardess, and be invited for a visit. I just don't know what to say?" Helen speaks with a warm smile, "Just say yes, darling, there's no reason why you can't come stay for a spell. We have plenty of room, and the 'lay of the land' will heal you and help you center yourself. You can swim in the creek and immerse yourself in its healing properties." Yanks smiles, and with misty eyes, he says, "Thanks, yes, yes, I would love to!"

Jack makes arrangements for Yanks to fly out on a date they both agree on, and Yanks stays at the Frye private residence, the Willow House, for several months. True to her word, Helen nurses Yanks back to a full recovery and Yanks remains close to both her and Jack for the rest of his life. Harriet too, is often at the ranch with the Fryes, and she is able to spend time with Yanks, riding and walking by the creek. Later, in the early 1960's Yanks dates another friend of Helen's, Santa Fe artist Doris Steider, who he met at the Frye Ranch through Helen.

Finally, on March 31, 1965, Yanks dies at just 48, his short life, no doubt, a reflection of the horrors he faced as a young man. Yanks was laid to rest with honors at the National Cemetery off North Guadalupe at Santa Fe, New Mexico. Yanks rejoined his brothers who suffered the Battle of Bataan debacle, cut down in their prime, many, never to see American soil again, except at death.

'July 7, 1946'

Jack is in Albuquerque on business when he learns Howard Hughes has crashed an experimental U.S.A.A.F. plane at Beverly Hills California, and is in critical condition at a Los Angeles hospital. Jack orders his Lodestar ready for a flight to California, departing within the hour. Once Jack arrives, he immediately rushes to Good Samaritan Hospital. He sits vigil outside Howard's room for 24-hours straight. Finally, only after Jack feels Howard is stable, he returns to the east coast in his Lodestar.

'Hughes- Slipping Over the Precipice'

The TWA Board of Directors cannot locate Howard Hughes. They need to approve funding for new planes. Jack is perplexed and laments about how Howard is always unavailable. Shortly after this, Jack and Helen are having lunch. Jack mentions the business crisis to Helen, knowing she and Howard keep in touch and she often knows where Howard is, even when no one else does. Helen states she will go retrieve Howard and bring him back to New York; however, first, she makes Jack promise that he will not have her followed, and the same goes for the TWA Board.

Shortly after, Helen secretly flies to Florida on the Lodestar. After landing, she takes a limo to a certain park lined with palm trees. She walks up to a secluded area where a man is sleeping under a park bench, covered with newspapers. Gently, she shakes him and says, "Howard, it's Helen." He opens his eyes and blinks in the bright sun. Slowly he smiles and reaches out for her hand. "Howard, you have to come with me. The board needs to talk to you, it's very important," implores Helen. She helps him up and they walk back to the limo where the driver helps the unrecognizable bum into the back of the car.

Helen and Howard go to a Miami hotel where she locates some clothes for him, Howard shaves and cleans up and then they fly back to New York City. After the Lodestar lands, a limo whisks Howard to TWA's executive offices.

Along with this bizarre incident, Helen begins to deduce Howard is slipping over the edge, with a similar event in Washington. One-day Jack asks Helen if she will deliver a valise of important TWA documents to Howard at his hotel in Washington. Helen's chauffeur Aubrey drives her across the Potomac and over to the Mayflower Hotel where the car pulls up in front. Helen takes the elevator up to Howard's floor and walks to his suite where she knocks softly. After hearing nothing, she calls Howard's name. "Howard, its Helen, I have some papers from Jack. Please answer the door. Are you there Howard?"

At last, the door opens just a crack, Howard, in a disheveled state, steps aside, as Helen enters the shadowed room. Helen is appalled at what confronts her—Howard is unkempt, looks like he has not changed clothes for a week, and everything in the room is covered with tissue paper. She looks at Howard, and he sees the puzzled look on her face. All he offers is, "Germs Helen, everything is contaminated." Howard asks Helen to set the papers on the desk and pull them out so he can see them. He then takes a tissue and turns them over one by one, not touching any of them. Then he says, "Yes, Yes, I'll take care of this Helen, thank you for coming over." Helen starts to leave but hesitates. "Howard, I'm worried," she protests, but before she can finish, Howard says, "I'm fine Helen, really I am." Helen looks at Howard compassionately and says, "O.K. Howard, I'd better go, but please dear, do take care of yourself and if you need anything, Jack and I are there for you, just across the river." Helen slips out into the bright hallway and escapes back into the hustle bustle of the real world.

Soon after, in one of many such charter and commercial flights, a TWA Constellation airliner sweeps cross-country with Jack at the helm with a load of celebrities from Los Angeles to New York City. Helen and several TWA Hostesses entertain the passengers, many whom Helen knows personally. Repeating a ritual Helen has performed many times previously on similar flights, the stunningly beautiful 'Mrs. TWA' walks up and down the aisles, charming the passengers and serving drinks. Dressed impeccably, her makeup and hair are flawless, and passengers are charmed by her wit and graciousness. This is the 'face of TWA' as Jack desires for his company.

Finally, Helen has a moment to take a plate of sandwiches up to the cockpit to Jack, the co-pilot, and engineer. "How 'bout some refreshments boys?" she inquires cheerfully as she enters. "Thank you darling," says Jack, "we were getting mighty hungry up here!" "There are sandwiches, coffee, and a bowl of Evangeline's chili for each of you. Be forewarned though, it's fiery hot!" Helen says. Jack turns to his crew chuckling, "I had our chef Evangeline flown down to Mexico so she could learn how to make it 'Texas Style'. It's delicious, and my all-time favorite! Usually, after each bite, you need two sips of beer, but we'll forego that in the cockpit!" The crew laughs and smiles. Helen leans in and kisses Jack, while the crew smiles enviously. The fragrance of her Park Avenue perfume lingers in the cockpit, long after she retreats to the passenger cabin.

'October 31, 1946'

Shortly after 12 P.M., Jack's Lockheed Lodestar 18 sweeps in for a landing at LaGuardia Airport, taxing to the TWA terminal. Before reporters can approach the Fryes, Harriet, or their V.I.P. passengers, they all duck into a limo, which transports them to Manhattan. This flight is in direct relation to the ongoing TWA pilot's strike. Shortly after, on November 2 the Fryes fly back to Washington D.C. again.

'November 4, 1946'

Helen has her chauffeur Aubrey drive her over the Potomac to visit Garnett Stackelberg at a Washington Hospital. Garnett is recuperating after the birth of her son, Sandy. However, Helen is alarmed to see Garnett is languishing, in part, because the infant was a rather large baby. As they visit, Helen tells Garnett she has the perfect solution for a speedy recovery and release! Helen has Aubrey drive her back to the Doubleday Mansion, after which she engages Evangeline to make some of her nurturing homemade chicken noodle soup. Helen and Evangeline take it back to the hospital, where Helen administers it to Garnett. The remedy is a success! In no time, Garnett rallies. She returns home with baby Sandy within days.

As result of this incident, Evangeline and Garnett become fast friends; thereafter, Evangeline caters parties for Garnett, and as well, special dinners for presidents and high-ranking political figures in Washington; her services sought by all.

'December 21, 1946'

Jack and Helen's long black Cadillac Fleetwood pulls up the drive to the White House. The chauffeur steps out and walks around to open the rear door. As he helps Jack and Helen out Jack turns and says,

"Please wait for us Aubrey, we won't be long. We'll be having dinner when this is over." Jack and Helen proceed to the entrance. Helen is wearing a three-quarter-length fur coat with matching mink hat over a tailored suit. Jack, as always, is dressed impeccably in a pinstriped suit and dark dress shoes, on this chilly day covered by a wool top-coat and silk scarf.

Jack is awarded the 'Medal for Merit' at this White House ceremony, this, the nation's highest civilian recognition for wartime service. Secretary of War Robert Patterson presents the award, as decreed by President Truman. In the accompanying citation, Frye is commend-ed for 'exceptionally meritorious conduct in the performance of out-standing service to the United States, from December 1941 to Au-gust 1945.'

Patterson reads the citation out loud, with Helen, TWA officials, and top-ranking military men like W. Stuart Symington (Assistant Secretary of War for Air) standing solemnly by. In part, the citation declares:

'As President of Trans World Airline, you made a noteworthy contri-bution to the success of air operations against the enemy as a result of your broad experience in the operation of commercial air trans-ports, and the force and vigor with which you addressed yourself to the critical conflict into which your country was projected.

'Even before the outbreak of hostilities, you established schools for the training of pilots and maintenance crews to insure successful fer-rying of material and personnel to the combat theaters. After the war began, you inaugurated air routes across the North and South At-lantic and from Northern Europe to bases in Africa. Thus, the net-work of air communications you established made the speedy ship-ment of mail, cargo and personnel necessary to carry out vital mis-sions for the armed forces.

'In accomplishing these projects you devoted yourself unselfishly and vigorously to the military necessities of the nation, and made a direct contribution to the success of the air war. Your conduct and achievements, your patriotic devotion, and your unselfish pursuit of the means to achieve victory in the air reflect the greatest credit on you and the government and the people of the United States.'

In depth, TWA, in performing its wartime service, completed more than 9,500 overseas flights, carrying tons of urgently needed military supplies. Mail, cargo, and thousands of high-ranking military personnel and wounded service men made up the passenger loads of TWA's wartime Intercontinental Division.

In accepting the award, Frye extends credit to all TWA, stating, "It is in recognition of the part played by all TWA employees that this award is given. I am proud to accept this honor," Frye continues, stating to Secretary of War Patterson, "and I am happy to have been able to serve the War Department."

Little known information follows as related by Jack Frye's family; however, I have never been able to substantiate it: 'Jack Frye was the only civilian readily admitted to the White House and the president's office, night or day, without question or restraint, during the war years.' This intimation has been recounted many times, by sources connected to Jack Frye.

Even though this unfettered access is unheard of in our current day, I have to say, security at the White House during World War II was quite lax. This concession was likely a result of Frye's relationship with both Presidents Roosevelt, and Truman, and his association with the Democratic Party. TWA, during World War II, was a vital asset of the United States and the airline worked closely with the military stateside and overseas. No other leader of TWA achieved this V.I.P. status or relationship with the highest levels of the United

States Government, except Jack Frye. This is an honor Jack earned—it wasn't bestowed on him frivolously.

Frye was a true patriot, and his lineage goes back to associations with George Washington and Thomas Jefferson. Frye, in the 1940's, was one of the most powerful and influential men of the Democratic Party. It was Frye who united with powerful peers to insure Truman captured the White House after Roosevelt's unfortunate passing. From 1941 on, Jack worked 24/7 with his contemporaries toward the war effort. This included committing all available TWA resources to serve our troops and setting up instruction centers to train U.S. service men in flying the larger support planes of the day. Many of these planes were airline flying stock, previously unfamiliar to military pilots.

One of the most famous facilities was the Eagle Nest Flight Center (more commonly known as the Jack Frye Training School) at Albuquerque, New Mexico. Jack Frye appointed TWA chief pilot, Otis Bryan (former Army pilot) to head the Albuquerque school, which became associated with many others around the nation. These training efforts greatly aided our military advancements in the Pacific and European theatre. Jack's military position during the war was Lt. Commander A-V (S) U.S.N.R.

In an unprecedented act of gratitude, Jack Frye was awarded the 'Order of Grand Officer of the Crown of Italy' by the Italian Government, for his invaluable aid and support toward rebuilding Italy's national aviation services after World War II. This honor was little known and quite an honor for Frye.

One person privy to Frye's involvement in the war effort, was Washington D.C. insider, Baroness Garnett Stackelberg. The Baroness was a Washington Post correspondent, not unlike our current icon, Barbara Walters. Garnett's husband, Baron Steno Stackelberg, worked for TWA and the State Department; he and Jack were also close friends.

The Baroness related, to paraphrase, 'Jack Frye flew endangered people from behind enemy lines, the communists were killing off all the wealthy free-thinking families; they didn't want free thought. One of these men was my husband.' She continued, 'the Stackelberg family is forever grateful to Jack Frye and his efforts.' Garnett also said Jack knew her husband 'long before I came on the scene'. In regard to the war effort she said, 'there was a plane named after Frye that went behind enemy lines'. This is a mystery; however, I have heard mention of a plane called the 'Frye Interceptor' but have never uncovered any details.

Frye's activities in the World War II were top secret, and since Frye worked directly with the President's office, uncovering the details of these operations is difficult at best. The only parties I'm aware of who were privy to Frye's involvements were Presidents Roosevelt and Truman, Helen Frye, and Steno and Garnett Stackelberg.

Perhaps, we can now better understand why Jack Frye was awarded the Medal for Merit, even if the classified details have never been fully disclosed to the public at large.

'January 1947'

At the snow-covered Sedona ranch Willow House, Jack talks to Helen about the anguish of having to leave TWA because of Howard. Jack stands in front of the red rock fireplace and stares at the crackling flames as he exclaims, "I built that airline, God damn it, from the ground up. I am TWA, and that S.O.B. is trying to take it all away from me! This will destroy the company and hurt a lot of people!" Jack continues heatedly, "Howard's henchman, Noah Dietrich has succeeded in blaming me for the pilot's strike, and the grounding of the Connies! Howard or Noah, neither one, knows a damn thing about running an airline! To make matters worse, Howard is never available when he's needed!" Jack turns to Helen, "Working with Howard has been an exercise in futility!" Helen is quiet as she watches Jack, his face beet-red as reflected in the firelight. She soothes him gently saying, "Jack, I am sorry darling. Howard has become such an enigma since the accident, and certainly, he is so very unpredictable. I never liked that Dietrich, how dare he interfere with the airline. I remember when Howard said you had total autonomy. I wish I could help in some way sweetheart." "Thanks darling," Jack says, "I guess things will never be as they were in the past, and frankly, I weep for the future of TWA if Howard's going to run it!"

Jack walks over to the bar and makes them both a fresh drink as he continues, "Helen, I'm going to take that C.E.O. position in New York City with General Aniline that Harry offered me. They are the largest film company in the world, with their only rival being Kodak. I'll make a lot more money with them than I ever did with TWA, not that it is much more than a bittersweet consolation," Jack adds with emotion. "Helen, my whole life has been the airline industry. I just don't know how to go on without TWA."

At this, Jack sits down next to Helen. "Please darling," he implores, "say you'll move out to New York City with me, at least part-time," he touches her hand as he cajoles, "to keep me company and entertain for Aniline." Helen looks into Jack's longing eyes. "Of course, honey, I'll consider it, and certainly I'll socialize with you as I can."

Helen looks away though at the fire before she continues, "But Jack darling, you know I don't want to live in the city again. For years, you told me if you ever left TWA, we could spend more time here at the ranch. I want to do just that Jack, and devote myself to finishing our new house. I'm exhausted with all the politicking and entertaining that is demanded of me with TWA." Jack leans closer as he says softly, "I understand all that Helen, but I love you, I need you, and I don't want to fly out here all the time just to spend a few stolen moments with you! Surely you can understand that Helen. I want to be here too, all the time, but I can't. Someone has to pay the bills. When money starts growing on trees, we won't have to do this anymore. I also won't have the luxury of being in flight all the time if I leave TWA either." Helen says nothing, she feels so conflicted and torn. "When will we ever get to experience Sedona as we have always dreamed," she laments to herself.

After a long pause Jack pulls his hand away from Helen's, "I need some air Helen. Let's talk about this later darling." He sets his drink down, grabs his buckskin jacket and leaves the cottage. The crisp air, heady with juniper, wafts around him as he follows the creek path down the hill. Trudging through the falling snow, silence drops over him like a blanket. In his mind, Jack knows he's at a threshold in his life—but what path should he choose? He feels lost and alone, abandoned by TWA, and abandoned by Helen too.

'January 16, 1947'

(In part, as below, Jack writes Meem with concerns about inflation costs of the Sedona house.)

TRANSCONTINENTAL & WESTERN AIR, INC.

1740 G Street, NW

Washington 6, D.C.

OFFICE OF THE PRESIDENT

Dear Mr. Meem:

"I am sorry to be so late writing to you about your letter of November 19 which Mrs. Frye forwarded to me. As you know, I was tied up in a pilot strike and since then, have been battling a financial crisis in TWA along with our chief stockholder, Mr. Hughes.

I would like the opportunity of discussing this matter in person with you but since I cannot be certain when this can take place, will have to write you instead.

Knowing that you are completely fair and reasonable, I would like to frankly set forth our views concerning this matter.

When we started on this project, we had in mind spending not more than forty of fifty thousand dollars altogether. Since the war came along, we have regularly stated that we did not expect to build until normal building conditions and costs again prevailed. Our references last summer, to building in the spring of 1947, were based on the assumption that this condition would be reached by then—"

With Kindest Regards,

Jack Frye

'May 1947'

By spring, the Fryes are moving out of the Washington mansion. Furniture, covered with white sheets, adjoin packing boxes positioned around the rooms. Movers are rolling a grand piano out the front door to a waiting moving truck. Helen is walking along supervising, "And when you get to our Georgetown house, boys, the housekeeper will help you place the piano."

Evangeline walks up to Helen, "Can I have a moment Mrs. Frye?" "Why, of course darling," says Helen as she nervously watches the movers slide the piano down the brick steps. Evangeline continues, "Howard has asked Aubrey and me to come work for him as personal chef and chauffeur, but we just don't know what to do." Helen pauses a moment before she responds, "Evangeline, I think that would be a wonderful opportunity for you both dear, you should take him up on it." Evangeline continues solemnly, "Well, he did offer us double-the-pay, but Helen we just wouldn't be happy leaving Washington, and certainly we can't work for a man who is responsible for Mr. Jack leaving the company he built up." Helen looks at Evangeline intently. She reaches out and holds her hand while saying with emotion, "Evangeline, you are an absolute dear, and I treasure you and Aubrey so very much, but you have to think of your future, not your kind sentiments. This may be a golden opportunity for you both!"

After Helen and Jack's personal furnishings are moved to Georgetown, the remainder of the furniture and trappings (previously purchased by TWA) are auctioned off. Helen attends the sale and purchases a majority of the items. Then she proceeds to have the furnishings delivered by moving truck to Garnett who had just settled into a large residence in Washington D.C. Garnett is in need of a large amount of fine furniture to fill her and Steno's new home and is thrilled at the gesture.

Garnett had been a loyal and dear friend to Helen, and after she married Steno, he had been a great asset to TWA. The Fryes were indebted to the Stackelbergs, as it was the Baron with his European connections, which greatly aided TWA's acquisition of their overseas routes. The last Viceroy of India was the Baron's cousin. Helen and Jack felt offering Garnett the furnishings was the least they could do, especially since Helen traveled all over the east coast buying it all specifically for the mansion.

A page turns, Jack and Helen's sojourn comes to a close at Washington, and certainly, much was accomplished. The time was nigh to move on to New York City amid the fray of life at Sedona.

Chapter 10

House of Apache Fires

'May 27, 1947'

The Fryes arrive at Santa Fe by private plane and check into their suite at La Fonda Hotel for two nights. The purpose of the visit is bittersweet; however, they are set to meet with their architect one last time. Mutually and amicably, they end a business partnership and friendship, which started in 1941, and lasted the duration of the World War II.

The original projected build-cost in 1941, for a home at the Sedona Ranch of $40,000 to $50,000, as determined by Frye, pre-Pearl Harbor, had escalated to $125,000 by summer of 1947 post-war. Furthermore, the remote locale of Sedona was a considerable challenge for Meem at Santa Fe. This, coupled with the square footage, originally at 4200 square feet, which had grown considerably, as much was added during the war, with little thought to the end product by the Fryes.

Therefore, the final projected cost for Meem to build at Sedona is quite a surprise for Jack Frye. It's worth mentioning that $125,000 in 1947 equates to $1,355,000 in our current time frame. It wasn't that Jack didn't have the money. It was more so that he would never spend that kind of money in a remote place like Sedona, when his employ as a C.E.O. in New York City necessitated a residence at Manhattan.

The delay in construction from 1941-1947 was caused by Jack's frantic work schedule with TWA, government square-footage restrictions during World War II, war-time building material shortages, and Meem's involvement with wartime government building contracts. The Fryes constantly desired to move forward, but it was just not possible.

With this last impasse, Helen was devastated, as it was she, who poured her heart and soul into the house. Jack was often too busy with TWA to immerse himself in the details of the enormous remote project.

After the final conference with Meem, at La Fonda, both parties continue to try to resolve the issues that face the project. Finally though, by June, Jack decides the process is unproductive and sends the following Western Union Telegram from Flagstaff, Arizona, to John Gaw Meem at Santa Fe, New Mexico. The telegram states clearly and concisely as follows:

1947, Jun13, A.M. 10:05

-BELIEVE WE CAN SECURE CONSULTING ENGINEER FROM PHOENIX MUCH CHEAPER THAN DENVER DUE DISTANCE SO DO NOTHING UNTIL FURTHER ADVISED-JACK FRYE

Later, John would write an inner-office memo about his last meeting at La Fonda, with the Fryes, "We therefore departed very good friends."

Shortly after, Jack immediately launches construction with a local contractor named Elmer Purtyman, and local labor, instead of a building crew from Santa Fe. In conjunction with postwar shortage of skilled labor, the Fryes rely on the Yavapai-Apache who live on a reservation near Camp Verde, Arizona some thirty miles south of the Frye Ranch. These Native Americans are excellent stonemasons.

'October 1, 1947'

Jack Frye is invited to the White House Rose Garden, this time when Truman offers another Medal for Merit to Colonel Louis Johnson, United States Secretary of War, Commander of the American Legion, and an executive with General Aniline and Film Corporation.

Of course, Frye is C.E.O. of General Aniline and Film, and he and Johnson are close friends.

'October 11, 1947'

Jack and Helen are in Kansas City for the weekend. Helen flies out to Phoenix, while Jack flies on to New York City. Helen stays in Phoenix Monday night the 13th and continues to Sedona by Tuesday. Helen settles in at the ranch supervising the house construction, while Jack remains in New York City tied up with G.A.F. Jack promises Helen he will be out as soon as he can get away.

Walking through the now launched Sedona ranch house, Helen surveys the week's construction after workers have left for the day. She wears dungarees with red and black wool shirt-jacket and matching silk scarf tied around her neck. On her feet are Indian moccasin half-boots, custom-made for her at Santa Fe's Feldhake Shoe Store on the Plaza. Helen steps down into the sub-level of the building from the dining room to check the progress of the kitchen area and cupboards mounted that day. Near an outside wall and next to a counter, Helen is lost in thought as she thumbs through an architectural magazine of kitchen designs. Suddenly, Helen hears a sound. Quietly, she sets the magazine down and looks around herself cautiously. Seeing nothing out of the ordinary, she looks down toward the darkened flagstone floor. As her eyes adjust to the shadow, she sees something that grips her heart with terror, something that should not be there! Helen sees a lime-green Arizona Black-Tailed rattlesnake, about four feet in length, curled up at her feet. Frozen with fear, Helen gulps, "Where did that snake come from?" Helen dares not breathe as the snake silently observes her, his eyes glistening menacingly.

Finally, after what seems like an eternity, but really is just a few moments, the strangest thing happens. Native American music begins to permeate the room, softly, then louder and louder, with chants, singing, and drums. Helen is perplexed as she continues to gaze at the reptile. His eyes are cold and calculating; he hisses and rattles his tail. Helen's legs start to shake, and she fights to keep her knees from knocking. "Just strike dammit and get it over with!" she declares under her breath, hardly daring to move her lips! She waits for the inevitable, seeing no escape, knowing she will likely die from the venom being in such a remote region with no local doctors. For what seems like an eternity, Helen waits. She knows in her heart, this surely is her just punishment for cruelly tormenting all those snakes at the ranch with her bullwhip. "Jack was right!" she laments. "The snakes want their revenge!"

All of the sudden though, the snake stops rattling, he seems to relax a bit. At that moment, Helen hears a plaintiff male Native American voice fill the shadowed room. Speaking in broken English, he declares, "Why do you harm me? Why do you kill my brethren? I am the spirit of land, I am the water, I am the wind, I am the earth, I am the eagle, and yes, I 'AM' the snake! This is 'My' land." Helen is speechless, it's like the snake is actually speaking to her! "Please," the voice continues pleadingly, "this is sacred land, many moccasins have worn paths here. Weary, they found respite in this sacred valley. Don't defile my people, don't disrespect Sacred Spirit!" The voice pauses, before continuing, "Rejoice, rejoice and celebrate your association here, for you too, were once an 'ancient one' and a native of this land! When you strike me you strike yourself." At that statement, Helen feels a wave of anguish and regret move up though her bosom and she begins to weep. After a long pause, the voice continues lovingly, "I leave you now in peace and love. Dry your tears and rejoice at your connection here in this sacred place!" At that, the snake slowly slithers away, sliding right over one of Helen's moccasins, out the door, and up into the rear courtyard, disappearing from sight.

Helen collapses in tears, she grabs the counter for support. The experience moves her beyond words. She realizes she has undergone an epiphany. Finally, she gains the strength to make her way out the kitchen's front door and around to the cliff, which overlooks the creek to the west. Out in the open, Helen stands in silence, her face streaked with tears, knowing she just had a once in a lifetime experience.

In silence, with the late afternoon breeze tousling her hair, Helen watches the Indian workers camped down below on the edge of the creek, lit by the orange glow of the setting sun. She observes their flickering cook-fires and listens to their singsong chanting as they dance in and around the smoke. Helen looks toward the setting sun and decrees through joyous tears, "Thank you, 'Oh Great Spirit', thank you, you have spared my life! I will never again kill a living thing on this ranch, nor will I ever allow anyone else to do so! This land is sacred, more so than I ever dreamed!" Now, as a changed woman, Helen finds her way down the narrow path to the sandy beach of the riverbed below. As she walks she declares, "My heart is no longer afraid of the snake. Nothing will ever harm me on this sacred land again, this I surely know."

Helen reaches the bottom of the cliff and continues toward the Apache encampment next to the creek. The cottonwoods stretch out overhead like a canopy, and the shell of the unfinished house looms silent on the cliff above. The red-rock-spires serve as an enchanting backdrop, as Oak Creek gurgles and flows past the sandy beach. Helen pauses under a huge cottonwood. All of the sudden she is dumbfounded by the scene before her! A shiver runs through her from head to toe. Hit with a revelation, as if delivered by a bolt of lightning, Helen is stunned! "The dream on the train trip out to Reno in 1932! Oh my God, it's all here at my feet, the fulfillment of my vision!" Helen holds her hand to her mouth and her eyes fill with tears. After fifteen years, a vision becomes reality!

Helen pulls herself together and continues to the gathered workers. She seeks out the Native American who is supervising the rockwork at the house. As she walks up to him, she greets him saying, "Do you need additional blankets, or anything at all? I do wish you and your men would stay up at the bunkhouse Jack and I had built for you." Helen points up toward the Willow House, which resides in the meadow above the riverbed. The kindly old Indian replies, "Our needs are simple Mrs. Frye, we require little, just food, song, and the sandy earth for our bed." Then, the Indian suddenly points up at the incomplete house on the cliff as he exclaims, "Look!" Helen looks up and observes the last blood-red rays of the sun illuminating the incomplete house like a smoldering ember, while campfire smoke obscures it intermittently. The Indian speaks again as he points emphatically, "House of Apache Fires!" Sure enough, Helen understands, she nods her head, "What a shimmering vision!" she exclaims with wonder. "I think I will call it just that, 'House of the Apache Fires', as it surely is! Thank you, my friend." Helen reaches out to hold his hand and says passionately, "Goodnight and sleep well, this is your land, your destiny, I am the visitor here." She turns away with tears in her eyes disappearing into the shadows of the Arizona Cottonwoods.

As Helen walks up the rise, a blanket of cool descends over the valley, amid the singsong chanting and drums of the Native Americans, which pulses and permeates the evening silence along Oak Creek.

'June 1948'

The Fryes move into the red rock ranch house, which is still in a state of construction, accompanied by Helen's new secretary-assistant Rosie Targhetta, and fulltime live-in cook Jane (Rosie's brother Joe is ranch foreman).

During this time, Jack's responsibility as C.E.O. with General Aniline and Film consumes his time. His office, at 230 Park Avenue, at the Vanderbilt New York Central Railroad Building, is a faraway place from the quiet serenity of Smoke Trail Ranch at Sedona. G.A.F. places a limo at his and Helen's disposal, night and day, to chauffeur them to and from their Manhattan penthouse and social gatherings. Whenever Jack can steal a few moments, he flies out to the ranch, usually in route to Los Angeles on business. This gives Helen and him a few stolen moments. Meanwhile, Helen spends as much time at the ranch as possible overseeing construction of their new dream-home, this, amid her social obligations with Jack at N.Y.C.

Chapter 11

A Fork in the Road Appears

'Spring of 1950'

Jack goes out to dinner alone in New York City at 21 Club. A beautiful woman spies him from across the room where she is sitting with her girlfriends. They are conferring together about 'catching a wealthy man.' They look over at Jack and joke about how he looks 'loaded'.

One of them whispers, "Why, that's Jack Frye from TWA, now he's C.E.O. of Aniline Film Corporation. He's filthy rich and loves the girls!" Another says, "But, he's married to Helen Vanderbilt." A third one replies, "Yes, but I hear she spends all her time out west at their ranch and leaves him out here all by his lonesome!" Finally, one of the women gets up and swishes over to Jack, "Why, hello darling," she coos, as she opens a diamond-studded gold cigarette case. "Do you have a light?" Jack smiles, looks her up and down, and reaches for his lighter. He asks her to sit down.

At that same moment, Helen is at the ranch in Sedona entertaining guests. On the grounds of the Apache Fires house, a sudden storm blows up disrupting her dinner party. The brisk thermals destroy the gala, tables tumble over, and a glass pitcher of margaritas smashes on-to the flagstone patio. Helen's guests grab their drinks and run for cover into the house. Inside the haven of the stone building, they gather at the picture windows watching the violent thunderstorm sweep through the ranch. Below, Oak Creek becomes a raging tor-rent of muddy red water while the cottonwoods bend and sway in the downdrafts. One of the guests turns to Helen and says with a sympathetic smile, "It appears darling, Mother Nature is trying to ru-in your lovely party!" At that instant, lightning strikes a giant cot-tonwood on the other side of the river, 'BOOM'! The lights go out and the guests shriek with fright!

Late that evening, Helen tries to call Jack as she does every night. The telephone in their New York City suite rings and rings with no answer; finally, at 4:00 a.m., Helen gives up. She knows deep in her heart, something is terribly wrong. With a sick feeling in her gut, she cries herself to sleep. An emptiness as deep as the ocean swallows her up and consumes her in blackness.

'April 1950'

Jack flies out to Sedona, arriving on a Trans World plane at Winslow. Helen is waiting at the airport in their 1948 Pontiac convertible. Jack greets her and they kiss warmly, Helen slides over on the red leather seat so Jack can drive. The car pulls out on Route 66, across the high desert, dropping down through Flagstaff and icy Oak Creek Canyon, to the sunshine of the Sedona Ranch.

Later, inside the House of Apache Fires, Jack, who has now changed from a suit and tie to western duds, stands in front a crackling fire in the master bedroom suite, holding a scotch, while Helen sits on sofa with a martini. Jack watches Helen intently as he says, "Helen, I can't keep flying out here all the time, and you say you don't want to keep traveling back to Manhattan."

Helen hesitates a moment before saying softly, "Well Jack, we've always commuted, it's just the way our marriage has always been. We are both happiest out here in Arizona." "I know, I know Helen," Jack replies impatiently, "but, it's just not working, especially now that I'm no longer with TWA and not in the air all the time." He continues more heatedly, "I'm just too tied up in New York City to come out here constantly, surely you can see that?"

Jack takes a deep breath before he continues gently, "Helen darling, I love you and I miss you, you have to come out permanently. Your place, as my wife, is at my side in Manhattan." Jack pauses a moment before he continues, "We can come out to the ranch whenever we can get away from my business obligations, that will just have to do."

Helen doesn't say a word. Instead, she rises and walks over to the picture windows while lighting a cigarette. Finally, she turns back to Jack saying, "I can't live in the east anymore Jack, I'm just too burned out from the TWA years. I just can't do it, I'm truly sorry darling."

Jack is quiet as he looks at the flagstone floor. He scuffs at a charcoal stain with his polished cowboy boot. For several moments neither say a word, the only sound is the juniper fire crackling and popping. Finally, Jack looks up at Helen, obviously stunned by her reply, "I guess that's your answer then Helen, and I must say, I'm the one who's sorry!" his voice trembles betraying his pain.

Without another word, Jack sets his drink down on an end table; he doesn't look at Helen again as he walks toward the door. "I have to get out of here, I'm going riding." He grabs his coat and walks out the front door to a saddled horse, which he mounts.

Jack rides away in a cloud of red silt, leaving the knoll where the house rests behind. He rides faster and faster, down a steep trail to the river at breakneck speed, straight into the water of Oak Creek, then, he turns the horse and rides along the edge of the creek through the shallows. Furiously he spurs his horse on, while water splashes all around him soaking his clothes. Jack's face is dark and full of sorrow. He chokes back his tears. He has lost so much and feels he can't seem to regain his losses.

At the House of Apache Fires above on the cliff, Helen stands in silhouette at the large picture window

overlooking the creek. She watches Jack ride wildly through the shallows, her misty eyes mirror her troubled heart and she raises her hand to her mouth, as her chest heaves uncontrollably.

'May 31, 1950'

Helen pulls away from the House of Apache Fires, dropping down to the creek, across the ford and on toward Sedona, while Jo Stafford sings 'Haunted Heart' on the car radio. As Helen winds her way through the red rocks, she laments to herself about how much she misses Jack. "I'll fly out next week," she says to herself, "we'll have a wonderful time and go to all the clubs, Jack will be so pleased." Smiling she says, "I miss him and love him so." The wind whips at Helen's curled hair, pulled up and tied with a silk scarf. Dark sunglasses with round lenses shield her eyes, as the Pontiac convertible winds through the red rocks. On an errand to town, Helen has an appointment with her friend Faye Crenshaw about a Forest Service land trade with the Frye Ranch.

Finally, Helen reaches her destination. She pulls up and parks in front of Faye's new realty office in uptown Sedona. As she steps out of her convertible, several reporters rush out of the shadows to confront her. One of them says, "Mrs. Frye! Mrs. Frye! Please, can we have a word with you?" Helen, caught off-guard, responds guardedly, "Well, of course, I guess so." Helen surveys the men with caution.

"Mrs. Frye, can we get a statement from you in regard to your husband filing for divorce this morning at Prescott?" Stunned beyond words, Helen's face falls at the revelation, she is speechless. Another reporter fires a question at her, "Mrs. Frye, what do you have to say about your husband's supposed engagement to the 28-year old showgirl, Nevada Smith?" Finally, Helen regains her composure. She pushes briskly past the impertinent men toward Faye's doorway. "Please", she utters plaintively, "have a heart boys, I had no idea!"

At that moment, Faye rushes out, her face ashen, "Helen darling, come on in here, right now!" Faye tries to shield Helen as the reporters block their escape. At last, Helen turns and pleads, "I have no comment, now please let me through, you are both very rude!" One of the reporters snaps several photos of Helen, 'poof' 'poof', at last they step aside. Sedona locals gather to stare at the scene and whisper while pointing. Helen hides her face with her handbag and quickly ducks into the office. Faye slams the door behind them and quickly shuts the blinds from within.

Left on the sidewalk outside the office, one of the reporters declares, "Why, she had no idea, poor gal, and her husband chasing after that showgirl, young enough to be his daughter she is. Come on, let's get these photos back to Phoenix." The two reporters retreat to a black sedan, identified with 'United Press' on the door. Quickly, they back out, do a U-turn, and head back to the valley with haste.

Headline- 'Decree Granted Industrialist Millionaire Frye, Appears Prescott Courthouse, Helen Vanderbilt Frye- No Show'

'June 26, 1950'

In late afternoon, the unfinished House of Apache Fires rests in hushed silence; a monument to lost dreams and memories, a legacy to what was—what can never be.

Forty-one-year-old Helen Frye wanders the empty rooms of the unfinished home, dressed to perfection, looking like she just stepped off Park Avenue. Gracing her lovely figure, is a three-quarter length burnt-orange cocktail dress with full-petticoats, that swish as she walks. With hair coiffed and make-up flawless, she waves a matching orange silk scarf back and forth, as she strolls through the empty dream house.

From the servant quarters, on through the kitchen, the clicking of Helen's matching burnt-orange silk high heels echoes through the silent house as they tap tap on the flagstone floors. Stepping up into the grand-living room, Helen pauses in front of her nearly life-size painting hanging in its niche. Gently, she caresses the frame with manicured red-nailed fingers. Closing her eyes, she remembers when she sat for it in 1942, she sees it hanging over Jack's desk at his executive offices in Washington D.C. for the duration of the war.

Helen turns, and with misty eyes she looks over at the bank of windows framing the grand vistas of Sedona and the valley below. She revisits the conversation with their Santa Fe architect in regard to the bigger-than-life view, a view she and Jack thought might give their children inferiority complexes. The children, she never realized. Helen grimaces, and her heart aches in knowing she is barren, the pain almost more than she can bear. Unconsciously, her hand rises to rest on her aching heart.

Continuing her tour, Helen climbs the stairs to the south wing. She pauses on a landing, which leads to a doorway on her right. She gazes into Jack's office, never used, yet filled with his essence. As she closes her eyes, she remembers the day Jack, cigar in hand, stood in front of her gesturing how he wanted to furnish the room, books lining one wall, the other reserved for all the signed photos given him by his contemporaries. On one side, Helen watches Jack measure for an executive desk with shelves adjoining to display the silver trophies he had won in his early years of aviation. For a moment, Helen distinctly smells the fragrance of his cigar; however, when she opens her eyes, the room, devoid of life, fades back to emptiness.

Finally, continuing to the master bedroom suite, Helen pauses in front of the fireplace mantel. She remembers, as her hand caresses the polished wood all the fires that burned within, fires now cold, embers black and gray. Walking past the hanging bed, empty, it swings gently and creaks softly as her full-dress brushes it. Helen stops in front of the grand picture windows. Her tour finished, she pauses a moment to take in the magnificent views. In the glass, she observes the reflection of a middle-aged woman standing before her, beautifully dressed and vital. "I don't feel vital," she answers to her own thoughts, "and I sure don't feel desirable or attractive, especially not today." Helen's red swollen eyes stare back at her from the vast void beyond.

In her heart, Helen realizes she played her hand and lost. "I should have folded, my losses were not worth my bluff," she laments to herself. "Jack was always the better poker player." She takes out a gold cigarette case, flips it open and removes a cigarette. Lighting it, she inhales deeply and pauses a moment, then exhales, as the smoke swirls around the room like a ghost. "We could have had it all Jack, but I just wasn't enough for you!" Suddenly, a tear wells up, escaping from the corner of Helen's eye, she whispers passionately, "You break my heart darling!"

Helen stands in the shadow of the empty room for a long time, staring out at the majestic views in a trance, remembering—a small figure as seen from below silhouetted in the massive window. As the light fades with the setting of the orange sun, Helen becomes but a shadow herself, swallowed up by the dark void of the empty house, consumed in a tomb of loneliness.

Chapter 12

Living a Life of Reflection

'Spring 1952'

Helen and her gal-pal Lynne Gray, visiting from New York City, drive out toward Big Park. They slow as they approach Bell Rock where Helen swings her convertible off the road and parks near the remote location of the film, "Pony Soldier." As they step out of Helen's Pontiac, their high heels settle into the red powdered dirt. Helen grabs her handbag out of the back seat saying to Lynne, "I wonder if he will remember me? I only met him a couple times, once on a celebrity charter flight, and another time at a party with Howard and Jack." Lynne replies, "Oh Helen darling, how could he possibly forget you!" Helen and Lynne seek out the location manager who directs them to sit down and wait, while he delivers a message for them.

Finally, after a few moments of watching the excitement around them Lynne exclaims, "Helen, look, here he comes!" As Tyrone Power walks up in his dashing red tunic he says, "My assistant tells me there are two beautiful women over here who want to meet me?" Then, he sees Helen, "Well, well, Helen Frye, it's been a long, long time. How are you darling?" In reply, Helen says, "Well Ty, I live out here now, and when I heard you were in town, well, I just had to stop by and say hello." Helen turns to Lynne, "This is my dear friend, Lynne Gray from New York City. She's a big fan of yours." Ty replies, "How do you do Lynne, and thank you for coming out." He takes Lynne's hand and kisses it, "I hope you are enjoying your visit?" Then Ty turns to Helen, bowling her over with his bigger than life charm he says, "And tell me Helen, are you a big fan too?" Even though

Helen is quivering inside, she responds coolly as she observes him. "Well, that depends darling," Helen says with a twinkle in her eye, "can you do more than act?" Ty lets out a big laugh as he replies, "I'll tell you what ladies, we're winding up today's shoot, so how 'bout we all have dinner after they cut me loose?" Helen replies, "I'll up you one darling, why don't you come out to my ranch and we'll have a re-al 'western night' of it?" "Will there be roping?" says Ty inquiringly with a wry smile. "Well", says Helen, "that surely depends on 'what' you want to rope darling!" At that, Lynne's face turns red, "Helen, really!" she protests embarrassingly. Ty laughs heartily and winks at Helen.

That evening, at the House of Apache Fires, Helen, Lynne and Ty are finishing their steaks. They're seated on the north patio overlook-ing Cathedral Rock, next to the built-in barbecue. Ty turns to He-len and says, "Well, Helen, you and Jack certainly built a stunning palace up here in the red rocks. I'm very impressed, and I'm just as impressed with your cooking too." Helen responds as she pours Ty another glass of wine, "Yes, Ty, it is beautiful here, that's a fact, but very lonely when compared to life in the city." Ty smiles and says, "Well, I like it." He lights a cigarette, "I crave a piece of the western-outback, and you seem to have found yourself a right nice chunk of it." "Really now Ty, you're starting to sound like one of your western characters," says Helen with a laugh.

With this last comment Lynne speaks, "Helen dear, I think I'm all done in. The flight out here really wore me down, I'm going to turn in and read for a while." Ty replies, "It was so nice to meet you Lynne." He reaches over and squeezes her hand as she gets up from the table. Lynne says, "Thank you Ty, the honor's all mine! I do hope I'll meet you again before I leave," Lynne turns to Helen and says, "Goodnight Helen, I'll see you in the morning." Helen bids her goodnight. "And please dear," Helen says, "let me know if you need anything, anything at all."

Helen turns to Ty, "I wonder if you are up for a walk down along the creek, it'll be picturesque!" Ty turns and observes an enormous moon rising over Cathedral Rock, "That'd be nice Helen. I don't know what's more stunning tonight, you, or the moon over the red rocks?" "Oh, come now Ty, stop waxing over the moon and let's get down to the creek!" Helen laughs as she grabs him. Arm in arm, they step down the front flagstone stairs to the path that leads to the creek below the cliff, while a symphony of coyotes howl in Frye Canyon from back behind the sprawling pueblo house.

'April 5, 1952'

Under a canopy of cottonwood trees in the shadow of Oak Creek Canyon, Ty turns off Highway 89A northbound, down a narrow dirt lane toward the creek in Helen's convertible. Helen is sitting beside him holding a cigarette and Lynne is in the back seat by herself. Ty is dressed in a tan suit with white shirt and cravat, while Helen and Lynne are dressed for a night out in smart cocktail dresses. A floral scarf holds Helen's long curls up off her shoulders. The car's soft suspension lurches and bumps along the red rock road bordered with lush green vines. After a few moments, they come to a stop in front of a Hansel and Gretel-like red rock cottage.

Helen reaches over and blows the horn. Within a moment, the door opens, and Helen's friends, George and Madeline Hunter Babbitt come out to greet them. Ty helps Lynne out of the back seat while Helen hugs Madeline, then she turns and introduces everyone, "This, darlings, is Tyrone Power, and of course you know Lynne," Helen says warmly. "Well, this IS a treat!" says George as he reaches out to shake Ty's hand. Madeline steps up, holds her hand out to Ty, smiles warmly and says, "Welcome Ty, this is such an honor." Then she turns to Lynne and they embrace. "I'm so pleased you could come up Lynne, it's lovely to see you again! You know dear, George and I would love to have you anytime!" Lynne replies, "Thank you Madeline. I would stay up here if Helen would ever let me out of her sight, even for a moment." They both laugh as Madeline continues, "Please, please, come on in. Let's have some drinks and hors d'oeuvres before we leave for dinner."

As they all enter the charming summer home with its beautiful carved doors and woodwork George says, "I thought we could all go up to the Spanish Inn at Flagstaff for dinner, it'll be fun. Don't you agree Helen?" "Yes, yes George, that's a lovely idea and it'll give Ty a chance to see the Canyon on the way up!" Helen says with a smile.

'1953'

On one of Tyrone's trips out to see Helen, he and Helen drive over to Sycamore Canyon to explore Geronimo's Cave. This sacred cave, in somewhat of a secret location, is largely unknown to most, sitting above the gurgling flow of the Verde River under an umbrella of cottonwoods. Both Helen and Ty are dressed in Western duds, fancy cowboy boots, jeans, buckskin jackets and silk scarves at their necks, Helen's scarf is scarlet, Ty's is buff. Helen and Jack's dog Copper accompanies them on this outing.

In the shallow cave, they examine the ancient walls smudged with charcoal and talk for hours, lounging on the sandy floor. The sound of the creek below permeates the cave along with a cacophony of birds and crickets. At the heat of the day, they skinny-dip in the cool refreshing waters of the Verde River. The day is perfect and not one other person intrudes on their special afternoon together.

Early one morning, at the House of Apache Fires, in Helen's private upstairs studio, Tyrone stands at the French doors looking out at the view of Cathedral Rock. "I still can't believe you live in such a spectacular setting Helen." He turns and looks at Helen, who is slowly dressing in the finest black stockings, panties, and brassiere. As she fastens her hose, Helen looks up, "Yes Ty, it's beautiful here. That's why it was so hard for me to leave and move back to New York City with Jack in '49'." Helen pauses as she pulls on a white linen skirt. "I realize, in hindsight, I made the wrong decision, but I just hated the thought of leaving the ranch for that concrete jungle!"

Again, Ty looks back out at the view of upper Oak Creek Canyon, illuminated by the early morning sun, which is slowly claiming the shadows. "No one can blame you for that Helen, no way!" Ty says. "Except, maybe Jack?" Helen answers. "Now come on lazybones, put some clothes on and let's get cracking. I'd like to reach the Grand Canyon for lunch."

Late that same day, after returning from the Grand Canyon, Ty and Helen walk back into the living room of Helen's home below the studio. As Helen makes them both a drink, Ty wanders around while he lights a cigarette. Commenting, he says, "Helen, you're truly such a gifted artist. How many years have you painted?" "Well," says Helen, as she hands him a drink, "I attended the Art Institute of Chicago, and then, well, I was sketching and painting even before I married Vanderbilt." Ty replies, "Well, I dare say Helen, this house looks like an art museum. How do you find time to work on all this?" He waves his hand at the paintings and sculptures. "Darling, you coming from Hollywood just have no idea how much time a divorcee' has on her hands in a place like this!" says Helen with a laugh! She continues, "Now come on sweetie. Let's go upstairs and watch the sunset, and then, perhaps a ride and a midnight swim?" They both leave the house and climb the stone stairway up to the studio, hand in hand.

'January 1955'

Helen and Ty are at Wickenburg, Arizona having an early dinner. "I'm so happy we drove over here for a dinner and it was so tasty too!" says Helen. Ty replies, "Yes, and far from the prying eyes of Sedona, nice to have a little privacy for a change! You're right about Sedona Helen, when you say it's a very small town!" Helen lights a cigarette as she addresses Tyrone, "Yes darling, you think they gossip about you? Well you have no idea how they like to talk about me and all the supposed men I entertain, night after night, in my boudoir!" They both laugh heartily as Helen continues, "Are you sure you have to fly back to Los Angeles tomorrow?" Ty replies, "Well, as much as I hate to leave you Helen, I do have to get back to work. I was wondering if instead of heading back to Sedona, we could drive down to Scottsdale and stay tonight, I can leave in the morning from there." Helen smiles at him as she blows smoke across the room. She puts her cigarette out in an ashtray. "I think that would be lovely dear, just lovely!" she coos.

Standing in front of an open slider with just a pair of slacks on, Ty draws on his cigarette. He stares down at the palm trees surrounding their Scottsdale hotel. As he exhales, he observes other guests at the pool, without turning he says, "Helen, I've never in my life, even with all the women I've known, met a woman with the sexual prowess and allure you possess! You actually wear 'me' out!" He turns and smiles as he walks over to the rumpled bed. Helen watches him from their love-nest. She reaches for a cigarette, taps it gently on the night table and lights it. Ty kneels down next to her and reaches for her hand, "Helen darling, will you marry me?"

Helen is stunned; she never expected such a proposal. She smiles as she exhales, "I do hope my darling, you're not just marrying me for my sexual prowess?" Ty laughs as he replies, "Well, uh, for your cooking too, sweetheart!" Helen grabs a pillow and hits him over the head, "You brute!" she exclaims. Ty continues, "Seriously though Helen, do you think you could ever be my wife?" Helen smiles at him radiantly, and with only the slightest hesitation she says, "Yes, yes, of course, I'm thrilled, I would love to marry you sweetheart! What woman wouldn't Ty?"

Later that afternoon, Helen drops Ty off at Sky Harbor in her 1953 pale-green Pontiac convertible. As he starts to step out of the driver's seat, he leans over to kiss Helen passionately. A baggage man waits for the two politely at the curb. "I can't wait to get back and ask Linda for a divorce sweetheart, and I am so anxious to tell all my friends about our engagement!" With that, Helen stops smiling, she reaches up with her ruby-red-nail index finger and touches it gently to Ty's lips, saying, "Shhh, shhh, my darling." She shakes her finger at him from side to side saying, "You mustn't tell anyone yet, I don't feel the timing is quite right. Why not wait until the divorce papers are processed?" Ty replies, "I guess you're right Helen, but I can't see any problem. After all, Linda and I are both unhappy and I've wanted a divorce for some time now." "Just trust me Ty," Helen replies solemnly.

Several days later, on an unusually warm day, Helen is sunbathing on the sky terrace of the House of Apache Fires, nude. Her chaise lounge, positioned next to a crackling fire in the rooftop fireplace, is within reach of a pitcher of margaritas. Next to the chaise are her high heels, a wrap, and a black telephone, which suddenly starts ringing. Helen sets her drink down along with The New Yorker magazine she is reading and answers it.

After a click, Helen hears the voice of Ty, which sounds strained, "Hello? Helen?" he questions. "Why, hello honey," Helen purrs lovingly, "I was waiting for your call!" Ty continues, "Helen," he hesitates, "I have some bad news. I don't even know what to say, but well, Linda, I did ask her for a divorce, but she told me she's pregnant!" Ty sounds totally defeated. Helen is silent as she pulls on her wrap and slips on her heels. Finally though, she responds quietly, "Ty darling, of course you know that's the oldest line in the book?" "Yes, well I certainly wondered about her timing," says Ty, "and this is not the first time she has claimed such a thing, but I feel I have to see how this plays out never-the-less." Helen again is silent.

At last, she speaks, "Well, what can you do?" Helen's heart is on the floor. Ty continues, "Helen, you told me you didn't ever want to be the 'other woman' so I can certainly understand at this point that you may have misgivings about our relationship." Ty is quiet for a moment before he continues gravely, "I feel like I've let you down Helen. I'm desperately sorry darling." Helen pauses briefly, then she says gently, "Ty, in this case, I think perhaps we should continue to carry on the way we have and be thankful we can share our love for each other and all the good times. I am sorry, really I am, but I did feel somehow this was not the right moment for us. So perhaps we should just re-group and see what happens from here."

Chapter 13

Reunion

'Fall 1957'

Returning from Sedona, Helen swings her convertible down into the ranch. As she pulls past the Willow House, her ranch manager steps out to stop her. Helen rolls to a stop as she greets him, "Hello Walter, how's it going today?" Walter approaches the car, with concern, he says, "Helen, there was a man out here today, but I wasn't able to get down here from the cliff to see who it was, he didn't leave a note." "What did he look like?" responds Helen curiously. "Well Ma'am, he was a big man, over 6-feet I reckon, and filled out too. He went up to the Apache house and then he drove back on down here to the Willow House. Finally, after looking around a bit, he drove on out. Oh, and he was driving a big fancy car, a Cadillac I think."

After a pause, Helen replies, "Well Walter, thanks, I will ask around and see if we can figure out who it was. Certainly, it's unusual, someone driving all the way down here, uninvited, and snooping around on top of that! By the way, tell Betty hello for me and I'm looking forward to the potluck Saturday night at the creek." "We are too, Helen, see you then," Walter replies, as he walks away to the barn.

Helen drives on up to the Apache Fires House. As she drives across the ford, it dawns on her who the tall stranger was. "It's Jack!" she cries out loud with glee. Her heart starts pounding madly. "Walter has never met him or he would have known!" Helen is very excited, "Why would Jack come back? What's going on with him?" she muses.

That afternoon the phone rings, it's Jack, 'Helen, I'm in town, up from Tucson, would it be O.K. if I dropped out to visit?' Helen rushes around getting ready while she listens to Jo Stafford sing 'Long Ago and Far Away' on the radio. In front of a dressing table mirror, Helen brushes her auburn hair and fixes her makeup. Carefully, she pulls on a beautiful virgin-white dress embossed with teal firebirds. She adjusts herself in front of a full-length mirror and dons several beautiful ancient Native American Indian bracelets and rings. Sitting on a sofa, Helen leans over and slips on the red leather strapped high-steps Jack bought her fifteen years ago.

At last, Helen hears a car below, she rushes to the west window and watches as a red '56 Cadillac passes through the lower ranch, cross the creek, and on up to the house. Helen rushes over to the east window to see the car parking behind the house. Hidden behind the curtains, Helen watches as Jack gets out. At that moment, with racing heart, Helen steps out the upstairs studio doorway and strolls across the deck to the stairs. Slowly, Helen descends the stone steps gracefully, as her dress billows out around her like a bell, exposing her black panties and hose.

Jack, who has just reached the stairs below, pauses, as he looks up at her, his mouth falls open. As Helen reaches the bottom step Jack says, "Helen, you're still just as beautiful as I remember, stunning, just like you were on the staircase in our mansion at Washington!" Helen smiles warmly; she notices his eyes are misty. She reaches out her hand to him, "Welcome back Jack," she says with emotion. He looks around and says, "It's good to be back Helen. I always loved this property so much, and I've never found anything to replace it!" For a moment, Helen feels a lack of empathy. Before she can stop herself, she blurts out coldly, "Well, Jack, you should have stayed! Nobody made you leave!"

It's obvious her words are a direct hit; a shadow passes over Jack's face and he looks away. "Why did I have to say that?" Helen laments to herself. She watches Jack closely, he looks tired, worn out, and beaten down. With pain in her heart, Helen realizes now is no time for anger or resentment. She may never have the opportunity to be with Jack again. With that thought, all Helen's anguish melts away. She decides she must make the best of this evening, for she knows in her heart, regardless of the past, she is still passionately in love with Jack. "I love this ranch too, Jack, and I certainly wouldn't have it if it weren't for you my darling!" Helen responds sincerely. Jack looks at Helen; his face quickly lights up. Helen reaches out, takes his hand, and leads him into the dream house they built together. "Come on darling, let's have a drink, then I'll make you some dinner. After we eat, you can tell me all about your exciting life!" "Thank you Helen, I'd like that very much! My God, I've missed you; it's nice to be home again!"

Helen walks over to the bar and fixes Jack and her a drink. Jack says, "That martini pitcher sure brings back memories Helen. I'm glad you are still using it, I served two presidents out of it." Helen turns and hands Jack a martini, she smiles saying, "I'd forgotten the history of that beautiful pitcher Jack, and yes, I do treasure everything we owned together and the memories too." Holding their drinks, the two wander around the house together and talk about how it all came about. They end up in the kitchen where Helen prepares dinner. She throws steaks on the barbecue outside the kitchen, when they're ready, she and Jack carry the food up to the sky-terrace to eat in front of a crackling fire. As they dine, they watch the sunset light up the red rocks from the ranch all the way to the top of the canyon, like a magnificent painting.

"The views here are unsurpassed Helen, I've never seen anything like it!" exclaims Jack emotionally. "Yes Jack, the views are grand, but more so when they are shared," says Helen as she looks deep into his eyes. Finally, after the sun sets, the crimson light fades to a rosy afterglow. At that point, Helen says, "Let's go downstairs where we can be more comfortable, we'll light a fire."

Jack starts a fire in the master-bedroom suite, while Helen fixes them both another drink. Then, she walks over and tosses a Jo Stafford record on the phonograph. She lights a cigarette, and throws open the windows, which overlook the creek. Cool air washes through the stuffy room along with a chorus of crickets and frogs, while Jo's whispery words, 'haunted heart won't let me be, dreams repeat a sweet but lonely song to me,' wafts through the room and spills down to the riverbed below.

Jack and Helen settle down on a sofa in front of the juniper fire as Jack starts to talk. The words tumble out as if he has waited a lifetime to share what is in his heart. Jack relates to Helen he has resigned from Aniline and is living back in Arizona. He's trying to launch an aircraft manufacturing facility at Tucson, hundreds of people will benefit from the venture. Then, he pauses, he takes a deep breath as he starts telling Helen about his marriage and how it had all been a huge mistake—a complete disaster. His tale of woe spills forth as Helen listens intently. The scenes of Jack's life play out in front of Helen spilling forth like a Technicolor film.

'Queen Mary, North Atlantic, July 1951'

'The Queen Mary comes into view on a placid ocean at full steam, voyaging under the command of Captain Harry Dixon. At the Captain's table, elite guests are sitting around making small talk at dinner. Jack and his stunningly beautiful young wife, the 29-year-old red headed Nevada Smith are seated on the side, with the Captain at the head of the table. Nevada is dressed in a white-satin gown with a white mink stole tossed over the back of her gilded chair. Bedecked in jewels, purchased by Jack, guests can't help but be dazzled by her eye-popping 117-carat Argentine Tourmaline, 10-carat diamond ring, and 40-carat diamond bracelet, all of which adorn her knock-out figure.

A porter walks up to the table and hands Jack a telegram. After reading the message, Jack turns to Nevada and discreetly says, "Nevada, all these train and passenger ship trips are murder on my business. I have an emergency meeting; we may have to 'fly' back to New York City instead of taking the Queen Mary." Nevada turns to Jack obviously irate. Sharply she retorts, "No!" Becoming overly agitated, she continues, "I just won't have it Jack, you promised me a cruise, 'over and back'. On top of that, you know damn well I'm afraid of flying and I absolutely loathe air travel, I will certainly NOT fly back! I could care less about your damn board meeting!"

Jack protests, "Please Nevada, not here, can't we talk about this in our stateroom?" However, Nevada is not to be quelled. Her voice rises as she screams at Jack, "I will not calm down you bastard. I hate your God-Damn obsession with planes!" Jack looks at the other guests, obviously mortified, and then he looks over at Captain Dixon, his face flushed with embarrassment. At that moment, Nevada rises in a huff, knocking her drink into Jack's lap. She throws her napkin down and storms out of the Grand Salon, screaming obscenities at Jack as she leaves. The dining room guests are aghast over this scene, as they whisper to each other. Jack's face is ashen, he gets up, first he apologizes to Captain Dixon, then to the Captain's guests. "I couldn't be more apologetic for this disruption, please forgive my wife and continue with your dinner. Excuse me please."

Jack leaves the dining room and follows Nevada to their stateroom that is near the Captain's quarters. Once there, he finds Nevada has locked him out, he knocks and knocks to no avail. Nevada screams and yells from inside, "Get the hell away from me you bastard!" Nevada flings a crystal vase full of flowers at the cabin door. Jack jumps back suddenly, as the sound of glass crashes just inches away from where he stands. At last Jack gives up and secures another stateroom for the night.'

'Christmas Eve 1954'

'A black 1952 Cadillac Fleetwood limo is idling in front of a fashionable townhouse at 246 East 49th Street in snow-shrouded Manhattan. A chauffeur is standing at the rear door of the car, as he opens it, Jack Frye steps out dressed in a camelhair topcoat and scarf. The chauffeur helps Frye to the sidewalk covered with ice and snow, and then walks around and opens the trunk. He removes shopping bags full of Christmas presents and follows Jack to the front door of the townhouse.

As they enter Jack says, "Please set the packages over there on the hall tree, the servants are off this evening." The chauffeur complies, then turns to Jack and asks, "Will you be needing me anymore this evening Mr. Frye?" Jack smiles and says, "No Frederick, I'm in for the evening, thank you." Jack reaches into his overcoat and pulls out an envelope which he hands to the chauffeur, saying, "Merry Christmas!" "Thank you, Mr. Frye, and Merry Christmas to you and Mrs. Frye too!"

The chauffeur retreats as Jack shuts the door quietly behind him. Jack shakes the snow off his topcoat and hangs it up. As he turns around, he notices Nevada in the living room, pacing back and forth, puffing on a cigarette. She appears to be in a rage. "Where have you been?" she demands sharply. Jack replies as he walks into the room, "I ran into Morton Downey and his wife Peggy, we had dinner together." "You what?" screams Nevada as she glares at him with smoldering eyes, "how dare you go out with them and don't include me!" "Nevada, you yourself told me you didn't want to go out this evening, and I wanted to eat before I came home," responds Jack. "You're a selfish bastard Jack Frye!" screams Nevada as she storms out of the room.

Jack shakes his head as he retrieves his packages and places them thoughtfully under a magnificent 15-foot Christmas tree. After doing so, Jack goes up to the bedroom suite and starts getting ready for bed, he is exhausted and has had a long day. From there, he walks into a room where his daughter Nevajac is asleep in a small cradle-bed. He caresses her hair and kisses her gently on the forehead. He scoops her up in his strong arms. Jack takes her into the master bedroom suite where he places her in another similar cradle-bed in a corner; the child is half-asleep. Jack covers her lovingly, kisses her, and says, "I love you my darling, Merry Christmas!" Jack walks over to the doorway, calling down to Nevada, "I'm going to bed now, I'm exhausted, I brought Nevajac in here with me." Nevada calls up drunkenly, "I don't care what the hell you do Jack! You've ruined 'my' Christmas!" Jack enters the bathroom, opens the medicine cabinet and reaches for a prescription bottle. He draws a glass of water, takes a sleeping pill, then goes back into the bedroom and crawls into bed; he's asleep immediately.

In the living room, Nevada claws through the presents under the tree like a wild woman; sparkling jewelry adorns her wrists and hands. Nevada mumbles to herself, "Where's that diamond necklace? How dare Jack not buy me that sparkle I found on 5th Avenue last week?" With a lit cigarette hanging from her mouth she continues, "I'll show that bastard!" Nevada drags the tree skirt out in the middle of the room and gathers all the presents into the center. She picks up the bundle, carrying it up to the master bedroom. She sets it down gently on the bed where the sedated Jack is asleep. The bundle comes undone as it settles, and the Christmas packages glimmer and sparkle in the shadowed room. Nevada reaches in a nightstand, removes a can of lighter fluid and sprays it all over the presents. She takes the lit cigarette from her mouth and flips it into the center of the heap. Suddenly, the paper and packages erupt into a burning inferno, with flames ten-feet high. Nevada jumps back and stands in the doorway with a wild look on her face, the back of her hand over her mouth as if to protect her face from the flames.

The heat and explosion of the fire awakens Jack. With a look of confusion and terror, he jumps out of the bed, which is now engulfed in flames. Jack quickly gathers the burning bundle of packages up in the blankets and tosses it all into the bedroom fireplace. Then, he grabs a blanket off a chair and smothers the burning embers glowing on the carpet. He looks over at his daughter Nevajac, who is terrified and screaming, gathers her up and carries her to her own room where he sets her down gently in her bed. Jack walks back to Nevada and confronts her. "Why, Nevada, why?" he says in a defeated tone. Jack is not angry, just very sad and disheartened. He grabs his robe; donning it, he reaches out to Nevada and leads her like a child out of the disheveled smoke-filled room to the living room. The Christmas tree twinkles in a corner and several lamps are on. Jack helps Nevada over to a sofa where he sits her down. Then he kneels beside her. Looking up at her face, he says gently, "Nevada, we have to get you help, this simply can't continue, especially now that we have Nevajac. You could have killed us both, let alone, burned the entire building down." Shaking his head, Jack reaches for a telephone next to the sofa, "I'm calling your doctor." Jacks voice is emotionless and reflects his feeling of helplessness.'

'Washington D.C., 1955'

'At a lavish hotel in Washington D.C., several people sit in a baroque drawing room. Jack's sister Sunny, seated on a gold leaf and salmon colored satin sofa, adjoins her husband Les Thomas, while Jack sits close by in a matching King Louis salon chair. All guests are enjoying cocktails and hors d'oeuvres before dinner. A tipsy platinum-blond Nevada is standing on the other side of the room, making herself yet another drink at the bar. Sitting next to Sunny is Nevada's astrologer friend who accompanies Nevada everywhere like a shadow. Sunny and the astrologer are visiting when the astrologer suddenly leans in and whispers to Sunny smugly, "Yea, I'm the one that told Nevada if you want to hold on to Jack you have to give him a child! How clever was that huh?" She continues, "You know, of course, their marriage is a wreck!" Sunny is stunned at this admission. She studies the crass woman coolly and quickly glances over at Jack. Thankfully, Jack had not heard the comment over his conversation with Les.

A moment later, Jack looks up at Nevada, as she stumbles back over to the group. He says, "Nevada, don't you think you should lay off the liquor? Surely, it won't help, you feeling sick and all. And don't forget, we're all going out to dinner soon." Nevada gives Jack a scornful look, sarcastically she replies, with slurred words, "I'm just fine darling, not that you care," she adds acidly. Nevada sits down abruptly and sloshes her drink on the sofa. She brushes at it drunkenly. Jack turns to everyone and says, "Nevada has been ill for a week or so. Because we are here for two weeks, and I didn't know who to contact,

I called Harry Truman, and he graciously connected us with his own personal physician. Talk about an honor!" Jack's guests all smile and murmur politely, 'isn't that nice, etc.' Jack continues, "And, we were also able to catch one of Margaret Truman's performances too." With that, Nevada pipes in acidly, "Yea, Harry's precious daughter actually thinks she can sing! What a laugh!" Jack gently admonishes her, "Nevada, you shouldn't say that, especially in regard to the fact that Harry offered you his own physician. That was quite a favor on his part. You're being disrespectful."

Nevada's face turns crimson. She stands up, walks over to Jack, heatedly, she exclaims, "Fuck you Jack, and to hell with the President's doctor! He's just another quack as far as I'm concerned!" Then, she slaps Jack hard across the face, sloshing his drink on his slacks. Jack is stunned and says nothing. The room is stone silent. On the sofa, Sunny's mouth falls open, and her eyes are as wide as saucers. Nevada makes an exit, passing the fireplace, she throws her drink in and glass explodes all over the hearth. Meekly, the astrologer gets up and follows her out of the room. Finally, Jack regains his composure and wipes at his trousers with a napkin, his hand shaking. With flushed face and grave voice, Jack turns to his guests and says, "I thought all this was over, her wild outbursts, with the therapy and all, obviously not. I just don't know what to do with her anymore." He shakes his head, rises, and he too leaves the room.'

At the Apache Fires House darkness has descended over Jack and Helen as they sit on the sofa, the fire has gone out, leaving only an orange glow. Jack speaks softly as he stares into the embers, "The only good thing to come out of all this is my daughter Nevajac." He pauses, then continues, "Nevada, well Helen, to be frank she's mental. The doctors say manic-depression and an alcoholic. Sadly, we've been separated for years. I can't live with her, I never could, yet she calls me relentlessly, she won't leave me alone. The only people I ever mentioned any of this to is my executive secretary Jean Phillips and Sunny." After a moment of silence, Jack turns to Helen and says sincerely, "Helen, I am truly sorry, I don't know why I told you all this, it just came out, I guess I have no one I can confide in, please forgive me. You didn't need to hear any of it."

Helen looks at Jack, she is stunned at his revelations and her heart is heavy with compassion. Finally, she responds, "There's nothing to forgive Jack, I'm just happy you feel you can still talk to me. I'm here for you. As for Nevada, well, certainly, I had no idea, but I've heard stories from our friends and read different newspaper comments. Frankly though I'm just flabbergasted! Obviously, your life's been a living hell!"

Helen gets up, throws a couple logs on the fire, and walks over to the grand picture windows overlooking the valley below the House of Apache Fires. Her image reflects in the glass at twilight with the backdrop of the now roaring fire. In silence, she lights a cigarette, draws it in, and exhales toward the large picture window. At last, without turning, Helen says crisply, "Jack, you're too good of a man for all this nonsense, no one could dispute that! I'll say one thing and I'll say it only once!" In an incensed tone Helen continues, "I knew when you got tangled up with that two-bit stripper she was nothing more than a low-class gold digger and no good could possibly come of it! However, I stood back and let you make your own mistakes. Eventually I thought, perhaps it wasn't so bad letting you go as you gained a child, something I," Helen's voice cracks with emotion, "something I just couldn't give you Jack." Helen turns around to face Jack, her eyes misty, "I'm so sorry you got hurt darling."

Helen walks over and sits beside Jack. She reaches out and holds his hand, "Jack, we've both been hurt. I was devastated when you left, I spent many years filled with hatred for that little home-wrecker. You know Jack, it wasn't just the pain of you leaving me, it was the added pain of you leaving me for a younger woman." At that comment, Helen notices Jack's eyes are watery, and his lip is quivering, as he stares into the fire with silence. Suddenly, his chest starts to shake as he begins to sob, no longer able to hold back his emotions. Helen, in seeing this big strong man cry is overwhelmed. She leans in and takes him in her arms, the two embrace as soul mates, reunited at last with their tears. Helen whispers soothingly, "There, there my dear, it's all in the past now, the only thing that matters is that you're here, your back home in the house we built. Let's see what we can do with our future from here on out."

After a few moments, Jack pulls himself together saying quietly, "Thanks Helen, I don't deserve your kind sentiments." Continuing, in a stronger voice, he says, "I'm divorcing Nevada and she's not going to raise Nevajac, she's just not capable of being a good mother. I've arranged for my father to take the child during our impending divorce and then she will live with me. I must protect her. I'm well aware of Nevada's motivations and why she married me."

At about midnight, Jack gets up to leave. He is staying in town and has to return to Tucson in the morning. He and Helen agree to stay in touch; they have a lot to work out, and much to resolve. Jack pauses a moment, as he leans back on the driver's door of his Cadillac. A serenade of crickets and night sounds surround them in the starlight. He says, "Helen, you and I shared the 'Camelot Years of TWA', no one can ever take that away from us! When I left you, I threw away the most precious thing in my life. I was married to TWA, *and* you, somehow I lost you both."

Suddenly, Jack pulls Helen close, kissing her gently on the lips. After a moment, he releases her and steps into his car. He starts the engine, turns and smiles, then, he's gone, down the hill, through the creek, and into the night.

Helen feels an emptiness clutch her heart as she watches the Cadillac's tail lights disappear into the darkness. Somehow, she feels time is not on her side. Helen looks up at the twinkling canopy of stars spread out over the ranch and wishes a wish, "Let this be the moment I have yearned for, the moment I have dreamed about, let Jack and me be together again. I love him, I have always loved him, I will never stop loving him." Helen turns and walks quietly back into the shadowed house. The massive wooden door shuts behind her taking all the light with it.

'May 1958'

Sitting at the kitchen nook in the Apache Fires, Helen is drinking a cup of coffee and reading a magazine in front of the cook stove, which is popping and cracking with the morning fire. The telephone rings, it's Ty. "Well, hello darling," says Helen, "I haven't heard from you for a long spell. How are you?" "Well," says Ty, "I've been so busy out here," he pauses and then says sincerely, "how are you Helen, are you O.K.?" "I am perfectly divine," says Helen. Ty seems relieved as he continues, "I do have some news dear, are you sitting down?" "Yes," says Helen, "please do tell!"

"Well, Helen, you know, since Linda and I divorced I have dated a lot of women. And you, my dear Helen, have continually refused to take me up on my offer!" "I know, I know," Helen replies, "but I have learned to enjoy our friendship just the way it is." "Well," continues

Ty, "I've met someone!" "Really?" says Helen, "anyone I know darling?" "I doubt it Helen, her name is Debbie Minardos," responds Ty. "Is she a knockout?" says Helen. "Yes," Ty says, "she's beautiful. We're going to be married!" "Well then," Helen replies, "I'm so happy for you, for you both!" Ty responds, "Helen, I knew you'd feel that way, you've always been such a special friend to me, someone I could really trust!"

Helen pauses for a moment, then says, "I have some news for you too, Ty. Something amazing has happened. Jack and I are seeing each other, and he has asked me to marry him!" "Jack?" says Ty, "Oh my God, Helen, that's wonderful, I can't believe it! How did all this happen?" Helen continues, "Well, he's been up many times, and he's separated from his wife, they haven't been close for some time. In fact, Jack wanted to leave her years ago. But, guess what? All the sudden she told him she was pregnant! Now, does that sound familiar dear?" Ty laughs heartily, "Yes, too much so!" "Either way," says Helen, "they had a child, and that's the only thing that's kept them together. Jack is just miserable. Once they're divorced we will re-marry."

Tyrone is quiet for a moment, "Helen," he pauses, "I say this from the bottom of my heart because I know both you *and* Jack. There are not two people who are meant to spend their lives together more than you and Jack. And I know you have always considered him the 'love of your life'. I'm so happy for you, and you both have my heartfelt blessing! Please tell Jack hello for me!" Replying lovingly, Helen says, "Thank you Ty, that means a lot to me and I hope you will be just as happy with Debbie!"

'November 15, 1958'

After a day of shopping in Scottsdale, Helen walks out to her convertible and places an armload of packages in the back seat. As she steps into the car, she takes a newspaper tucked under her arm, and opens it. She sits down on the leather driver's seat as she scans the front page, the headline reads, 'Cinema Idol-Tyrone Power Dead, Heart Attack at 44.' Helen puts her hand over her mouth and starts sobbing softly.

Chapter 14

The Last Day- February 3, 1959

33-years to the day Jack founded Standard Air Lines

Helen awakes after a restless night; the morning sun is rising, illuminating the cracks and crevices of the House of Apache Fires. Helen gazes out the window of the studio over her Oak Creek Valley. The crimson towers usually feed their beauty back to her soul, but not today.

Helen had always been a spiritual person, knowing things, but not always knowing what the things represented. The day is dark, as is her mood, she feels empty inside, but why? She and Jack were going to be together again. No, not just together, they were going to spend the rest of their days at each other's side, married. No more mistakes, he 'needs' her. "Do you know how that makes a woman feel?" Helen chides herself. "Jack wants you back!" Helen was on cloud nine in regard to their future. Jack was her soulmate; the essence of this lifetime was the culmination of their existence together. This time she would do it right, "I will not make any mistakes," she says to herself. "Why then am I so depressed," questions Helen? She makes her way down to the kitchen, as she starts the coffee, she feeds Brumbo and the other dogs. A chill takes Helen and she shivers, she pulls her sweater tight and throws a couple more sticks in the cook stove. The room fills with orange flickers of light and warmth.

The phone rings, it's Jack, right on cue. "Helen, I love you," are his first words. Still in Tucson, he calls every day, when he didn't, Helen always knew where he was and what he was doing. They had shared so much together; it was as if they had never been apart. "I love you too, Jack, more than ever," Helen replies. "What's on your plate today?" Jack asks. "Well, I have to run into town and take care of some errands, and then, I'll be back out here later," says Helen. "Well, I have a dinner this evening, I so wish you could be with me darling," says Jack in his Texas drawl. "Now, honey, you know I don't enjoy those fund-raisers anymore. I would bore all your friends to death," replies Helen. "You would charm their pants off," says Jack, "just like you always did!" He continues, "I am meeting with one of your old friends." "Who?" Helen replies. "Howard," Jack responds, "he has indicated he may come on-line with the Safari project at Tucson." "Well, darling, as much as I would love to see him, I think business is business," Helen replies. "I miss you so much Helen," Jack whispers. Eventually, they hang up and go about their busy days.

Late in the day, after errands in Sedona, Helen drives back out to the ranch. The sun is sinking fast, betraying the time of the year and highlighting the forever-vistas. Helen just can't get into it though, she has felt disconnected all day, sad for no reason, blue without cause. She parks her station wagon and walks into the master bedroom suite of the house. Instinctively, she reaches for a cigarette from one of the end tables, she lights it, and takes a long draw. As she exhales, the smoke flows out into the suite. In the shadows, it swirls around, painting the room misty in the early evening light.

Helen sighs deeply as she stands in front of the massive plate glass windows. She smokes her cigarette silently as she watches the sun sink low in the sky. Her diamond bracelet, a gift from Jack, sparkles in the sunset. She notices movement in the shadows below and observes deer foraging for dinner.

In downtown Tucson, Jack finishes up his conference at the Pioneer Hotel and walks out into the warm afternoon sun. He strolls over to his rented Fairlane-500 sedan, removes his jacket, gets in and throws his briefcase and jacket on the passenger-side. The car starts with a groan; he merges into traffic east to his hotel.

Driving north on Alvernon Way, Jack turns right, into the driveway of the Lodge on the Desert where he has a suite. He parks, grabs his jacket and briefcase, walks down the back garden path to his room, where he unlocks the door, and enters a suite decorated in Southwestern décor. Two rooms appear, a sitting area with a desk, adjoined by a large bed, with an adjoining bedroom, and hallway to a bathroom.

Jack throws his briefcase and coat on the bed, while reaching for a cigar off the bedside stand, which he unwraps and lights. As he puffs on it, he sits on the edge of the bed and removes his shoes. Standing in front of a full-length mirror, Jack removes his shirt, revealing a furry chest. He unbuckles his pants and lets them drop to the floor, where he retrieves them, folds them, and lays them on the bed. Glancing at his reflection in his boxers, Jack sucks in his stomach, and says, "Still looking good for 54!" He turns and walks into the bathroom, snags the light switch, leaves his cigar on the counter ashtray, and steps into the shower. After showering, he dries off and throws the towel on the toilet.

Jack walks back out to his bedroom, where he carefully selects just the right outfit for his next meeting. From an open drawer filled with perfectly creased and stacked boxers, he picks a pair and pulls them on. At the closet, Jack observes a dozen Park Avenue suits lined up with matching shirts and slacks. He selects one, which he lays out carefully on the bed. Slowly and meticulously he dresses. From a dresser, he selects a pair of socks from a drawer, and from the bottom of a closet, he selects a pair of polished cowboy boots. He walks over to the dresser, reaches for his inscribed Rolex, a gift from the company after he did advertising for them, and slides it on his wrist. He turns to the bed, organizes his briefcase, looks over the room, shuts off the light and walks out the door. As Jack shuts the door, he hangs a 'Maid Service' sign on the doorknob.

Walking out to his car, he pulls out into traffic heading south on Alvernon Way to the airport. After about 15-minutes Jack passes a sign stating, 'Tucson Airport', he drives around the terminal and across a stretch of tarmac to a row of offices and hangars.

After Jack parks, he walks into a 1950's style low-slung office with words, 'Frye Aviation & Safari Aircraft' in crimson-red letters displayed across the front glass. Entering the office, he pauses in front of one of two desks. Jack's secretary looks up and says, "Good afternoon, Mr. Frye." Jack replies, "How are things going out here today?" "Well," the woman says, "Nevada called again, she needs money, and Helen called as well, would you like me to call either one back for you?" "Yes," Jack says, "please call Helen and put it through to my office." "Yes sir, Mr. Frye," the young woman replies efficiently as she picks up the phone. Jack walks through a door which says, 'Private Office, Jack Frye,' shutting the frosted glass door behind him.

Within the hour, Jack joins his friend Robert Schmidt, Tucson's Airport Manager, and they climb into Jack's Helio Courier H391B

STOL plane. After settling in, Jack starts the single engine, and the plane taxis out on the runaway and takes off, it climbs quickly over saguaro, which peppers the surrounding desert. The Helio reaches altitude and establishes a holding pattern over the small city.

Finally, Jack turns to Robert and says, "Bob, I wanted to get you in the air in order to talk about the Helio project. I don't want anyone to know of this meeting, absolutely no one." Bob replies, "Why, of course Jack." Jack proceeds, "I think I have solved our funding issues. I have lined up a partner who will open all doors which are closed." As the two fly over the Catalina Mountains and Tucson, the plane's engine drowns out any further discernable words.

After the flight, and back at the airport, the two old friends visit next to the Helio. Jack reaches out to Bob, shakes his hand and pats him on the shoulder while saying sincerely, "Bob, you have been my best ally and friend through all these difficult negotiations and I want to thank you with all my heart." Bob smiles warmly and says, "Of course, of course Jack, you don't need to thank me for anything, it's I who should thank you, and the City of Tucson! You have a history here and your legacy of aviation in Arizona will always be treasured by the citizens of this state."

Jack leaves the airport, heading south he drives through empty scrub desert. Finally, he turns on a private road and passes a sign, which reads, 'Air Force Plant 44'. As Jack continues up the long narrow drive he passes more signs displaying, 'H.M.S.C', 'Restricted', 'Military Facility', etc., and another 'No Public Access'. The Fairlane 500 slows as it approaches a guardhouse in front of perimeter fencing and an entry gate. A guard in uniform exits the smoked-glassed building with clipboard, he asks for a name and the purpose of the visit.

Jack replies, "Jack Frye", before he can utter another word, the guard snaps to attention, curtly he responds, "Yes sir—Mr. Frye! Please drive right on in. Continue down the main road to the very end, there you'll see a large hangar on the left, park there and enter the door on the right." Jack thanks the guard as the electric gate slides open. The guard replies, "The pleasure is all mine Mr. Frye!" Jack drives on out of sight amid military-like buildings and hangers.

Jack pulls up to the hangar indicated by the guard and parks. Stepping out, he grabs his briefcase, and walks over to a small door. Opening it, he enters a dark void; he notices several aircraft parked in the shadows. Jack sees a light at the far end, down a long hallway. He continues to walk toward the light, his cowboy boots echo on the concrete floor. At the end of the hall, he stops in front of a door to an office, partly ajar, a sliver of light escapes.

Jack knocks twice on the door. He hears a voice say, "Come in." Jack pushes the door open and walks into the poorly lit room. At the far end is a desk, lit by a reading lamp, adjoined by several lime green military-issue chairs. There is a man sitting behind the desk, but Jack can't see his face, as he is cloaked in shadow. The man looks up as Jack walks in, he slides his chair back and walks into the light, he's tall, with a mustache, and limps slightly. When the man reaches Jack he extends his arm and says, "How you doing Jack? It's really good to see you my friend!" Jack extends his hand and smiles, "Good to see you too, Howard, it's been a long time."

They both walk back to the desk and Howard asks Jack to sit down. The first thing Jack says after getting a better look at Howard is, "Gee Howard, you look mighty rough, are you sure you're feeling O.K.?" Howard flinches a bit replying, "Well Jack, things have been a little tough for me after the accident and all, but I'm doing fairly well." He opens a drawer and pulls out a bottle of whiskey with two glasses. Howard says, "Let's have a drink Jack, to aviation," he pauses, "as we knew it old friend." Touched by the proposal, Jack replies, "Sure

Howard, thank you, we've shared a lot, haven't we?" Howard says, "Yes, we have Jack." With an unsteady hand, Howard pours whiskey in both glasses and hands one to Jack. After they take a drink in silence and reflection, Howard takes a deep breath and says, "Well Jack, what can I do for you?"

Jack opens his briefcase and starts showing Howard different files and blueprints for the new Frye Safari transport, and the proposed joint Safari-Helio aircraft factory. The two huddle over the drawings and blueprints, conversing together with muddled words. After 30 minutes or so, Jack shuts the briefcase and shakes Howard's hand. Howard closes by saying, "You've got a great design here Jack, it all sounds good to me. You can count me in, I'll have the papers drawn up and sent to your office for review." Jack replies, "I knew you would want to be in on this Howard and I thank you for your help."

At this, Jack gets up and starts for the door, he pauses though as he looks Howard over carefully. "You know Howard I have a really great doctor in California. You should consider seeing him, he has helped Helen and me in the past, and likely he can help you too. His field is totally different than a normal G.P., Endocrinology, leading edge."

Howard hesitates, finally though he responds, "Well Jack, if you say he's that good, then I believe you." Jack asks if he can use the phone to call the doctor, then he takes a little black book from his breast pocket, retrieves a number, and calls Dr. Charles H. Carpenter in Glendale.

The phone rings several times and picks up, Jack says, "Hello Charles, this is Jack Frye." After he listens to Dr. Carpenter for a moment he continues, "I have Howard Hughes here, I wonder if you would be willing to see him some time? I thought maybe you could help him." After inaudible words, Jack continues, "O.K. Charles, that sounds good. Howard will call you later after I leave, so he can speak to you in private." After Jack thanks Dr. Carpenter, he asks about his family, etc., he says goodnight and hangs up. He turns to Howard, "It's all set up. All you have to do is call." He writes the number down and hands it to him.

Jack and Howard leave the room and start for the hangar's exterior door. Suddenly, Howard stops, he turns to Jack in the shadows, "Jack," he says, "I, I want to say I'm sorry. I should have said it a long time ago, but I, well, I didn't ever find the right opportunity." Howard's face is full of compassion as he reaches up and touches Jack's shoulder. "Howard, you don't need to apologize for anything, it was all just business," Jack says. "I know, I know Jack, but I shouldn't let other people tell me what to do. When I fired you, I let Dietrich manipulate me. You were one of my best friends and a great business partner. We shared the infancy of flight together, the glory of TWA, there aren't many of us still around you know. In addition, ever since you left TWA, well, as you likely know, we've struggled. I'd do anything Jack to have you back at the helm." After a moment of silence and obviously deeply moved, Jack replies sincerely, "I'm speechless Howard, thank you, your words mean a lot to me, more than you'll ever know my friend."

The two aviation legends continue to the hangar door where Jack pauses, he turns to Howard and says quietly, "Howard, people really care about you. Please take care of yourself, O.K.?" Jack then rests his hand on Howard's shoulder, and pats him on the back. "Thanks Jack, I have too few real friends, and by the way please give my best to Helen," Howard says. Jack smiles and says, "I will Howard, and come up to the ranch anytime, we would love to have you!" Jack pauses, then continues, "I haven't divulged this to many people Howard, but Helen and I are going to be re-married, as soon as I divorce Nevada."

"Well, well, congratulations, Jack!" Howard says with a big smile, "and the same for Helen too! I feel you two were meant to be together, and frankly, I never understood your parting." Jack smiles softly and looks down, "In retrospect, neither do I Howard, neither do I." Jack leaves the hangar and walks over to his car, "Goodbye old friend," he says over his shoulder, as he gets in.

Jack drives away as Howard stands in the parking lot watching, in a moment though, he retreats back into the shadow of the doorway where his form fades to black. From the shadows, he stands in silence, as the car's taillights disappear.

Within 10 minutes, Jack is driving north on Palo Verde Boulevard. Enjoying the evening air, he puffs on his cigar. He feels good, finally, his struggle is over, all will move forward now. Three-long-years of trying to raise money for a new airplane manufacturing plant are behind him. As Jack drives on, he flashes back to earlier that day in the cockpit over Tucson.

The cockpit side window is slid open and the cool breeze wafts around Jack's content face as the engine drones happily along. He's in the air, the place he has always felt most at home. The scene fades as Helen's radiant face appears. Jack reaches out, takes her hand in his, and kisses it gently. Jack feels a warm glow of love permeate his body from head to toe.

'6:49 P.M.'

Jack's car, seen in overview, enters the intersection of Ajo Highway, from the south. From the west, a speeding station wagon approaches and flashes past a stop sign heading directly at Jack's Fairlane 500. In seconds, blinding headlights wash over Jack's car, with no time to re-act, Jack yanks the wheel of the heavy sedan. In an instant, the two cars connect with a deafening crash; the sound of tinkling glass per-meates the night and Jack plunges into a black void.

'6:50 P.M.'

After the horrific collision silence descends on the scene, while sev-eral witnesses run to the intersection to help. The driver who hit Jack, a woman, is screaming and crying in her car, as a small crowd gathers. Several people help her out of the crumpled station wagon; she struggles to stand, amid beer bottles, that clatter out onto the ground. The good Samaritans lead the woman to the side of the road; she mumbles incoherently in a drunken stupor.

Meanwhile, an attendant from the nearby Flying A service station runs to the comatose Jack, who lay in a heap on the highway, 30 feet away from his crumpled sedan. The attendant is horrified at what he finds. He starts yelling frantically, "Help, anyone, help, call an am-bulance, this man is hurt really bad!" He quickly takes off his jack-et, rolls it up, kneels down and gently places it under Jack's head. He holds Jack's hand and tries to make him comfortable. "Help is on the way sir, please hold on," he urges.

After what seems like an eternity, the sounds of wailing sirens per-meate the silence from the north. Within moments, a Pima County Sheriff's Department cruiser is first to arrive, soon after, another po-lice car, a wrecker, and finally a Cadillac ambulance. The red strobe lights from the emergency vehicles cast an eerie glow on the blood-soaked scene. The officials find Jack barely conscious, covered with blood, and mumbling indiscernible words. Police officers retrieve

Jack's wallet from his slacks and discover his identity, while other officers question the female driver, who is unhurt, and help her into the back of a police cruiser.

The officers soon discover, even though the station wagon approached a stop sign, the car didn't slow down. Instead, it proceeded to impact the side of Jack's car toward the left rear at a high rate of speed. The impact spun the station wagon around, while Jack's impacted sedan continued to roll down the road for 178 feet. Finally, his sedan came to rest 40 feet out in the desert scrub and sand. Jack was no longer in the Fairlane, however, as the impact ejected him 30 feet, depositing him into a heap in the middle of the blacktop highway. Obvious to the officers is Jack's own car ran over him, crushing his 6-foot frame; further, it is discovered the driver who hit Jack never applied the brakes, as there were no skid marks—the 4,000-pound car rammed Jack at near full-speed.

Fatefully, another driver, Howard Blackmore, witnessed the entire incident. Blackmore traveled into the same intersection, right before Jack, and turned right (westbound) on Ajo Highway. Because of his optimal placement, Mr. Blackmore observed the entire accident and he could not help but observe the speeding wagon race by him on Ajo (eastbound). He stated to officers he realized as he watched the speeding car flash past on his left, it was not going to stop at the intersection behind him. Helplessly, he watched another car approach (Jack's) and observed in horror as the speeding station wagon impacted with a deafening crash. Blackmore quickly pulled off the highway and ran back to the scene to assist, his heart pounding at the experience, something he said he would never forget.

White-attired attendants lift Jack on a stretcher and wheel him toward the waiting ambulance. After a few moments, they slam the door and jump in. Gunning the engine, the massive '58 Cadillac leaps away, its siren screaming into the night. An idling police cruiser leaves the scene within moments, racing ahead of the conveyance, it provides escort to a distant hospital. The destination is St. Mary's, several miles to the north, about a 20-minute drive down the dusty rural roads of South Tucson.

Inside the ambulance, the attendants are well aware the man's life they are transporting is slowly ebbing away. They try to make him as comfortable as possible for the long journey. Jack, barely conscious, shuts his eyes and flashes back on his life. The scenes play out like a fast-moving film: from his youth, growing up on the Texas Panhandle, to his first ride in an old Jenny biplane, his embracing of aviation, his triumphs with TWA, and on to his wives. Suddenly, the scenes stop flashing; Helen walks out of a swirling mist and reaches out to Jack with outstretched hand, her face full of love and compassion.

Before Jack can grab her hand, the Cadillac lurches into the entrance of St. Mary's and the flashback fades. Jack grimaces with pain as he tumbles back into unconsciousness. The ambulance pulls up to the emergency entry and backs up, while a medical team rushes out to assist. Jack is unloaded and wheeled into a waiting operating room lit with a soft green glow.

For an hour, the doctors and nurses evaluate Jack's injuries and try to sustain his weak life force. The St. Mary's hospital priest is summoned, even though Jack is not Catholic. As the white-collared holy man holds Jack's hand, he hears Jack say, "Please, please help me Father!" The priest squeezes Jack's hand saying, "They're doing all they can my son, God is with you now." A nurse squeezes his other hand, and leans in as Jack mumbles, "Call Helen."

In spite of the dedication of the doctors and nurses, they are unable to save Jack, his injuries are just too severe. Unable to find a pulse, after several minutes, the resident physician states, "We can do no more." The death is called at '8:35 P.M.', a result of massive internal and external injuries. The hospital team backs away in reverence as a nurse pulls a white sheet over Jack's now lifeless body. The priest stays behind for a moment to offer a prayer and then he leaves the room with bowed head.

Then something miraculous happens. Unseen by physical eyes, a beam of light flashes from the ceiling down to Jack laying on the operating table, as a portal opens between our physical world and the other side. Slowly, an orb of pulsing color rises out of Jack's lifeless body and soars up through the ceiling, following the beam and disappearing. In an instant, the light flashes out as if a switch is flipped off.

God has called this great man home. A light extinguished in our world is re-illuminated in the heavens. Jack Frye is dead at just 54, it's over.

'Apache Fires House- Sedona'

In the kitchen, Helen pours herself a glass of red wine as she tends to dinner. She is alone tonight, and lonely. Jack would call late, after he meets up with Howard, and tomorrow he is off to Dallas. Suddenly Helen wishes she had driven down to Tucson and attended the dinner, or had Jack fly up and get her. It would have been a nice change. "Why do I have to be so anti-social?" she chides herself. Burned out from the TWA years, Helen prefers only intimate gatherings, close friends, and warm sharing at Sedona.

Helen turns from the stove, her full dress with petticoats brushes her wine glass sending it tumbling. Helen turns to look just in time as the goblet falls downward. In slow motion, the glass smashes all over the flagstone floor. The late afternoon sun, orange red, shines through the window, transforming the spilled wine into an appearance of blood, flooding over sparkling shards of glass.

Suddenly, Helen feels dizzy; she grabs the corner of the table to steady herself. In a trance, Helen observes the surreal scene. Putting her hand over her mouth, a cold chill flashes through her from head to toe. Startled, she starts shaking uncontrollably. The incident, certainly a premonition, leaves Helen feeling stone cold in her gut. After a few moments, she snaps out of it. "Damn-it, pull yourself together woman, it means nothing!" she concludes. However, Helen knows better; with shaky hand, she picks up the daggers of glass as one of them slices her finger. "Ouch", exclaims Helen as her finger turns red. The sun has disappeared and the room is now in shadows. Always psychic, Helen knows in her heart there is some deep meaning to this incident. But she can't quite discover the key, it's like a veil has been pulled over her all day, and she is not intended, not meant, to know what all the signs mean. Helen's looks over at the clock on the counter, observing 6:50 P.M.

Later, sitting at the kitchen nook, Helen picks at her simple dinner; however, she now has no appetite. She climbs up to the master bedroom suite, walks over to the phonograph and puts on a Jo Stafford 78 record, 'Stardust', and settles herself by the fire. As Jo's voice wafts through the stone house, she makes herself another drink and lights a cigarette. The dancing flames always relax her and make her feel better, but not tonight. Inky darkness shrouds the House of Apache Fires, as the fire plays out on the walls and through the windows with its dancing yellow fingers. Helen, her face warm, and body buzzed from the bourbon, dozes off, while a dream overtakes her mind.

'Helen and Jack are flying in their plane for what seems like an eternity, over country Helen does not recognize. She and Jack are both young again, it's as if it were back in 1941, before the war. The plane, silver-orange in the sunset, drones on over valleys and mountains. Helen looks over at Jack, his presence so powerful to her. She feels weak around him, overwhelmed with love, filled with admiration. Suddenly, Jacks looks over, he reaches for Helen's hand, covering it with his. Their eyes lock and they smile, Helen feels her heart jump and tumble. "Where are we going?" she inquires. Jack doesn't answer though, he turns away and focuses on his flying.

Finally, they start circling a small airport. "Are we going to land?" says Helen. "Yes," Jack replies, "it's time." They descend over a desolate airstrip in the middle of nowhere; Helen has no idea where they are. Jack guides the Lockheed down settling onto the runway. After they taxi a minute or so, he parks, and kills the engines. Silently, he goes through a shutdown procedure.

Then Jack turns to Helen, his eyes are full of sadness as he says compassionately, "I love you Helen, don't ever forget that." Helen, startled, replies with a quavering voice, "Well, I love you too, Jack. I always have, desperately, you know that darling." Jack gets up, opens the fuselage door and helps Helen to the ground. They walk over to a small abandoned office. "Where is everyone?" says Helen, puzzled. "Probably all have moved on," Jack says mysteriously. Then, he turns to Helen and implores, "Helen, I have to leave you here." "Why Jack? I don't even know where we are?" says Helen, who is growing increasingly uncomfortably. "You'll be fine darling, don't ever forget that," he says. Then, Jack reaches out and gently takes Helen's hands. At that moment, he gazes into her eyes, Helen feels his strength flow into her, words are not necessary, as their eyes convey to each other many lifetimes of partnership. Jack pulls her close and holds her in his massive arms. They embrace for what seems like an eternity.

In Helen's heart, she knows it was Jack she was meant to meet in this lifetime; she was born to be with him. Gently, Jack pulls away. He kisses Helen on the lips, turns, and walks out on the tarmac back to the plane. Helen is alone. Perplexed she watches Jack. When he reaches the Lockheed, he steps in and secures the cabin door behind him. In a moment, the starboard radial whines, as it turns over, then the port. Finally, the Electra Jr. is purring with a low rumble which slowly increases to a full roar. Jack releases the brakes and the plane picks up speed and pulls out on the runway. Jack looks out at Helen, throws the cockpit window back, and waves, his face full of love but yet a certain sadness. At this moment, Helen feels the emptiest feeling she has ever experienced, as if someone has taken a trowel and scraped her insides out. She grimaces with pain and puts her hand over her stomach. The plane rolls down the tarmac, faster and faster, suddenly, it lifts off and climbs out into the rose-hued horizon. Soon, just a gleaming silver speck, it disappears.

All alone now, Helen gazes around her. The airstrip is forlorn, unused, and windswept. She sees a hanging sign flapping in the wind, it reads, 'Last Stop'. "What an odd name," she muses. On the horizon, inky clouds boil and erupt, washing away the rose-hued glow, with shadow and gloom.'

A bell starts to ring loudly, "What's that?" thinks Helen. Suddenly, she awakens to the telephone, the noise assaults the still evening. Helen reaches over to answer it, thinking, "What a bizarre dream?" The clock next to the telephone shows, '8:45 P.M.' Placing the receiver to her ear, Helen listens, as anxious words pour forth.

"Helen? Helen?" a voice says, "I have some bad news." After a pause, the voice continues compassionately, "Helen, Jack is gone." Shock starts to consume Helen and she hears only a few more words. "He, tonight, terrible car accident, he died at St. Mary's, at Tucson. Helen? Helen? Are you still there?"

Helen was not there, she can't believe what she is hearing, the room starts spinning as she drops the receiver. Helen sinks to the floor, slipping into a whirlpool of darkness. Amid this Helen hears herself screaming, "No! Oh my God no, he can't be gone!" Helen surrenders to the darkness; her body lay in a crumpled heap on the cold stone floor. Eventually, the fire fades to smoke, and the silent House of Apache Fires closes in around her like an icy grave.

Around midnight, the dancing smoke of a cigar wafts through the room. Dipping and swirling in the twilight; it drifts toward Helen and settles around her. The cigar smoke permeates Helen's consciousness, she stirs and calls out longingly, "Jack? Jack? Is that you darling?" Helen listens intently, but the silence of the dark house ignores her plea, the cigar smoke lingers. Finally, Helen rises, shakily, she lights a cigarette and fixes herself a strong drink. Walking over to the phonograph, she sets 'The Nearness of You' on the turntable. Helen re-lights the fire, sits down on the sofa and listens to Jo Stafford's voice sing, "when I'm in your arms and I feel you so close to me." Slowly, Helen draws in on her cigarette with shaking hand, the tip, orange, in the shadows.

In her mind, she starts to replay the phone call from Howard. He related Nevada hadn't been called yet. "So, this is how it all ends?" Helen muses. "For the last eight years of my life I dreamed Jack and I could correct the tragic end of our marriage, re-unite, and find some common ground we could share. Both of us accepted we made a horrible mistake. Yet, now Jack is gone, how can this be? Helen often worried Jack would perish in a plane crash—but a car, impossible!" she exclaims. "I can't live without him, I can't!" Then Helen remembers the dream, "Jack said I would have to 'walk alone now', oh my God, the dream!"

Until dawn, Helen sits and watches the fire, the flames flicker and claw at the darkness. Finally, sunlight invades the dark valley and erases the night's horror.

The ensuing days are a blur. Helen receives many phone calls and flowers, hesitantly though, she wonders, "Do I dare attend the funeral at Tucson? After all, I'm the 'ex-wife' now, many know me as Jack's 'former' wife, but few know Jack and I had planned to re-marry. Jack is separated, and he leaves a young child behind, a child that had been such a worry for him." Helen decides she will go to the funeral; however, she will keep a low profile, a few mourners will understand her presence, and certainly, she owes it to Jack. The phone rings, 'Howard is sending a private plane to Sedona and has arranged for a car to pick her up at Tucson, the decision is made.'

'February 7, 1959'

As Helen's private plane lifts out of Sedona, winging its way over the southern deserts, Helen speaks not a word. Sitting next to the pilot, she is alone now and lost in thoughts of the man she had loved and lost, not once, but twice. As Helen observes the rising sun illuminate the desert horizons the words of the poem, 'Funeral Blues' by Wystan Hugh Auden, floods through her mind in all its solemnness. A sunbeam finds its way into the cockpit; it explodes in a radiance of color, as it contacts a tear slowly rolling down Helen's cheek.

Landing at Tucson, a limousine awaits Helen at a secluded area of the tarmac. In hushed silence, Helen is whisked through the bustling streets, isolated from normal people, all living another busy day. At last, the limo pulls up to the funeral home. Mourners observe a beautiful well-dressed woman in black step gracefully out of a Cadillac, her face shrouded in a cloak of veils. Quietly, she slips into the service and sits inconspicuously in the back. Several people whisper, "Why, that's Helen Frye!"

After the service, unobtrusively, as if she were never there at all, Helen slips away. The funeral-goers witness a tall man with a mustache talking to an elegant black-shrouded figure in a corner of the quite garden. He embraces her gently as she leans on him heavily; he guides her to the waiting limo where the woman collapses into the shadowed interior. Howard leans in and speaks to the driver, Jack's de-facto wife and soul mate is whisked away, a shadowy vision of refined elegance, a testament to love.

'February 8, 1959'

A long red 1959 Cadillac convertible pulls up in front of Jack's Tucson airport office. Nevada Frye, dressed like a movie star, with her astrologer pal, step out and enter the office. As they come in Jack's secretary looks up with surprise, "Why Mrs. Frye, I didn't expect to see you out here today. I just didn't know what to do, so I went ahead and opened the office." She pauses, saying sadly, "I'm so sorry about Jack, it's devastating." Nevada looks at her coldly, stating bluntly, "Pack up your things and get out, you're fired!" Taken aback, the secretary's mouth drops open; however, Nevada doesn't miss a beat, she points at the door and screams, "Get out! Get Out! My attorney will handle your final pay!"

With that, Nevada and her astrologer go into Jack's office and slam the door behind them. Nevada fires off a command to her accomplice, "Start searching through everything and look for anything that has money attached to it." Nevada walks over to Jack's desk, "I know there's a safe in here," she says as she pulls open the middle drawer. With her bejeweled hand, she feels for something hidden up under the drawer. She rips out a paper taped within, displayed on it are account numbers and the combination to a safe.

"Bingo!" she exclaims, "got it!" From there, she twirls around and starts tearing pictures off the walls. On the third one, she finds the safe. Nevada turns to her accomplice who has paused to watch, "I have to destroy that trust before the attorney gets here, and I bet I just found it!" she exclaims with glee. Nevada twirls the tumblers, and then pulls the handle, the safe opens with a long squeak. Inside are stacks of bills in bundles, about $100,000. She quickly stashes this all in a straw satchel, then she grabs a stack of paper work and starts leafing through it all—mineral rights, bank accounts, real estate titles, oil interests, stocks and securities.

Finally, Nevada pauses at one large brown envelope, which reads, 'In the event of my death give this to my attorney'. Nevada opens it and finds the Will, and a Trust, too. She unfolds them both and quickly starts reading the Trust. "So, you thought you would leave your millions to Nevajac," she says sarcastically, "and appoint a guardian for her care? Not on my life, you bastard!" She takes the trust over to the garbage can, lights it on fire, and drops it in with a whoosh. "Now, there 'IS' no trust," she says confidently with a laugh. Just then, there's a knock on the door, it's Jack's attorney.

Shortly after, Nevada's attorney and the astrologer are waiting outside the office by the Cadillac convertible. Nevada calls out the door, "I'll be out in a minute, I just have to make a quick phone call." Nevada dials a number, it rings on the other end, Jack's sister Sunny, her voice very quiet and filled with grief answers. Nevada tells her coldly, "I've just gone through Jack's affairs with his attorney," she pauses, "Sunny, Jack died broke, penniless, I don't even have the money to bury him. There are a couple insurance policies though, one's for you, as a matter of fact."

On the other end of the line, there's awkward silence. Finally though, Sunny replies, "Well, Nevada, I'm just flabbergasted, I don't know what to say. I never knew Jack was having financial problems?" After another uncomfortable pause, at which Nevada says not a word, Sunny continues awkwardly, "Please, if you want me to pay for the funeral, I'll do so gladly, anything to help you."

"Thanks," says Nevada, "that would be nice." She hangs up with a wry smile and walks out of the ransacked office leaving the door wide open. Once in the car, she tells the attorney she will be in touch. As she pulls away Nevada says quietly to her friend, "We're flying over to Jack's office at Ft. Worth immediately. I've got to secure Jack's estate and start hiding his assets!"

Chapter 15

<u>**New Beginnings**</u>

'**1962**'

High on a cliff overlooking the Frye Ranch, across the valley from the House of Apache Fires, Native American Indians have gathered for a cleansing ceremony. Helen stands aside as the medicine men and dancing Indians bless the location of her new home, seeking harmony of marriage for the new dwelling and the overlook. Helen sits in the afternoon breeze, listening intently to the chanting and drums. Watching the dancers, the music stirs her soul as she sways gently back and forth. The pinnacles of Sedona spread out below and in front of her like a magnificent painting by the Creator himself. On this beautiful red rock outcrop, Helen will design and build her retirement home.

After the ceremony, an old medicine man comes over to her and speaks, "Spirit grateful for you asking harmony and peace here. This place sacred, new home be more than dwelling, it be place for Native American energy to manifest, to unite with earth. This land ancient burial ground, it home to Great Spirit! You protect! Apache Fires house, new house, sacred, filled with spirit! Walk in peace and love! Spirit not harm you or those who respect and honor ancient ones who dwell here!"

Then the old man turns to the sky, and with a wave of his hand he declares, "Spirit offer you sign!" Helen looks out over the valley, from side to side and all the way to Cathedral Rock, she sees dozens of large birds soaring on the thermals, black hawks, several eagles, and red-tailed hawks. Helen puts her hand over her mouth, never in all the years she has lived at Smoke Trail Ranch has she seen such a display. "How beautiful, I will name this house the 'Wings of the Wind', Helen says with passion. Then she turns to share the revelation with her Native American friend, but he has mysteriously vanished.

'1970- Spiritual Liberation for a Price'

Helen is in Sedona shopping at Ida's Health Food Store, owned by Bert and Ida Powell. Her friend Ida introduces her to a young man working at her store. "Helen, meet Marc, he's working here for a while." Helen turns to the young man who reaches out to shake her hand. "Hello, my name's Marc Slater, I'm very pleased to meet you Mrs. Frye," he says. "Why hello Marc, I don't think I've seen you around Sedona before?" Helen is overwhelmed by the man's presence, she had always been psychic, and sensed this person was the real deal, an enlightened man on a path of pure light.

Suddenly, Helen feels a jolt of electricity from head to toe, her knees buckle. She turns to Ida, "I have to sit down dear," she says quietly. Marc stands back and watches silently. "My Lord Helen, whatever's wrong," Ida exclaims! "Just give me a moment," says Helen, as she looks over at Marc who is quietly observing her. Marc then walks over and says, "Mrs. Frye, can I get you a glass of water?" "No, thank you," says Helen, "but you can give me your hand, and please call me Helen." Marc extends his hand; which Helen takes in hers. As if in a trance, Helen says in a monotone voice, "You have lived many lives; many people have come to you for guidance and spiritual enlightenment. You are nearing the end of earth's path, soon to walk with those that no longer dwell in the vibration of our planet. You will touch many lives, walk many paths, but your purpose, as is mine, is to help those who have been cast aside, those ancient ones who live on the Mesas. It is those who offer you their essence and sustenance." Helen pauses, "It's time for you to leave Geronimo's Cave and come to stay at the Wings of the Wind. Our paths were meant to cross, and we are destined to share our spiritual journey and share sacred knowledge."

At that, Helen slumps over. Ida is taken aback by this outburst and rubs Helen's hand, "Darling, are you O.K.? Helen? Whatever happened?" Marc stands by with peace on his face, the look of a person who knows his path is being fulfilled. He addresses Helen saying, "I will gather my things and be over this evening."

Late that night, Marc is fast asleep in the guestroom of the Wings of the Wind; he awakens to the sound of chanting and the beating of drums. Startled, he sits up in the darkened room, the window is open slightly and the evening breeze is wafting through the drapes. He looks toward the moonlit terrace and sees the shadows of Sedona monoliths bathed in moonlight, he listens closely, trying to pinpoint the origin of the sound. The disturbance becomes louder and louder, the sound of an Indian ceremony, a cacophony that fills the bedroom.

Marc gets out of bed, gingerly, he creeps toward the door, opening it a crack, he peers out. He sees nothing, yet the sound is right on him. He opens the door wider and steps out in the hallway. Suddenly, out of the shadows, a medicine man appears, dancing and swaying, chanting and singing, followed closely by other Native American dancers. They nearly pass right through Marc, seemingly, oblivious to his presence. Startled, Marc jumps back into the doorway. The procession of specters disappears, amid drums and chanting, right through a wall!

Silence descends over the house; the sound of crickets resumes and waft through the open windows. "Jesus!" Marc exclaims, as he shakily walks down the hallway and out into the living room. He sees Helen coming his direction from the master bedroom. She notices Marc standing in the middle of the darkened room, with a soft smile, she says quietly, "You see them too, you hear them, don't you?" Are you scared?" she adds. "Yes Helen, I see them, and no I'm not scared. It just startled me as I was asleep," replies Marc. Helen continues, "They come all the time Marc, I'm the only one who ever hears and sees them. This building site is the location of an ancient healing ground for Native American Elders. I was aware of this when I built here, and had the site blessed first." Marc says, "I knew this was sacred ground, I had similar experiences at Geronimo's Cave." Helen replies, "Yes Marc, Tyrone Power and I spent time exploring that sacred cave once." Marc responds with surprise, "I had no idea you had been there, or that you knew him?" "Oh yes, we were engaged," says Helen nonchalantly, "but it didn't work out. His wife Linda wouldn't give him a divorce." "I'm sorry Helen," says Marc. "Don't be," Helen replies, "Jack was meant to be the last one." With that, Helen walks back to her room, she calls over her shoulder, "I'll see you at breakfast." The bedroom door shuts softly behind her.

One morning, Helen and Marc are sitting on the terrace of the Wings, watching a magnificent sunrise. Helen turns to Marc and says with passion, "Marc, you are the most wonderful friend I have had in ages." Marc responds, "We are merely rekindling our past alliance Helen, walking together again for a short time, to re-connect."

Later that evening, after retiring to bed, Marc hears soft crying, he sits up and rests on his elbow. With a perplexed look, he rises and grabs his robe. Exiting the guestroom, he looks for the source of the sound. As he enters the living room, he sees Helen sitting on some cushions in the middle of the floor crying. Around her are dozens of photos of her and Jack, their planes, and the people they knew. Helen reaches out for a photo of her and Jack holding each other. Marc hears her whisper painfully, "Why did you leave me Jack? Why did you abandon me, not once, but twice?" She continues softly, "My heart is broken Jack. I have nothing to live for if not for you." She gently kisses the photo, "I've never stopped loving you my darling."

Suddenly, Helen is startled as she looks up to see Marc standing in the shadows at the edge of the room. "Oh Marc, I am sorry, I must have awakened you," her voice trails off, her eyes far away and misty. Marc walks over and helps Helen to her feet, "There now, Helen, don't cry, you and Jack are soul mates, he's still here, I feel him. He's waiting for you." With that, Helen's chest starts shaking as she weeps softly. Marc pulls her tenderly into an embrace, "Come on," he says, "let's get you to bed, you're going to be O.K."

One day, Helen and Marc are riding near the House of Apache Fires. "Do you want to see it?" says Helen. "I would love to Helen!" Marc says excitedly. They dismount and walk to the front door. Helen, with Marc's help, pushes the heavy door open. As Helen walks in she says, "This was Jack's and my dream home Marc, unfinished, but still filled with memories." "Yes, I feel it Helen, this is a sacred place, full of Indian spirit, and Jack, he's still here Helen." Helen turns to Marc, softly she says, "You aren't just saying that are you Marc?" "I would never say anything I did not feel, Helen. His presence is here, he's waiting for you," Marc replies. With that, Helen turns away, she touches a hanky to her eye, as she continues their tour of the rambling old house.

Later, after sunset, Marc and Helen find their way to the upstairs sun-terrace. "Jack and I would lay up here, au naturel," Helen says with a smile of remembrance. "Jack too?" Marc questions. "Yes, we were both naturists, in private of course," says Helen, "our help was not allowed up here." "I can see why!" replies Marc with a laugh. They both sit on the edge of the red rock parapet. "Just relax Marc and sit quietly. I want to show you something special."

Helen and Mark sit down on a ledge, slowly, Helen raises her hands to the west, the summer breeze gently tugs at her hair and clothing. Suddenly, Marc sees the glow of a blue light start to appear over the valley below. He looks at Helen who is lost in trance, and then back at the shimmering light, which soon becomes a glowing ball of indigo blue. As he watches the ball grow in size, it starts to float over to where they are sitting at the House of Apache Fires. It hovers over their heads, turning the house a surreal reflection of blue. Then, it disappears in silence through the roof, and into the house below them.

Helen slowly comes out of her trance and looks over at Marc. "Well, what do you think Marc?" "My God Helen, what was that?" says Marc excitedly! "I don't know for sure Marc, but it's somehow connected to the essence of the ancient ones who inhabit this property, those who came before the Native Americans." She continues, "For years, there has been a legend of the blue light which haunts this valley. In time, after seeing the orbs a few times, I found I was able to make them appear. This land will not be at peace until it is returned to those who truly guard its essence; this would be the Navajo and Hopi." Marc is quiet for a moment, finally he comments, "That was such a beautiful experience Helen, thank you." Helen says, "Thank, them Marc! It's you they wanted to visit!" Marc turns to Helen with a smile, "Helen, you are the most wondrous person. I have never met anyone like you, and certainly few are blessed with your wise spiritual essence." Helen smiles, "Thank you Marc, but what walks within me, walks throughout eternity, the essence of light and love. I am but a vessel of expression for spirit."

Helen attends various mystical group meetings in Sedona looking for spiritual solace to fill her empty heart. She meets a variety of nefarious new-age practitioners, some seemingly pure, some outright charlatans. One day, Helen is riding on her vast Sedona ranch when she comes to the fringe area of another property. Several young college students are out hiking; they call out and greet her. "Hello," Helen calls in return, as she rides up to the group. After exchanging pleasantries, one of the young men turns to Helen with a charismatic, but shifty manner. In a smarmy voice he says, "So, you're Helen Frye? I've heard all about you!" Helen was intrigued, although there was something about the young man that made her uncomfortable. "Yes, I'm Helen Frye and I can imagine what you've heard from the locals," she replies. Continuing, she says, "You and your friends are welcome to come up to the Wings sometime to visit and I'll show you around my ranch."

Later, the charismatic young man comes up to the ranch alone. After he rings the bell at the Wings, Helen opens the door; puzzled, she looks from side to side, "And where are your friends dear?" she inquires. "They all went back to Flagstaff to school, but I was free." He reaches out to shake her hand; however, instead, he raises it to his lips and kisses it. "By the way, my name's Kenneth, but everyone calls me Kenny." Helen was charmed, "Pleased to meet you Kenny, won't you come in darling?"

Later that evening, Helen and Kenny walk along the creek under the sycamores lit by a setting sun. "I can't believe you're living out here all by yourself," says Kenny. Continuing he says, "Don't you ever get lonely for a companion?" Helen looks at him, taken aback by his frankness, "Well, it is isolated, but I love the serenity and spiritual essence of this land." Kenny turns to her, "I guess that's an answer," he says. Helen replies, "Well, what about you? Surely the girls are chasing you all over Flagstaff?" Kenny looks straight at Helen, he replies directly, "I'm totally unattached, I've been waiting for the right," he pauses, as he looks deep into Helen's blue eyes, "right woman." Before Helen can respond he grabs her hand and says, "Come on, I'll race you back up to the house!"

Helen and Marc are sitting out on the terrace one afternoon when Marc turns to Helen and says in a serious tone, "Helen, I would never interfere with your life, or tell you what to do, but I have to say, I feel very uneasy about Kenny. I just don't get a good vibe from him." Helen looks over at Marc as she lights a cigarette. After a moment, she blows the smoke out over the chasm. "I respect your opinion Marc, and you're not the only one to bring this up with me. Rosie mentioned it too. I think Kenny is just not easily understood by people." Marc continues earnestly, "Helen, it's more than that, he's up to something, there's something he's not revealing to you. I'm worried Helen, I'm concerned for your safety." Helen looks at Marc uncomfortably, "I hope you're wrong Marc, I," she hesitates, "I feel I need to see where this leads." Marc takes Helen's hand, "Helen, we've enjoyed the most beautiful friendship, strictly platonic, but somehow I feel he wants more than that from you," Marc pauses, "something akin to an element of control." He continues, "Helen, please just be careful. Your empty heart makes you a target for those, well for those that may not have your best interests in mind. You are just too kind and giving sometimes; to be frank Helen, sometimes you can't see the forest for the trees." Helen smiles at this comment and squeezes Marc's hand, "Thank you dear, and thank you for looking out for me. You are a dear, dear friend, and I love you."

One night, Kenny leads Helen by the hand into a large meeting hall at Sedona. "I can't wait for you to meet my friends," says Kenny. "They certainly all want to meet you!" Helen walks into a room where a group of people is gathered. One by one, they come out of the shadowed peripheral, gathering around Helen, who quickly becomes the center of attention. One of them, an older man, takes Helen's hand and says, "Hello Helen! We've been waiting for you." He guides her over to a podium where there are two seats, a throne-like gold gilded chair, and another adjoining it. He gestures for her to sit on the adjoining chair while he seats himself on the large one. The group gathers around, they fawn over Helen in the manner of a long-lost queen. The leader, Darwin Gross turns to Helen and says, "Let me tell you all about Eckankar, Helen. This is the answer you have been seeking!" Helen looks around at the people who have gathered at her feet, 50 or so, and then back to Darwin with a look of peace on her face. Kenny stands back at the edge of the group with a smug look of satisfaction.

Early morning at Wings of the Wind, Marc and Helen are sitting at the breakfast table. Helen sets a glass of orange juice down for Marc. He says, "Helen, we have to talk." Helen sits down and says, "Whatever is it Marc?" Marc continues, "It's time for me to leave." Suddenly, Helen's face darkens, "No Marc, I want you to stay, I've told you that, as long as you want," she pauses, "is it Kenny, is this about him?" "No Helen, my work is done here, it is time for me to move on, my path opens before me." Helen is quiet for a moment, "I understand," she says quietly, "I will miss you dear. You have been a beacon of light in my world." Helen rises and hugs Marc from behind, without another word, Helen leaves the room. Marc listens as she walks back to the master bedroom. After the door shuts softly, he hears the sound of soft weeping.

Helen becomes entangled with Eckankar—they had the all the right answers, but little integrity. Helen becomes a figurehead of the newage group. She had recently sold part of her ranch to a developer who defaulted on his plans to turn the property into a resort. Alarmed at the fate of her ranch, Helen tries to get the developer to sell the property back to her, but, she is refused. Helen soon devises a plan where Eckankar will buy back the property for $1,200,000. In 1974, at the Wings of the Wind house, Helen offers Eckankar two thirds of the payment, $800,000. She conveys they are to have the property, but it is to be used as a spiritual retreat for people seeking 'healing of the heart'.

High above the Sedona ranch, on a red rock overlook, Helen sits in a silk Caftan; she is talking to Eckankar followers about her beliefs in spirituality as they sit around her mesmerized. The followers see Helen as a den mother; indeed, Helen is given the title of Priestess. Helen has a smile on her face, with hands outstretched to the sky, the Sedona winds gently billow her Caftan as she tells them about the 'ancient ones' who guard the valley below.

By 1976, Helen has a 'Gift Deed' drawn up. At the Wings of the Wind, Helen is sitting on the sofa, she reaches down to the coffee table and picks up a document, which she hands to Darwin Gross. "Here, Darwin, this is the deed to my house, with one codicil, it's to be developed as a spiritual retreat for the Navajo-Hopi, as I envision. You are to make sure that access is always fluid and no one is turned away from experiencing the essence of the Wings. Native Americans are to be welcomed here—always!" Darwin takes the deed, looks it over, and with a smug smile says, "Why of course Helen, just as you say. And, of course, you have the legal right to remain here until your death." Helen replies, "That's just the way I want it Darwin, but as I said, Eckankar must follow through with my wishes—to the letter."

Chapter 16

Prophecy

'Fall of 1976'

Helen is down by the creek below the House of Apache Fires. A bonfire is burning in the clearing with about 20 Hopi and Navajo standing nearby. Helen is sitting on a rock watching a ceremony, which is cleansing the land and celebrating the union of the Native Americans with the valley.

Suddenly, the chanting stops. A sudden breeze blows through the trees and rustles the falling leaves, which flutter to the ground gently. The sun shines golden through the sycamores as the scene dons a surreal glow. One of the Native American youth walks up to Helen, he holds out his hand, "Grandfather offers you a gift of prophecy, please, come with me."

He leads Helen over to the fire where he helps her sit in the sand on an old worn Indian blanket. Then, from out of the group, comes a frail old Indian medicine man. He reaches out to Helen and starts speaking in broken tongue, "I have message for you, one that will reach across sands of time."

The old man stands before Helen and the flickering fire, everyone is silent with anticipation. He reaches toward the fire with open hands; it explodes toward the sky with sparks and flames. Then he speaks again, "This land, this land sacred, for many thousand years, my people, and those who came before, the Ancient Ones, have found peace here, have found portal to spirit."

He stretches his arm out toward Sedona as he continues, "This community, you call Sedona, it rests," he pauses, "in what white man call 'church' to Indian, it not in harmony with land!" Then he turns to face Helen, she watches his weathered face intently. "This land, land you call 'yours', not in harmony with Spirit. This group you call Eckankar, they defile land, not belong here! They claim, but not belong to them!" His voice rises, "Not Belong, No One!" He pauses as he takes a long, labored breath, "But," he says, as he looks toward the sun setting in the west, "This will not stand!"

Helen watches the old man with respect, her face full of love, as the late afternoon breeze caresses her white hair. Continuing, the old man points at the sun, "Many suns will rise and fall over this land. Spirit blow much wind through crack and crevice of cliff before prophecy rise out of red dirt!" He turns back to Helen, "People come, people go, houses be built, all intrude on sacred land." He pauses, as he moves his arms in a sweeping motion from embers to sky. The fire explodes, and an inferno of flame and sparks erupt up toward the heavens.

He continues, "One day man will come." He turns toward Cathedral Rock and with a sweep of his arm he points toward the eastern sky and gestures from horizon to horizon, "This man will be your son, he will know you and your man of flight, you have shared many lifetimes together as family." He looks back at Helen, he reaches out and touches her forehead with a weathered hand, "Just as your story forgotten, he will remember with passion, he will do a re-telling of you and your man's life, your discovery of this valley. People will have a knowing of what was, what is coming." He points up at the Wings of the Wind, "Another will assist him, he will share his understanding of your path, his knowing of you. Both will work to return this land to destiny and reuniting with people who share essence, the Ancient Ones."

The old man is silent now, his breathing labored. Helen watches him raptly as tears well up at the corner of her misty eyes. "Who, Grandfather, who will come?" Helen questions emotionally. Again, the old man speaks, "It will be many moons from now, long after you rejoin Great Spirit. Finally, he come, finally he remember. He stand right here in sand, he look up at house, his heart open, tears fill his eyes, he remember! You will assist as spirit. This will come to pass!"

At that, an Indian youth comes over and assists the old medicine man who leans on him heavily, worn out from his prophecy. He turns to Helen, "Grandfather tired, I must take him home now." The Native Americans quickly gather their belongings and trudge up the hill out of sight. Helen sits staring into the fire until it becomes nothing but smoking embers. Then she rises and walks up the hill toward her home, into the shadows, her mind filled with wonder.

'Discourse and Betrayal'

Arguing with Darwin Gross over financial expenditures, in the living room of the Wings of the Wind, Helen is pacing back and forth in front of the fireplace, puffing on a cigarette. Emphatically she tells Darwin, "There will be no more money!" Darwin consoles Helen and manipulates her like Rasputin, he implores that the group is low on funds, but soon money will be pouring in from wealthy new members! Feeling defeated and cornered, Helen writes out a check for another $100,000. "This is the last time Darwin, no more!" She states firmly.

That evening, Darwin is up at the House of Apache Fires, which he has claimed as his private residence. The valley of the ranch spreads out below the pueblo-home, leaving Helen's Wings of the Wind on the opposite side of the valley to emit the only other light in the area. By midnight, Darwin moves upstairs for an orgy with naked converts in the new Jacuzzi-bathtub he had installed in Helen's art studio, her most cherished and sacred space.

Holding the check up for all to see Darwin says, "I got another $100,000 out of Helen, and there's more where that came from!" A couple men, part of the Eckankar inner circle, joke about how they could 'off' Helen, eliminating her once and for all. "First though," Darwin interrupts, "Eckankar needs total control of Helen's estate, and I'll get it too," he adds with a wry smile.

Downstairs, in the sprawling House of Apache Fires, worker-ant members of the group are sleeping in every corner of the building, the once stunning home, now no more than a filthy flophouse is unkempt and littered with trash. Helen is well aware of the conditions at the house, certainly, many times, she delivers buckets of Kentucky Fried Chicken to the hungry members camped out there. It's obvious to Helen, the lower level converts are being treated as slaves, poorly clothed, housed, and little fed by Eckankar elite who control her property. Helen enjoys these youthful neophytes of Eckankar, many who have come from far and wide to partake of the essence of her property and commune with those of like mind, all searching for basic spiritual truths.

A major impasse develops between Helen and Eckankar when she discovers Eckankar plagiarized their core doctrines—a covert act which betrays the originality and provenance of the organization. Helen had believed Eckankar had all the right answers; but unfortunately, like all the other orthodox and mystic religions she had studied, Eckankar was just a sham, with a few gems of truth thrown in for effect. In her heart, Helen knows it's really more about the search; the answers as elusive as time itself.

Becoming increasingly distrustful of Eckankar, Helen is nervous and alarmed at her isolation. She finds herself trapped on property she no longer owns, wary of the course Eckankar is chartering with her ranch and their refusal to consider her expressed desires. Indeed, many members opt to flee the group during this time frame, but are stalked by threats regarding their safety, and forced to live under a veil of paranoia with fears of retribution. Afraid to talk, trusting no one, they wander aimlessly, realizing they are victims of a cult—a cult which solicited their membership but rejected their free thought and exit.

In regard to the ranch, Helen is tired; so many greedy people surrounding her want only her assets, coming in for the kill now that she is advancing in age. Helen knows these interlopers care nothing for her and are just ever so many wolves at her door. Helen needs an escape, a place she can retreat which will be isolated from the frenzy of the ranch, a place of peace and reflection.

By 1977, Helen launches the construction of a third home, this time on property she purchases from her close friend Faye Crenshaw, located at south end of the Village of Oak Creek. By air, the property is just a stone's throw from the Frye Ranch, just across the creek and to the east a couple miles. Helen can easily reach the parcel by fording Oak Creek at the Frye Ranch, and following Turkey Creek Trail to Verde Valley School Road.

Visiting the property, called the 'Ridge' many times with Faye in the past, Helen always felt it would be a stunning building site. One evening, Helen watches a magnificent western sunset from the parcel; at that moment, she decides to call her new dwelling 'Sky Fires'. In the surreal orange glow, Helen smiles at the synchronicity of the name as associated with the House of Apache Fires.

Helen designs her new home to be 'green' desiring it to blend in with the character and simplicity of Sedona's western ambiance. The architectural design is more so by inspiration than plan, with a ranch-style befitting the adjoining community, two-storied at the center, akin to an A-Frame, with two wings. One hidden feature is a subterranean Kiva-style meditation room in Helen's master bedroom, an idea she embraces as associated with her Native American friends. Unfortunately, Helen finds the walls of the sub-room vulnerable to seepage from Sedona's torrential summer monsoons. The room fills with water continuously; a boondoggle, which proves some ideas are more appealing in thought than reality.

By 1979, all construction ceases, even though Kenny hounds Helen to finish the house and bequeath it to him. His motivations are 'true to type' and borne out of greed. Oh yes, Kenny wants the property, but not if he has to invest money to finish it. Subsequently, Sky Fires is never completed. Eventually even, it burns in a mysterious fire in 1983, the remains bulldozed for construction of the showplace 'The Ridge at Sedona' golf course project. No trace remains today of this last Helen Frye expression. Rumors of this dwelling set on fire by disgruntled 'Eck' members who resented Kenny's ill-gotten gains are seemingly unfounded; however, he was in residence at the time of the fire.

Meanwhile, back up at the Wings, another heated argument ensues, the discourse wafts over the cliff and down to the canyon below. Kenny screams at Helen demanding more money. Helen retorts firmly, "I've given you enough!" The brash young man demands to know the status of her Will and other assets, at which Helen glaringly responds, "I've changed it and left everything to Eckankar, it's no longer your concern!" Kenny's face contorts in rage as he rants at Helen, "You did what, and you never consulted me?" Continuing heatedly, he screams, "You promised me I would be the sole beneficiary!"

Helen, though, has had enough. She reaches for a cigarette, and with smoldering eyes, she glares at Kenny as she lights it, "I will not be treated so disrespectfully in my own home. How dare you!" She points to the door, "Get out, you are no longer welcome here. I'm sick of your manipulations and deception, something I'm intuitive enough to know you will continue long after I'm in my grave!" Kenny rises to leave, but not before he hurdles another threat at Helen, "You haven't heard the end of this old woman. I'll get what I want in the end," then he adds with a smirk, "I always do!" As Kenny drives away in a cloud of red dust Helen watches from the Wings window with piercing eyes. She puffs on her cigarette with shaking hand and flips the deadbolt of her front door with the other.

Shortly after, Helen meets with her attorney and his assistant at the Wings of the Wind, the attorney notarizes a new Will for her. The Eckankar Will lays on the coffee table torn in half. The attorney asks Helen where he should file the new Will. Helen asks him to place the document in the Wings safe, stating, "No one has the combination, except Eckankar and me, but they won't have access to my home anymore." As the attorney leaves, he assures Helen she has made the right decision. "Rosie is the only person I can trust now, I know she will distribute my assets as I desire," Helen replies. At his car, the attorney implores Helen to leave the ranch, stating, "Helen you're not safe out here with these people. Is there any way you can come stay in town?" Helen declares, "No one will drive me off the land Jack and I bought together! I will die here!"

Chapter 17

A Dark Monsoon Builds

Despite Helen's effort at cures, even with a trip to a Mexico treatment center, and an array of natural remedies, her body slowly surrenders to life-robbing cancer. Helen develops a hideous tumor on her side but hides it from everyone with her kaftan. She refuses to go to a doctor and abhors western treatments, thus, her Hopi friends encourage her to go up to the reservation where a Hopi medicine man will attempt to offer her relief.

Helen contacts her good friend Oma Bird who owns the popular Oak Creek Tavern at Uptown Sedona. "Oma, can I leave my car in town at your house?" Helen implores. "Why of course dear, you need not even ask," Oma cheerfully answers. Oma has no qualms about helping her old friend, having known Helen for some 30 years, even having met Jack Frye and Howard Hughes at her Oak Creek Tavern one afternoon when they came in for gas. Helen explains the reason for her request as Oma listens compassionately.

The next day, Helen's Native American friends meet her at Oma's modest home on Van Deren Road, after which she and her friends start the journey to the Hopi Lands north of Flagstaff. After the end of a long journey, the group arrives at dusk. Helen is helped out of the car and over to a nearby chair adjoining some long tables. The sun is setting and no one is stirring; the rugged dirt streets are empty. However, out of the long shadows Native Americans start to appear with platters of food, which they place on the tables adjoining Helen. As they pass, they smile lovingly; several even, reach out to caress Helen's hair. Helen watches this gathering, this welcome celebration with misty eyes, her heart filled with love for these beautiful selfless people.

The Hopi revere Helen, having long since adopted her as one of their own. After a celebration dinner and honoring Helen with friendship, several Indian youth help Helen over to a mat by a roaring fire. Warmed by the radiant crackling flames, Helen soon forgets her excruciating pain. Coyotes serenade from a nearby hill, in Helen's heart, she is home, loved and complete. No one wants anything from her here.

Native Americans start gathering around Helen. Swooping and singing, they welcome her to their world, the Land of Hopi. Helen is overwhelmed and starts to cry; finally, the dancing ceases. An old medicine man hobbles over to Helen, he administers to her with herbs and talismans, while other elders gather around to assist. The dancing commences, accompanied by drums and chants. Hopi swoop and sing, as the ancient chorus wafts out into the starry night. Helen swoons with dizziness; the experience overwhelms her and disorients her. The fire roars higher, as Helen surrenders to the flames collapsing like a limp rag doll. Exploding in sparks and embers, the flames lick at the sky, reaching toward the Milky Way, which twinkles and snakes above the mesa.

High in the sky the sparks dance and join with another roaring fire, this one at the Wings of the Wind. Inside the pinnacle home, a roaring fire explodes out of the living room fireplace; the figure of a man silhouetted in front of the angry flames holds up a document. Laughing like a mad man, Kenny tosses Helen's latest Will into the flames like a sacrifice. Erupting and curling, the paper floats up the chimney, out over the canyon. Kenny exclaims maniacally, "Now, when the old woman dies, there will be no Will to find and she will die intestate! I'll befriend her family; we'll sue the estate and usurp Eckankar!" Laughing hysterically and with wild eyes he adds, "I will have what I desire Helen, and I'm clever enough to get it!"

Closure

'December 4, 1979'

Helen sits with misty eyes in front of plate-glass windows of the Wings of the Wind house, aside a crackling fire, a spent phonographic record spins on a turntable. Rosie enters the room, she walks over to Helen and adjusts her blanket, lovingly she kisses Helen on her forehead. As she leaves the room, Rosie walks over to a console and sets the needle at the beginning of the record again. Jo Stafford's voice fills the Wings, "Fly the ocean in a silver plane, see the jungle when it's wet with rain, but remember darling till you're home again, you belong to me," wafts out the opened windows, over the cliff, and down across the red rock valley below. Helen is nearly gone, almost in a coma; her breathing barely perceptible as her eyes stare out the large window, waiting for something, or *someone*.

Suddenly, Helen stirs, she murmurs softly, "I will never forget this ranch, I will hold it in my heart for an eternity!" In her hand, she holds a gold charm bracelet that glitters in the firelight. Gently, Helen fingers all the pieces—stopping at one in particular. Helen turns it over and reads the engraved words, 'To Helen, With Love Always, Jack, Xmas 1949'. Helen smiles lovingly, as a tear rolls down her cheek. She clutches the bracelet to her bosom. Slowly, Helen's eyes close, in slow motion, she slumps over and her hand falls to her side. The charm bracelet slips away from her lifeless hand and falls to the painted concrete floor with a tinkle. Breaking apart, the charms roll away in different directions.

In the Wings living room Helen's body rests in peace, on her face a smile of contentment and completion. Standing reverently nearby, the specters of Native American medicine men, hunters, and ceremonial dancers watch over Helen, guarding her as they await her exit. Slowly, an orb of pulsing color rises up and out of Helen's bosom.

Floating through the ceiling, the shimmering light soars out across the valley and descends into the House of Apache Fires.

In front of the fireplace, the shimmering image of Helen suddenly appears in all its glory, filling the room with daggers of rainbow brilliance. Within moments, a blinding presence of light enters the room from the long hallway. A hand reaches out, and with a masculine voice, the words, "I've been waiting for you Helen." Helen reaches out and takes Jack's hand; they explode in a pulse of rose and indigo blue. Speaking again with loving embrace, Jack says, "Now my darling?" "Yes, now my darling," says Helen, expressed with an eternity of love and devotion.

Hand in hand, Jack and Helen rise up out of the pueblo home as two golden orbs, climbing higher and higher into the starry night, they disappear into the heavens, eventually, indiscernible from millions of twinkling stars. In a silent celebration of farewell, a mass of blue orbs release from the lowland meadows of the ranch by the dozens. With an appearance of hot air balloons, the shimmering lights follow the two aloft to the stars.

The darkened House of Apache Fires, empty and barren, rests in stony silence on its promenade overlooking the ranch bathed in moonlight. Slowly, night sounds start to reignite the valley. Nature's orchestra of screaming frogs, crickets and night creatures rise in cadence, accompanied by the gurgling Oak Creek.

In the rushes, a band of Native American hunters with bows appears, forging through the reeds along the creek, walking along old Smoke Trail. Accompanied by the serenade of coyotes in the canyons beyond, they walk in filtered moonlight under the ancient cottonwoods and Arizona sycamores, disappearing one by one, into a mist, at the base of a cliff west of the house.

The End

Creator-Owner 'Sedona Legend Helen Frye'

The "Jack and Helen Frye Story"[1]

For photos and historical details of this work please see the comprehensive website cited above. Book cover image was taken by the author from Helen Frye's Wings of the Wind terrace out toward Cathedral Rock.

About the Author

Randall Reynolds grew up in the scenic Pacific Northwest communities of Corvallis and Bend Oregon. He relocated to Sedona Arizona in 1987, at 27 years old, later he lived in Tucson, and currently at Santa Fe New Mexico. With his love of Sedona, Randy volunteered with his spouse at Red Rock State Park (former Frye Ranch) in 2003 and 2008. With a background in the transportation and airline industry (UAL) Mr. Reynolds became interested in the Frye association with the property, a saga which had never been properly researched or developed. Caught up in a passion to get the story out there, Randall used his gift of word to create the phenomenal webportal: Sedona Legend Helen Frye, 'Jack and Helen Frye Story - The Camelot Years of TWA'. This effort evolved into the book project and a milestone event for Randy and his partner when they were passengers on Jack and Helen's former 1937 TWA Lockheed 12A above the coast of California. (Author shown at Red Rock State Park with Jack & Helen Frye's 'House of Apache Fires' in background)

Read more at www.sedonalegendhelenfrye.com.

About the Publisher

Distribution of historic information in regard to the Frye Legacy as associated with Transcontinental & Western Air, Inc., Jack Frye, and Helen Varner Vanderbilt Frye. This end is accomplished with the Sedona Legend Helen Frye website (The Jack and Helen Frye Story) and published book, 'The Jack & Helen Frye Story- the Camelot Years of TWA'.

Made in the USA
Middletown, DE
12 April 2023